I Am America Atlas

Based on the Maps, Prophecies, and Teachings of the Ascended Masters

ALSO BY LORI TOYE

A Teacher Appears

Sisters of the Flame

Fields of Light

The Ever Present Now

New World Wisdom Series

Points of Perception

Light of Awakening

Divine Destiny

Sacred Energies of the Golden Cities

Temples of Consciousness

Building the Seamless Garment

Freedom Star Book

I AM America Map

Freedom Star Map

6-Map Scenario

US Golden City Map

I AM AMERICA PUBLISHING & DISTRIBUTING
P.O. Box 2511, Payson, Arizona, 85547, USA.
www.iamamerica.com

I AM America Atlas © (Copyright) 2016; 2018 revised edition by Lori Adaile Toye.
All rights reserved.
ISBN: 978-1-880050-21-7

All rights exclusively reserved, including under the Berne Convention and the Universal Copyright Convention. No part of this book may be reproduced or translated in any language or utilized in any form or by any means, electronic or mechanical, including photocopying, recording, or by any information storage and retrieval system, without written permission from the publisher. Published in 2018 by I AM America Seventh Ray Publishing International, P.O. Box 2511, Payson, Arizona, 85547, United States of America.

I AM America Maps and Books have been marketed since 1989 by I AM America Seventh Ray Publishing and Distributing, through workshops, conferences, and numerous bookstores in the United States and internationally. If you are interested in obtaining information on available releases please write or call: I AM America, P.O. Box 2511, Payson, Arizona, 85547, USA. (928) 978-6435, or visit:

www.iamamerica.com
www.loritoye.com

Graphic Design and Typography by Lori Toye
Editing by Betsy Robinson

Love, in service, breathes the breath for all!

Second Edition

9 8 7 6 5 4 3 2 1

"Those who dwell among the beauties and mysteries of the Earth are never alone or weary of life."

- RACHEL CARSON

Contents

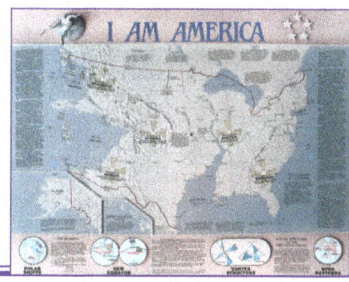

Section One: I AM AMERICA MAP

Introduction *17*	Northeast States *26*
I AM America Map *18*	I AM America Map Prophecies:
Prophecy is Not Prediction *19*	United States and Canada *26*
Pacific Northwest *19*	Great Lakes *27*
West Coast *20*	Mississippi and Missouri Rivers *28*
Southwest *21*	East Coast *29*
Timing and Timelines *21*	Southeast States *30*
Rocky Mountain States *22*	Alaska *31*
West North Central States *23*	Polar Shifts *31*
South Central States *24*	New Equator *31*
East North Central States *25*	

Section Two: FREEDOM STAR WORLD MAP

Freedom Star World Map *32-33*	Southeast Asia: *Political* *43*
Canada: *Earth Changes* *34*	Central Asia: *Political* *43*
I AM America Map Prophecies:	Central Asia: *Earth Changes* *44*
Alaska and Canada *35*	Region of Tibet: *Political* *45*
Canada: *Political* *35*	India: *Earth Changes* *45*
Greenland *36*	Australia: *Earth Changes* *45*
I AM America Map Prophecies:	Europe: *Earth Changes* *46*
Mexico, Central America, and South America *36*	Map of Exchanges Prophecies: Europe and Africa *46*
Mexico: *Political* *37*	Europe: *Topography* *47*
Mexico and Central America: *Earth Changes* *37*	Iceland: *Earth Changes* *48*
Central America: *Political* *38*	Middle East: *Political* *48*
South America: *Earth Changes* *39*	Middle East: *Earth Changes* *49*
China: *Topography* *40*	East Europe: *Earth Changes* *50*
The Greening Map Prophecies:	Russia: *Topography* *50*
Japan, Korea, China, and Australia *40*	New Lemuria: *Earth Changes* *51*
East Asia: *Earth Changes* *41*	Africa: *Earth Changes* *52*
North Asia: *Earth Changes* *42*	Africa: *Topography* *53*
North Asia: *Political* *42*	Antarctica: *Deglaciated Topography* *54*
Southeast Asia: *Earth Changes* *43*	Antarctica: *Earth Changes* *54*

I AM AMERICA ATLAS **9**

Section Three: SIX MAP SCENARIO

Map Number One 55
Prophecies 56
Mystic Message 58

Map Number Four 62
Prophecies 62
Mystic Message 64

Map Number Two 57
Prophecies 58
Mystic Message 59

Map Number Five 65
Prophecies 64
Mystic Message 67

Map Number Three 60
Prophecies 59
Mystic Message 62

The Sixth Map 67
A Genuine Prophet - Always Wrong 68
Spiritual Insights on Earth Changes 68

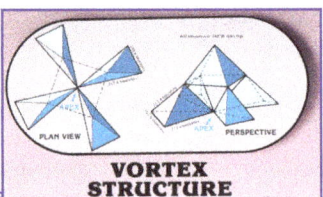

VORTEX STRUCTURE

Section Four: GOLDEN CITIES & US GOLDEN CITIES

Golden City Structure 69
What Exactly is a Golden City Vortex? 69
Ray Forces and Golden Cities 70
Arcing of Ray Forces to Golden City Vortices 70
The Five Golden Cities of the United States 71

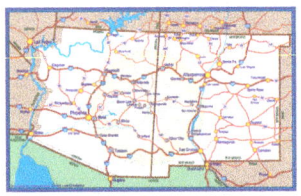

Golden City of Gobean
(Arizona and Montana) 71
El Morya, Hierarch of Gobean 71

Golden City of Shalahah
(Idaho and Montana) 74
Lord Sananda, Hierarch of Shalahah ... 74
Ascension Valley 75

Golden City of Malton
(Missouri, Illinois, Indiana
and Kentucky) 72
Kuthumi, Hierarch of Malton 72

Golden City of Klehma
(Colorado, Kansas, Nebraska,
and Wyoming) 75
Serapis Bey, Hierarch of Klehma 76

Golden City of Wahanee
(Georgia, South Carolina,
and North Carolina) 73
Saint Germain, Hierarch of Wahanee 73

Doorways and Star of Golden City 76

Section Five:
LAND OF CO-CREATION GOLDEN CITIES
CANADA, GREENLAND

Land of Co-Creation: Canada and Greenland	77
Lady Portia, Hierarch of Eabra	77
Archangel Zadkiel, Hierarch of Jeafray	77

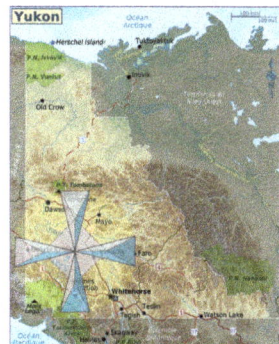

Golden City of Eabra (Yukon) 78

Golden City of Pashacino (Alberta) 80

Golden City of Uverno (Ontario) 81
Hilarion, Hierarch of Yuthor 81

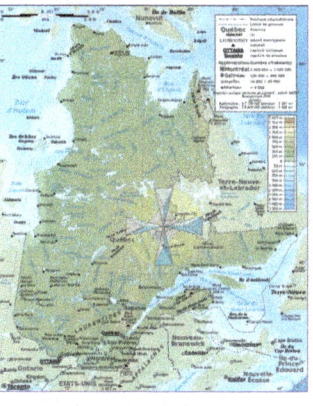

Golden City of Jeafray
(Labrador, Quebec) 79
Soltec, Hierarch of Pashacino 79
Paul the Venetian,
Hierarch of Uverno 79

Golden City of Yuthor (Greenland) 81
Deglaciated Map of Greenland 81

I AM AMERICA ATLAS **11**

Section Six:
CRADLELAND GOLDEN CITIES
MEXICO, CENTRAL AMERICA, CARIBBEAN

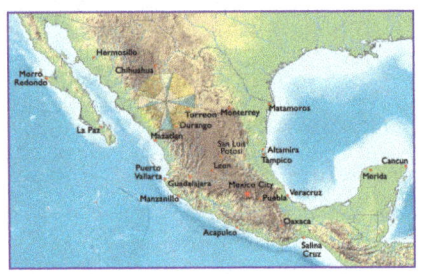
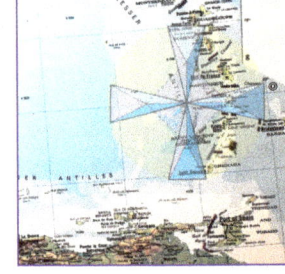

Golden City of Crotese (Costa Rica) *83*
Paul the Devoted, Hierarch of Crotese *83*

Cradleland Golden Cities Map *82*
Golden City of Marnero (Mexico) *82*
Mother Mary, Hierarch of Marnero *82*

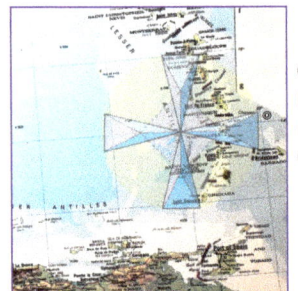

Golden City of Jehoa (Caribbean) *84*
Kuan Yin, Hierarch of Jehoa *83*
Petit Peton, Saint Lucia Island,
Golden City of Jehoa *84*

Peter the Everlasting, Hierarch of Asonea *82*
Golden City of Asonea (Cuba) *83*

Golden Cities of
South America *85*

Section Seven:
MOTHERLAND GOLDEN CITIES
SOUTH AMERICA

Golden City of Andeo (Peru) *86*
Goddess Meru,
Hierarch of Andeo *86*

Golden City of Braham (Brazil) *87*
Four Points of the Swaddling Cloth *87*
Goddess Yemanya,
Hierarch of Braham *87*
Goddess Pachamama,
Hierarch of Tehekoa *87*

Golden City of Tehekoa (Argentina) *88*
Valle Grande, Argentina,
Golden City of Tehekoa *88*

12 I AM AMERICA ATLAS

Section Eight:
GREENING MAP GOLDEN CITIES
AUSTRALIA, TASMANIA, NEW ZEALAND

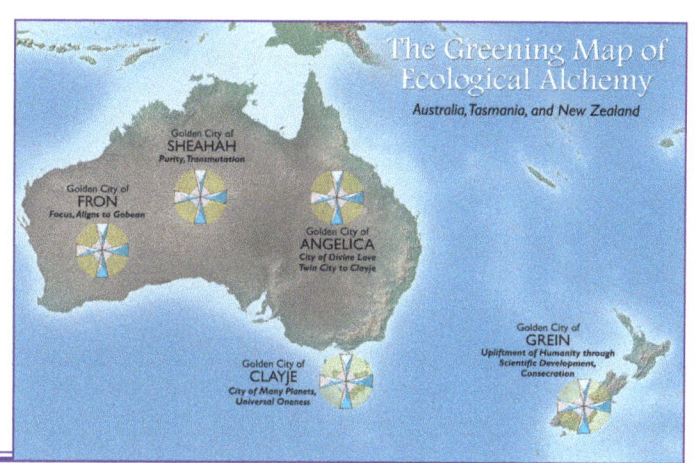

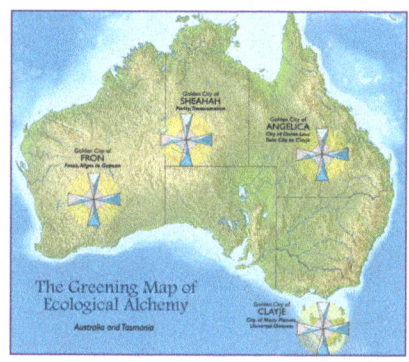

Greening Map of Ecological Alchemy Golden Cities 89
Australian Golden Cities 90

Golden City of Sheahah
(Northern Territory) 92
Elohim Astrea,
Hierarch of Sheahah 92
Uluru/Ayers Rock,
Australia 92

Golden City of Angelica
(Queensland) 90
Elohim Angelica,
Hierarch of Angelica 90

Golden City of Fron
(Western Australia) 93
Lady Master Desiree,
Hierarch of Fron 93
Aoraki/Mount Cook,
South Island, New Zealand 93

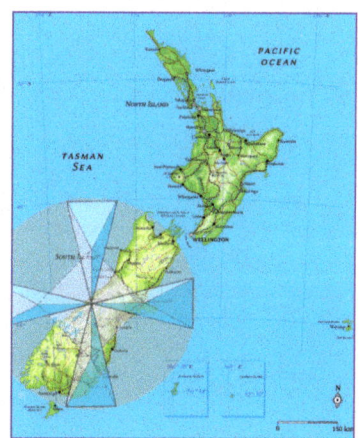

Golden City of Grein
(New Zealand) 94
Viseria, Goddess of the Stars,
Hierarch of Grein 94

Tasmania 91
Golden City of Clayje (Tasmania) 91
Elohim Orion, Hierarch of Clayje 90

I AM AMERICA ATLAS *13*

Section Nine:
MAP OF EXCHANGES GOLDEN CITIES
EUROPE, ICELAND

Map of Exchanges Golden Cities (Europe) 95
Archangel Michael, Hierarch of Stienta........................ 95
Elohim Hercules, Hierarch of Gruecha 95

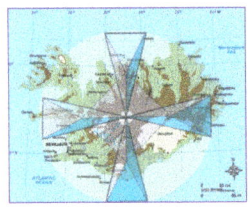

Golden City of Stienta (Iceland) 96
Lady Master Nada,
Hierarch of Denasha.............................. 96
Godfre, Hierarch of Amerigo 96

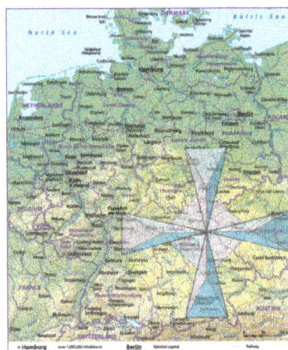

Golden City of Braun
(Germany, Czech Republic) 100

Golden City of Gruecha
(Norway, Sweden) 97

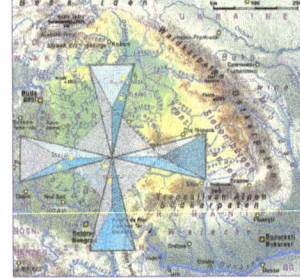

Golden City of Afrom
(Hungary, Romania)....................... 101
Seraya, the White Buddha,
Hierarch of Afrom 101

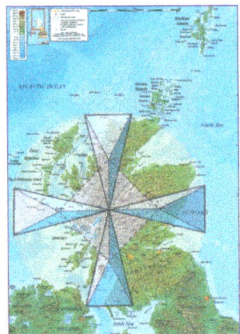

Golden City of Denasha (Scotland).......... 98

Golden City of Ganakra (Turkey) 102
Elohim Vista, Hierarch of Ganakra............................. 102

Golden City of Amerigo (Spain) 99
Mighty Victory,
Hierarch of Braun 99
Elohim Claire,
Hierarch of Afrom 99

14 I AM AMERICA ATLAS

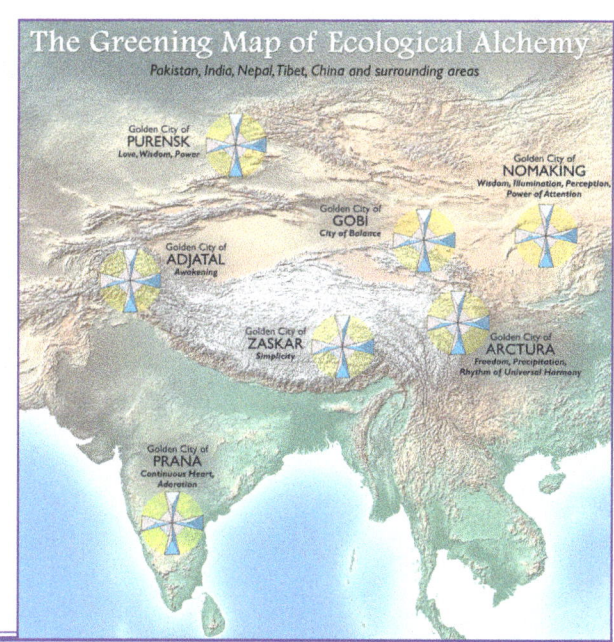

Section Ten:
GREENING MAP GOLDEN CITIES
PAKISTAN, INDIA, NEPAL, TIBET, CHINA

Greening Map of Ecological Alchemy Golden Cities (Asia) *103*

Golden City of Prana (India) *104*
Archangel Chamuel,
Hierarch of Prana *104*

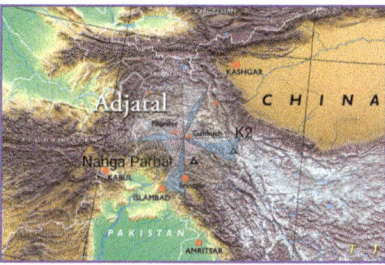

Golden City of Adjatal
(Pakistan) *105*
Lord Himalaya,
Hierarch of Adjatal *105*

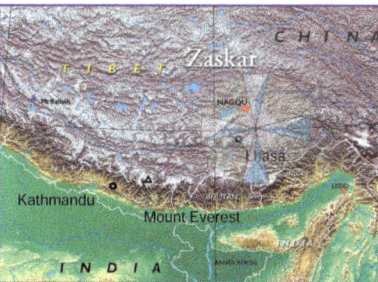

Golden City of Zaskar
(Tibet) *105*
Lady Master Reya,
Hierarch of Zaskar *105*

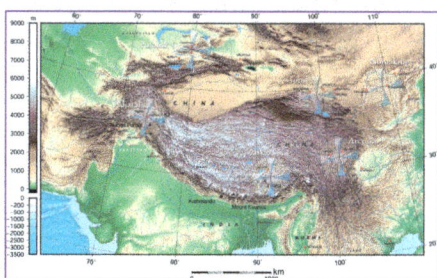

Map of Tibet and
Surrounding
Golden Cities *106*

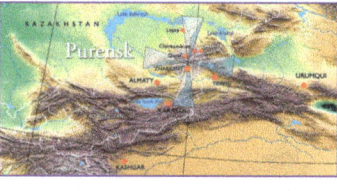

Golden City of Purensk (Kazakhstan, China) *106*
Divine Beings Faith, Hope, and Charity,
Hierarchs of Purensk *106*

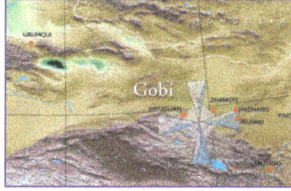

Golden City of Gobi (Tibet) *107*
Lord Meru,
Hierarch of Gobi *107*

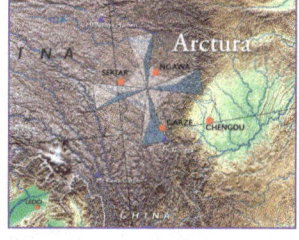

Golden City of Arctura (China) *107*
Elohim Arcturus and Diana,
Hierarchs of Arctura *107*

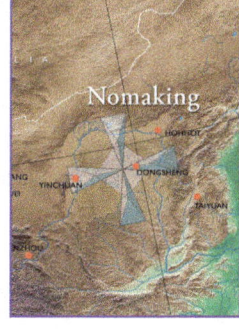

Golden City of Nomaking
(Inner Mongolia) *108*
Elohim Cassiopea and Minerva,
Hierarchs of Nomaking *108*
Five Pagoda Temple, Inner Mongolia *108*

I AM AMERICA ATLAS *15*

Section Eleven: GOLDEN CITY NAMES & MEANINGS

Golden City Names 109
Sonoran Desert, Golden City of Gobean 109
Meanings of the 51 Golden City Vortices 110
Qilin Mountains, Golden City of Gobi 110
Petroglyphs along the Snake River, Golden City of Shalahah 110
Ben Navis, Golden City of Denasha 112

Moraine Lake, Golden City of Pashacino 113
Neuschwanstein Castle, Golden City of Braun 114
Hanalei Bay, Kuaii, Hawaii, near the Golden City of Mousee 114

Section Twelve: MAP OF THE ANCIENTS

Map of the Ancients:
The Seven Rays and the
Nine Civilizations they
have formed. 116

Map of the Ancients:
The influence of the
Seven Rays on nations 122

The Churchward Map 117
Ameru 117
Ameru and the Right-hand Path 117
Lemuria 117
Atlantis Map by *Ignatius Donelly* 118
Ameru and the Rise and Fall of Atlantis 119
Temple Ruins at Chichen Itza 119
Land of Rama 120
Atlantis by *P. Kampankis* 121

The Colonization of Earth as Taught by Lord Meru 122
Ancient Timeline 123
Pangaea 124
North America Craton 125
Prehistoric Earth 126
Prehistoric Tectonic Plate 128
Flora and Fauna of the Ancient Lands
    of the Plumed Serpent 128
Ray Systems 128

INVOCATION OF THE VIOLET FLAME
    FOR SUNRISE AND SUNSET 129

AWAKENING PRAYER 130

GLOSSARY 131

END NOTES 144

END NOTES: *Illustrations of Hierarchs* 145

END NOTES: *Golden City Maps* 146

BIBLIOGRAPHY 148

RESOURCES AND READING 149

INDEX 151

ABOUT LORI TOYE 161

ABOUT I AM AMERICA 162

SECTION ONE

Introduction

THE FOLLOWING PAGES contain perhaps one of the best anthologies of Earth Changes Maps we have ever produced. In addition to large, easy-to-understand pictures, this collection focuses on the prophecies and spiritual teachings of the *I AM America* material. The first *I AM America Map* was published in 1989, and depicts prophesied Earth Changes events for the United States. Our second Map—the *Freedom Star World Map*—was published in 1994, and illustrates Earth Changes events for the entire globe. The *Six-Map Scenario* placed an emphasis, again, on the United States, and portrays six different Earth Changes scenarios with possible progressions of Earth Changes events. This prophetic Map was published in 1996. And all of the Maps contain the various sites of Golden City Vortices—geophysical locations of safety and spiritual sanction during the tumultuous *Time of Change*.

When we first began our work with these Maps, our viewpoint or interpretation of the prophetic information was somewhat literal. As our insight matured, we began to understand this knowledge as invaluable metaphor, which significantly deepened our spiritual growth and insight regarding the prophecies. This spiritual process of perceiving beyond the literal uncovered essential, yet hidden, esoteric knowledge and further revealed each Map's mystic messages. I've included some of this interpretative work in the text of this Atlas in the excerpt, "Spiritual Insights on Earth Changes."

If you are interested in learning more and want to read the prophecies that helped to construct these Maps, I suggest you read our prophecy series *New World Wisdom: Books One, Two, and Three*. In fact, these three books are a perfect accompaniment to this Atlas. These books were published previously as the *New World Atlas Series*, and we have recently refined and updated this series with new material. This spiritual wisdom from the Ascended Masters helps us to navigate the prophesied troubled times ahead through the development of our personal Mastery. The first book features the *I AM America Map* (United States, Canada, Mexico, Central and South America) and the spiritual teachings from this Map's sponsor, Saint Germain. You can learn specifics about this Map in the first section of this Atlas. The second book in this series features prophecies from the Bodhisattva Kuan Yin's *Greening Map* of Japan, Asia, India, and Australia. The spiritual teachers El Morya, Lady Nada, and Kuthumi sponsor the final *Map of Exchanges* in the third book of prophecies, warnings, and spiritual wisdom. Both the Greening Map and the Map of Exchanges are featured in the second section of this Atlas. Each one of these metaphysical Maps denotes a series of seventeen Golden Cities, which help to cultivate and guide human consciousness into *Unana*—unity consciousness, a vital precursor to the New Times. There are fifty-one Golden City Vortices throughout the world, and you can learn about Golden City Energies, their unique locations, and purpose throughout this Atlas.

This Atlas also contains close-ups of the five Golden City Vortices of the United States. You'll be able to view the highways and road systems in each of these Maps along with the esoteric imaging of arterial lei-lines, alchemic adjutant points, unique doorways, and ceremonial Stars (center) of each of the Golden Cities. If you want to learn more about Golden Cities and how you can tap into their life-changing energies, I suggest that you read any of the I AM America books in the *Golden City Series*. This list of books is available in the back of this Atlas.

In the final section, I am proud to release the first full-color version of the *Map of the Ancients*. This Map depicts a past epoch on Earth and the ancient, mythical lands of Rama, Mu, Lemuria, Ameru, and Atlantis. Originally shared in the Golden City Teachings to further illustrate the creative principles of the Seven Rays, Lord Meru's Map shows how our Earth may have appeared millions of years ago. And apparently Earth Changes have a profound impact on reshaping worldwide political and social structures, and their various cultures. I thank Penny Greenwell for her help with the production of the Map of the Ancients, and sculpting and painting yet again, another I AM America Map Model.

We first shared the I AM America Maps almost thirty years ago, and at that time we barely knew anything about global warming, then more commonly known as the "greenhouse effect." We had yet to experience hurricanes Andrew, Katrina, or Sandy. The theories of continental drift and plate tectonics were relatively new. Scientists had only recently noted the Cascadia subduction zone—a fault line that extends from northern Vancouver Island to southern California, but its Earth-rattling history and potential quake-making of 8.0 and higher is now a new finding. Back then the notion of polar ice caps melting was considered pure quackery, and now it is scientific fact.

Through I AM America we have always taught that "A Change of Heart, can Change the World." This is based on the philosophic ideal and metaphysical teaching that an empowered and positive collective consciousness can co-create a better world without the need for catastrophic or destructive change. However, we still face a systemic breakdown of our precious Earth through a "new normal" comprising extreme climate change events and Frankensteinian-engineered anthropogenic climate disruptions. At this point, humble, spiritual solutions may seem "too little, too late." The physicist Albert Einstein once said, "We cannot solve our problems with the same thinking we used when we created them." Simply stated: to change our thinking, we are faced with no less task than the transformation of self. So I reiterate, "A Change of Heart, *can* (and hopefully *will*) Change the World!"

Lori Toye

LEGEND: Earth Change · Golden City · New Times

PACIFIC NORTHWEST

States Include: Washington, Oregon, Idaho, Northern California, and Utah.

- Islands of Fortune
  Bay of Prosperity
  Blue Islands
  Snake Lake
  Mount Shasta Peninsula
  Pathway Islands
  Vancouver Island
  Tablet Islands

- Shalahah

- Weather Crystal
  Transportation Center
  Ascension Valley
  Lewisport (Lewiston, ID)

The Ever Present Now: Prophecy Is Not Prediction

In Hindu culture, when a teacher wants to place the emphasis on an important point, the information is repeated three times. I imagine this is done so that the message is forever imbedded in the student's memory. With this intention, I'll make this statement: "Prophecy is not prediction. Prophecy is not prediction. Prophecy is not prediction." Now that we have that out of the way, you're probably asking, "Why?" Western culture does not and maybe has never understood the difference between Prophecy and prediction.

When examining Western culture from a spiritual perspective, one easily leaps to the conclusion that we are a material society. Just look at the array of smart-phones, luxury cars, and ATMs on every street corner. Our "toys" are our measure of success and comfort, and this value system can and does stop spiritual growth and evolution. But, it is not really our obsession with materiality that blocks the view. Rather, it is our mind. It is the way that we see things. The Masters call it "The Point of Perception."

Remember the iconic story of the three blind men hanging on to the elephant? Since each is in a different position, each defines the elephant according to the piece he's touching—different from the other two blind men. When we are dealing with something as dramatic and looming as Earth Changes Prophecy, we similarly see things according to whatever small piece we are hanging onto—which may be different from what another person perceives.

When people first encounter an I AM America Map, they either love it or hate it. Those who love it feel hopeful and happy that a New Time is coming. Those who hate it simply don't believe it, and sometimes point out that the map is geographically impossible. Over time, I have learned whether someone loves or hates the map, or thinks it is possible or impossible is not important. The map is a powerful metaphor

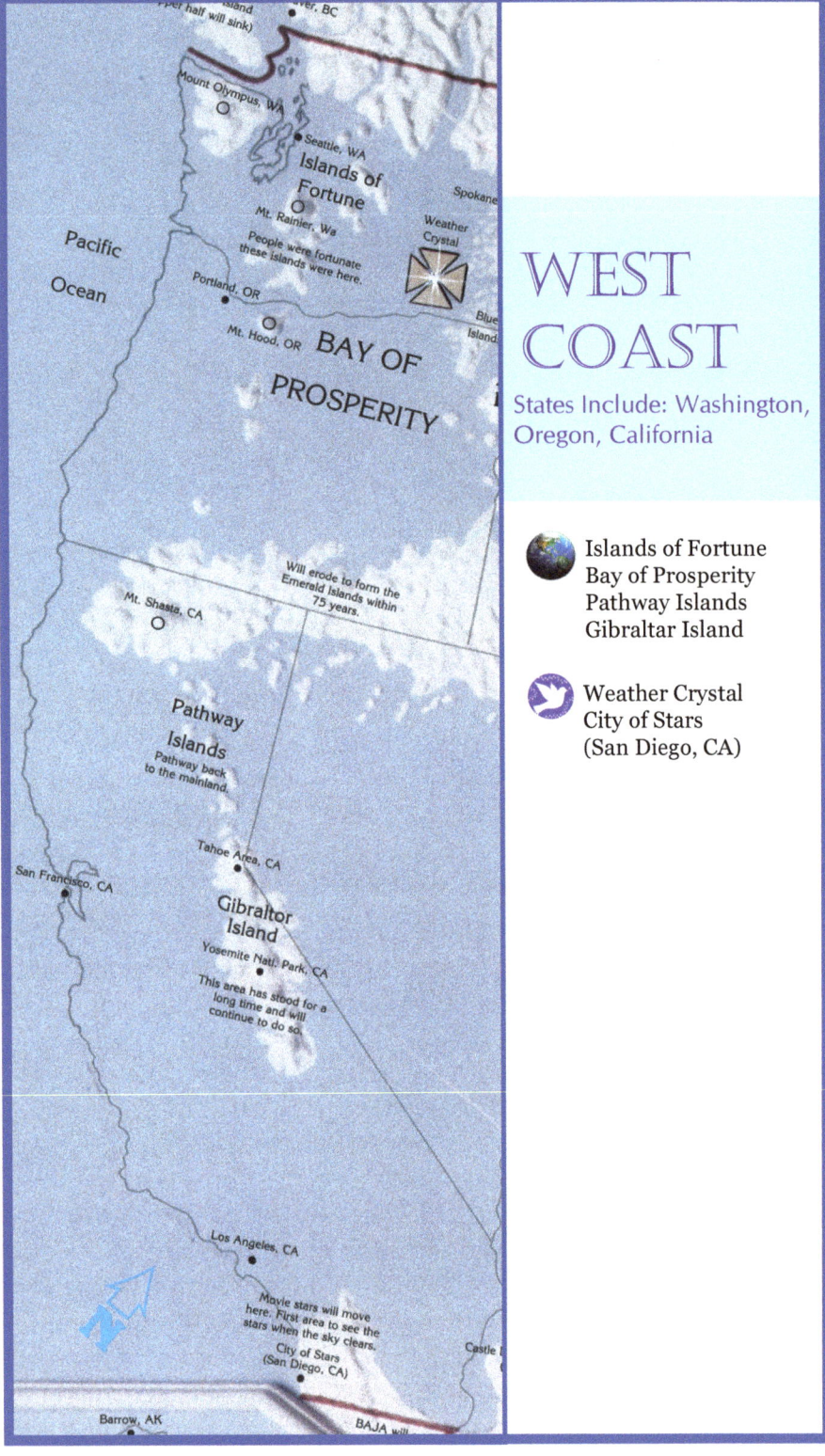

WEST COAST

States Include: Washington, Oregon, California

🌍 Islands of Fortune
Bay of Prosperity
Pathway Islands
Gibraltar Island

🕊 Weather Crystal
City of Stars
(San Diego, CA)

As I stated above, Prophecy is experiential. Throughout the years I've witnessed many people experiencing the tampering spiritual fires of Prophecy. Prophecy evokes fear and anxiety; the idea of losing anything we are attached to is horrifying. However, Native Americans encourage the process evoked by Prophecy—the letting go of the unessential—as purification. The visions and dreams of their prophets were the signals to do so and, through this process, their culture, their way of life, and their connectedness to Mother Earth were restored.

Eastern Indian Rishis heard the voice of the unconscious, and their position in their community as prophets and visionaries was considered invaluable. Once established on the spiritual path of listening to the inner-voice of wisdom, Prince Siddhartha, who later became known as the Buddha, denied an ego-voice that prodded him to: "Go back to the pleasures you have left behind." It was then that he declared that a philosophic "middle way" was the way one could be redeemed from illusion and experience unity. The Hopis say that humanity must "walk in balance," to prevent our world from experiencing calamity.

We westerners are fortunate to have one well-known body of spiritual teaching that could be classified as Prophecy: the Book of Revelations. When I was a little girl growing up in rural Idaho, we would listen to the radio every morning during breakfast. There was a program that came on before the news called *The Voice of Prophecy*. It was very evangelical and even my mother, who loves Christianity and is a devoted Lutheran, would roll her eyes when the show's song, which sounded much like a Sousa March and was sung by a barbershop Mitch Miller sort of trio, began, "Ring out the trumpet, and long live the King. Jesus is coming again . . ." None of us ever believed it. In Sunday school, I liked the idea that someday

of spiritual teachings, and therefore it releases the purifying, redemptive, and transformative experiential results of Prophecy—subtle yet extremely important.

Western culture's point of perception is extremely literal. We are over-identified with what we can only touch, see, smell, or hear, and unless we have scientific, empirical evidence, it doesn't exist. So why even deal with Prophecy? If "they" can't take it and make it into a date, a time, a correlation, a fact, a possible prediction, what good is it? But this thinking misses so much!

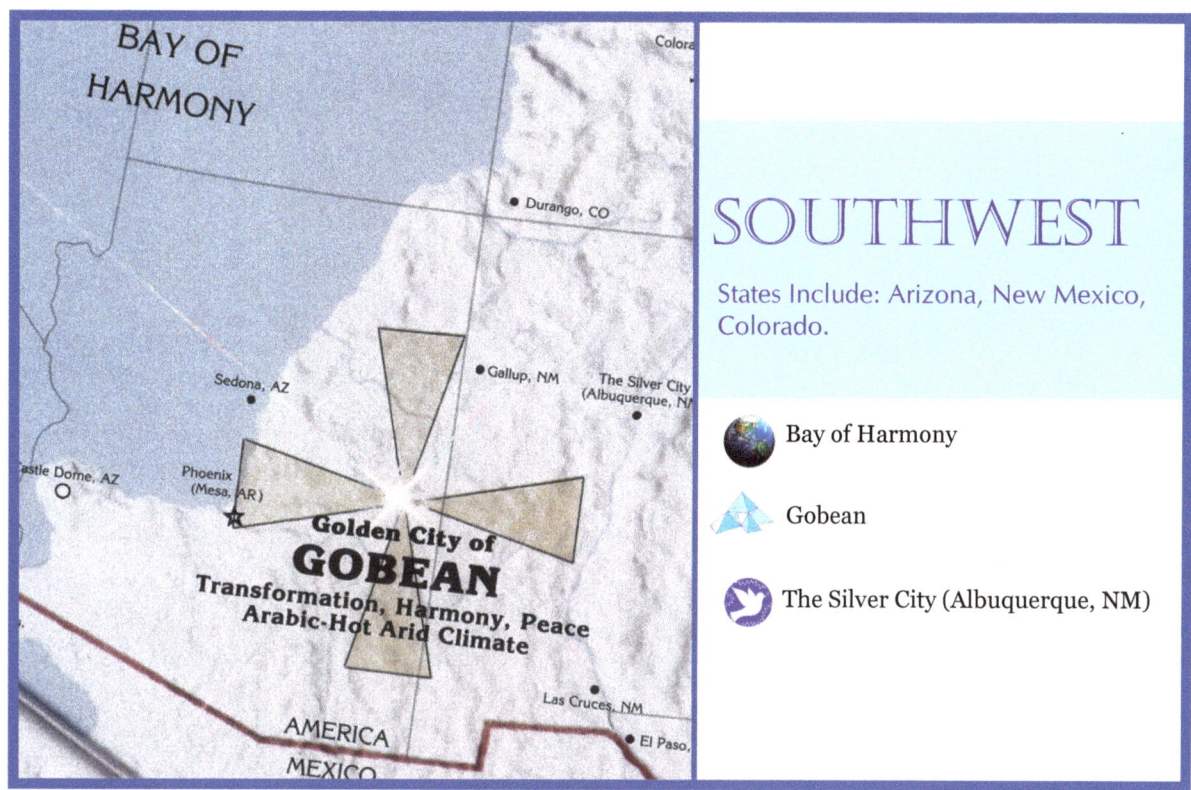

Heaven on Earth would come—but why did we have to fight the battle of Armageddon to achieve this?

Today, through the help and example of our Native American and Eastern Brothers and Sisters, I can see that Prophecy helps us to address the spiritual battle that is often waged within ourselves through the birth of our conscience and the redemptive power in our choice. Prophecy is truly the balance that blends human fate with free will. This occurs through Prophecy's physical, emotional, mental, and spiritual prodding, that inevitably initiates a reevaluation of our current choices. Again, the Master Teachers say that we have a choice how to react to Prophecy—through whatever "Point of Perception" we choose.

And so Prophecy is not prediction. Prediction is a declaration about the future; Prophecy, however, addresses possibility and the potential for change. One quick and easy way to tell the difference between Prophecy and prediction is that Prophecy always gives a way out, a solution so to speak, of what to do to avoid catastrophe. It's like the option clause in a business contract that allows you to reconsider a major purchase after twenty-four hours: the door that miraculously opens in the eleventh hour; the inner voice that tells you to turn left instead of right on your way home, thus avoiding a traffic accident. In a Prophecy, the end result may be conveyed, not fated—if the urging and prompting of Prophecy are heeded—and the results are transformative.

So don't get hung up on dates, earthquakes, shifting plates, and volcanic explosions. That's just the drama of the story to get you to change. The story is dramatic so that you won't forget it, so that it is imbedded in your memory. Prophecy is not prediction! Get the point? ⚜

The Ever Present Now: **Timing and Timelines**
Timing and Prophecy is perhaps one of the most difficult aspects to understand. Because the prophesied events are possibility, not probability, the timing of these events is always ambiguous if they do indeed occur and are not simply lessened or ameliorated. Prophecy is an emotional word picture that is intended to astonish and surprise and even incite deep-seeded concern. This process rouses suppressed, unconscious fears that we may hold or not be aware of, and this spiritual route accedes to their recognition, transmutation, and inevitable release. Of course, along with this inner process, we begin to change the way we perceive our lives and the situations and

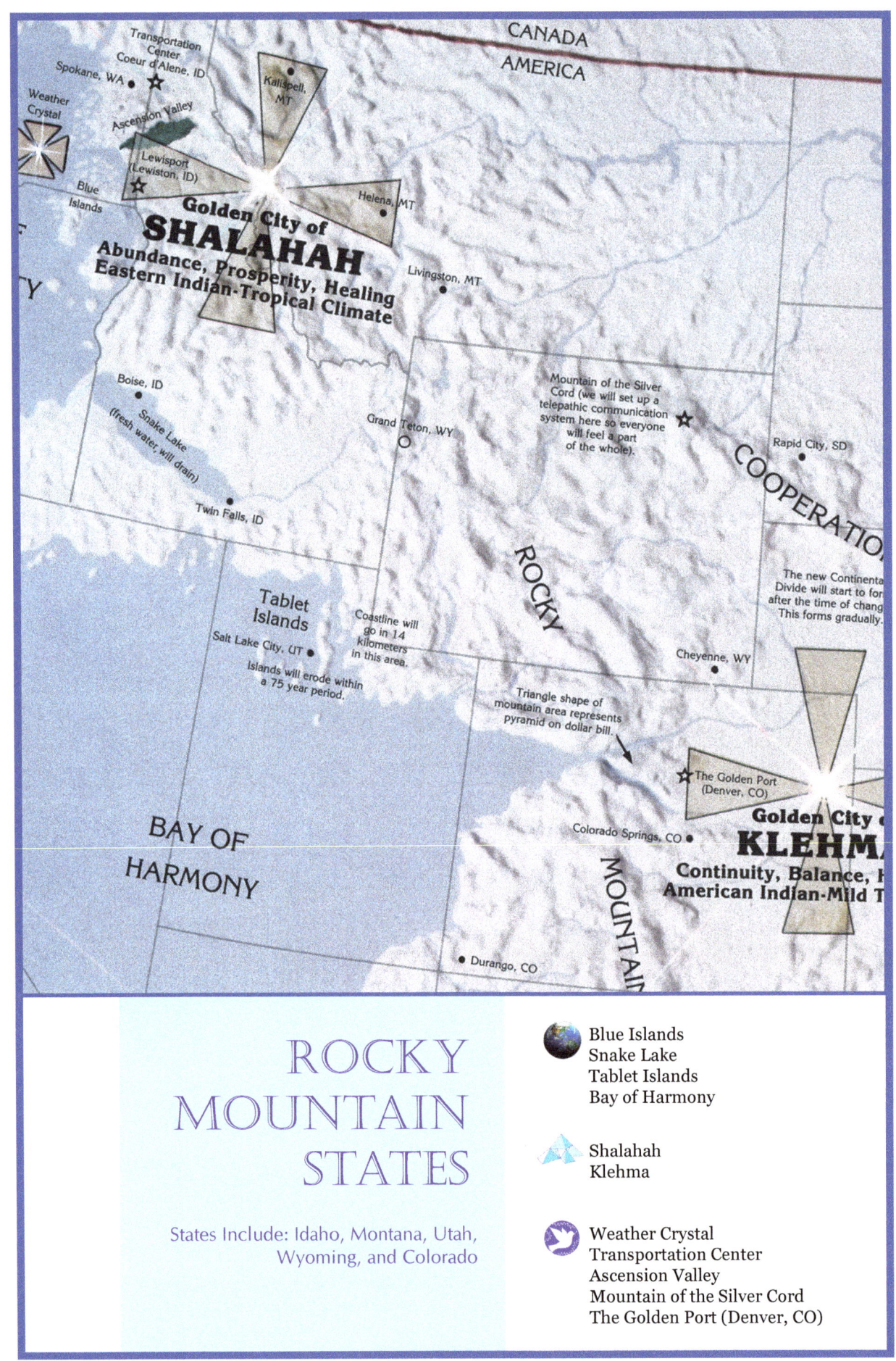# ROCKY MOUNTAIN STATES

States Include: Idaho, Montana, Utah, Wyoming, and Colorado

- Blue Islands
  Snake Lake
  Tablet Islands
  Bay of Harmony

- Shalahah
  Klehma

- Weather Crystal
  Transportation Center
  Ascension Valley
  Mountain of the Silver Cord
  The Golden Port (Denver, CO)

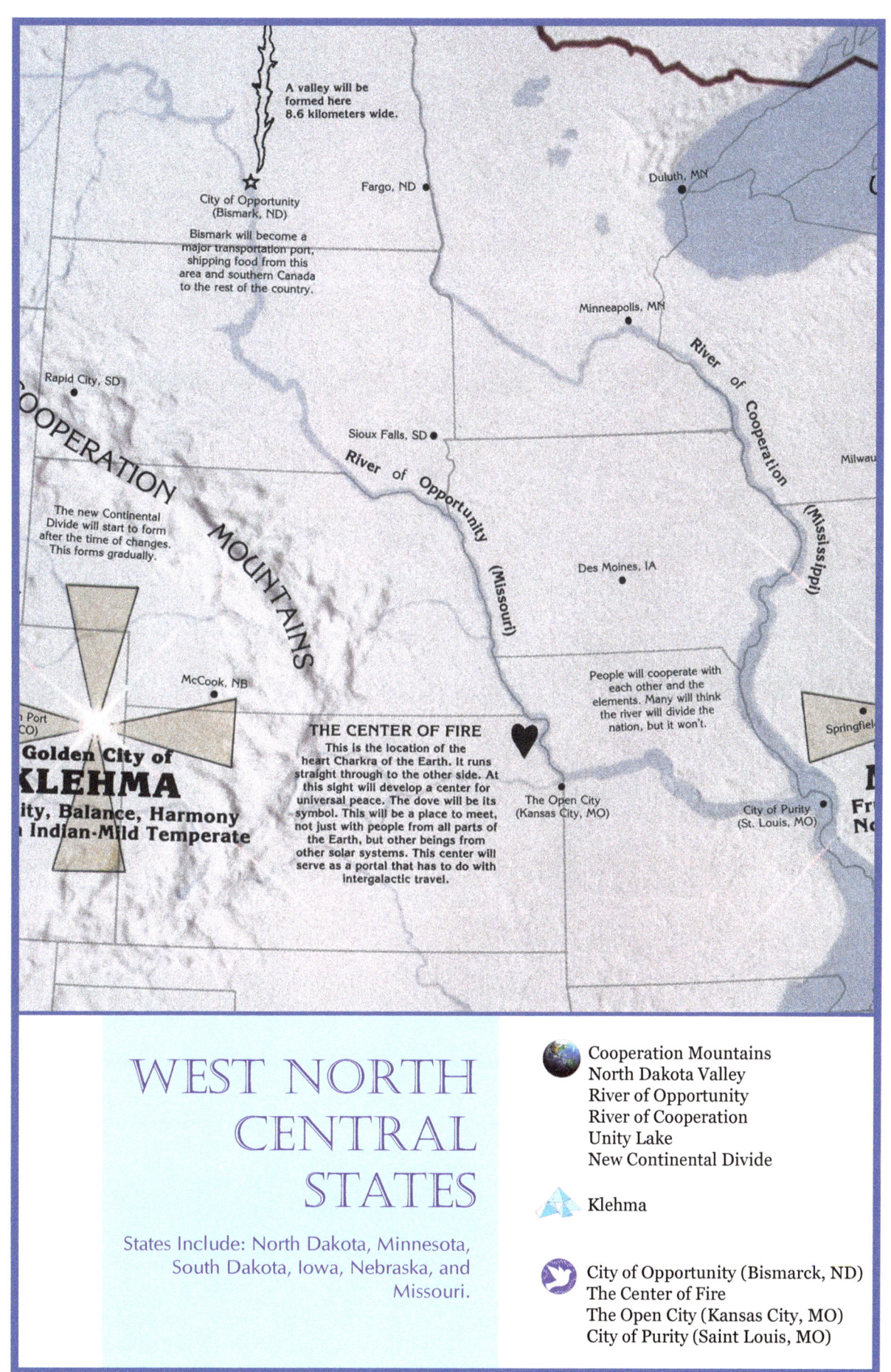

WEST NORTH CENTRAL STATES

States Include: North Dakota, Minnesota, South Dakota, Iowa, Nebraska, and Missouri.

- Cooperation Mountains
- North Dakota Valley
- River of Opportunity
- River of Cooperation
- Unity Lake
- New Continental Divide

- Klehma

- City of Opportunity (Bismarck, ND)
- The Center of Fire
- The Open City (Kansas City, MO)
- City of Purity (Saint Louis, MO)

SOUTH CENTRAL STATES

States Include: Oklahoma, Arkansas, Texas, and Louisiana

- Delta Area
- Harvest Bay
- Celebration Island

- The Silver City (Albuquerque, NM)

circumstances that surround us. From this viewpoint, Prophecy is a remarkable healing tool.

The Spiritual Teachers do not relate at all to our perception of time! There may be several reasons for this. First, their outlook comes from a different dimension altogether, and when they speak or recognize our perception of "time"—which is nonlinear to them—"time" morphs into an *ever present now*. Many occasions we've asked, "When will the changes begin?" And they most always reply, "The time is now!"

Second, most Spiritual Teachers will rarely, if ever, interfere with our karma; so warning us about events that will happen in the next year or so is really not their intention. After years of working with their teachings, I have found that they often edify the universal, or natural laws, and will suggest how we can best apply them for our individual spiritual growth and enlightenment. Since Ascended Masters are free from the wheel of karmic retribution, they clearly understand our distinctive free will and the innate power of personal choice, and they rarely, if ever, will med-

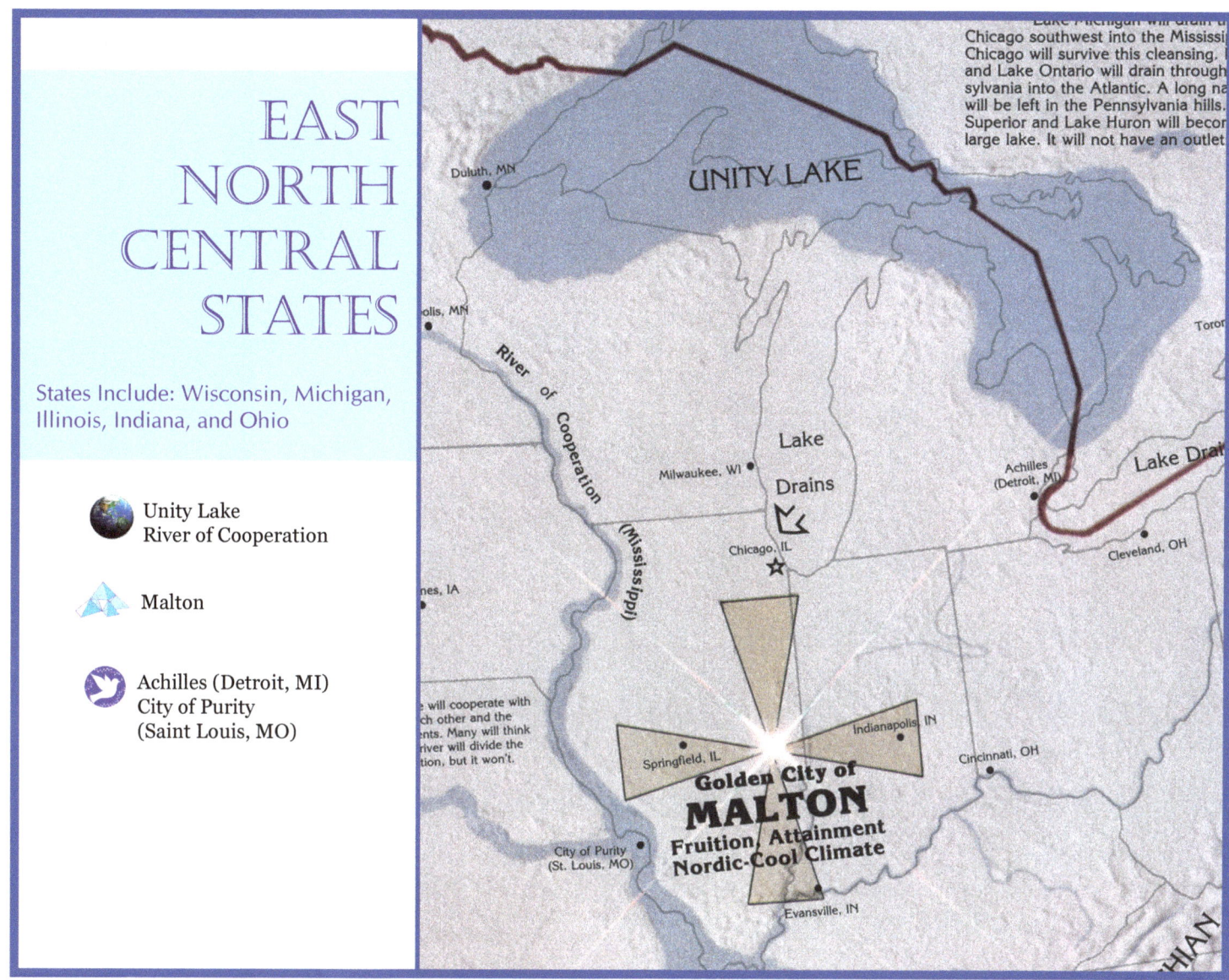

EAST NORTH CENTRAL STATES

States Include: Wisconsin, Michigan, Illinois, Indiana, and Ohio

- Unity Lake / River of Cooperation
- Malton
- Achilles (Detroit, MI) / City of Purity (Saint Louis, MO)

dle. It seems we are here on Earth to learn through vital, personal experience which is fundamental to our evolution and empowerment.

In my early days of trance-work, they clarified their position on the use of dates for prophesied events, and at that time it obviously flew above our heads. But my recent re-examination of this material illuminates and explains their use of dates. They describe dates as "reference points." A reference point is a position in the landscape of time, the ever present now, where one can evaluate or weigh probability. Ideally, this point is positioned so we can initiate comparison between actual events, prophesied events, and then weigh the possibility of their timing.

The I AM America Teachings do not place an emphasis on the calculated time of prophesied events; rather, their possible transformation and change. With this in mind, the few dates that we've published in our materials were given to compare actual events to assess possible outcome. I have no doubt that when the Master Teachers first shared the I AM America Maps, they had grave concern regarding Earth's possible future into the 90s and the early 2000s. Fortunately, we are obviously doing much better. This might be due to the overall growth of lightworkers, the nonstop prayers and ceremonies for Earth and humanity enjoined by all faiths and denominations, and the growth of the golden light on Earth from the Galactic Center. I also think that because we engaged in purposeful yet arduous scrutiny of Earth Changes possibility throughout this entire time frame, we were able to shape-shift a different reality.

Clearly, it isn't over yet. Every week I update my Earth Changes blog with the most recent information on global warming and climate change, alongside earthquake and extreme weather events. Sadly, this aspect regarding the prophesied events is escalating, and the latest terminology regarding Arctic ice-melt

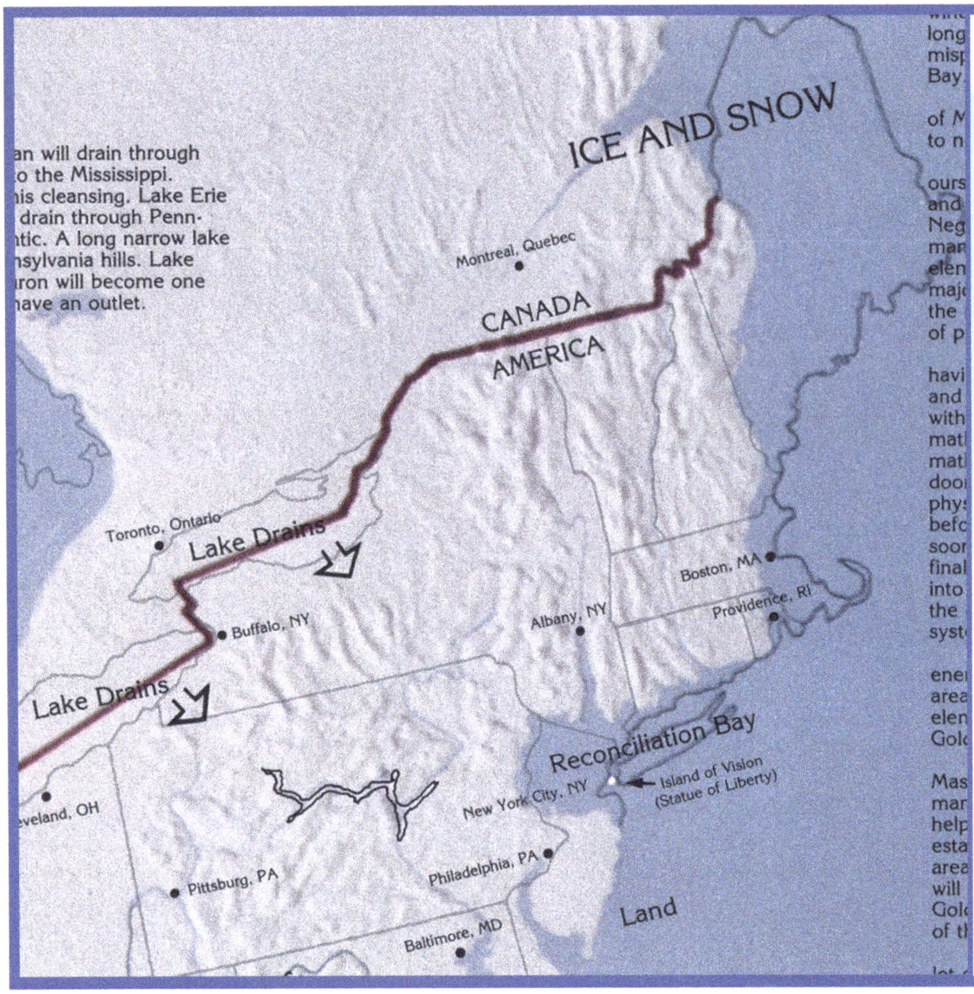

NORTHEAST STATES

States Include: Maine, New Hampshire, Vermont, Massachusetts, Connecticut, Rhode Island, New York, New Jersey, and Pennsylvania

🌎 Lake Ontario
Lake Erie
Upper Lake (PA)
Reconciliation Bay

🕊 Island of Vision

is now scientifically recognized as, "Rapid Climate Transformation." Many years ago I interviewed with a newspaper in Atlanta, Georgia. The reporter was keen and responsive to the message of Earth Changes Prophecy and asked me this question, "So if I understand you correctly, we should never disregard Prophecy; it is a spiritual teaching?" I whole-heartedly agreed and reminded her that it was almost impossible to update a Prophecy or alter the impact that its story may have on the consciousness of the listener. I smiled when I received a copy of her article, it was titled, "The Perpetual Warning." ⚜

Prophecies for the I AM America Map
Compiled from New World Wisdom, Book One
The United States and Canada—known by the Spiritual Teachers as the "I AM America Map."

United States
Every state in the United States will be affected by the changes. The first events start in the year 1992 and will continue for hundreds of years. During 1992, these events took place:

A 6.8 earthquake in eastern Turkey killed 500 people.

One of the most destructive hurricanes ever, Hurricane Andrew, raged through the Bahamas, Florida, and Louisiana.

Hurricane Iniki struck the State of Hawaii, Kauai and Oahu.

1992 Tornado Outbreak: November 21–23, eastern

Lake Michigan will drain through Chicago southwest into the Mississippi. Chicago will survive this cleansing. Lake Erie and Lake Ontario will drain through Pennsylvania into the Atlantic. A long narrow lake will be left in the Pennsylvania hills. Lake Superior and Lake Huron will become one large lake. It will not have an outlet.

GREAT LAKES

Lake Superior, Lake Michigan, Lake Huron, Lake Erie, and Lake Ontario

Unity Lake
River of Cooperation
Upper Lake (PA)

Achilles (Detroit, MI)

and midwestern US. This outbreak was the largest and longest on record.

All of the four elements will be involved during the changes: fire, water, earth, and air.

Prior to a mega-quake in Oregon, Earth is bombarded by a massive shower of meteorites. These numerous impacts cause an ash cloud to envelope Earth's atmosphere, and tremendous rainfall. We experience massive flooding all over the world. Rivers, seas, and oceans swell.

The increased water causes increased pressure on fault lines. This leads to massive earthquakes and mega-quakes.

After the strike of an asteroid, there will be many earthquakes in California. This will lead to massive earth movements that inevitably leave most of California under the Pacific Ocean. The Sierra-Nevada Mountains will become islands, and one large island containing the Lake Tahoe area, Yosemite Park, and Sequoia National Park will be formed. A peninsula of land will extend out to Mount Shasta extending near Crater Lake, Oregon. This peninsula later erodes into a series of islands. Surrounding the largest island that is fashioned from the changes in California—Gibraltar Island—are many smaller islands. These are called "The Pathway Islands" They are very stable geophysically and will exist for hundreds of years. These islands exist to the north between Gibraltar Island and the Mount Shasta peninsula. The Baja Peninsula slowly erodes into a series of islands which will be known as the "Diamond Islands."

In the Pacific Northwest, ash from exploding volcanoes will hide the sun for two years. Seattle will be covered by water. A new coastline in the Pacific Northwest covers most of the current state of Washington. This is due to a series of earthquakes and mega-quakes that occur throughout Washington and Oregon. Much of Oregon sinks due to a massive earth-

I AM AMERICA ATLAS *27*

quake. The new coastline extends west to La Grande, Oregon, where the Wallowa Mountains become a new chain of islands. The Cascade Range of mountains becomes islands. Mount Baker and Mount Rainier become islands. During the changes, Oregon becomes engulfed by the Pacific Ocean. This happens in several stages: first, the ocean laps into the Willamette Valley; then the ocean moves east, beyond the Cascade Range; the Wallowa Mountains become the new coastline near La Grande, Oregon. The Blue Mountains and the Wallowa Mountains become chains of islands.

The new Continental Divide of the United States starts near Livingston, Montana, as a new range of mountains, known as The Cooperation Mountains. The Bay of Harmony, which is formed by the Pacific Ocean covering much of California, Nevada, and the northwestern and western portions of Arizona, is a very shallow bay. It is almost impossible to navigate. The beaches are very gradual and the water is not deep, limiting the ships and boats in this bay. However, the waters of the Bay of Harmony create coastline cities of Phoenix and Sedona, Arizona.

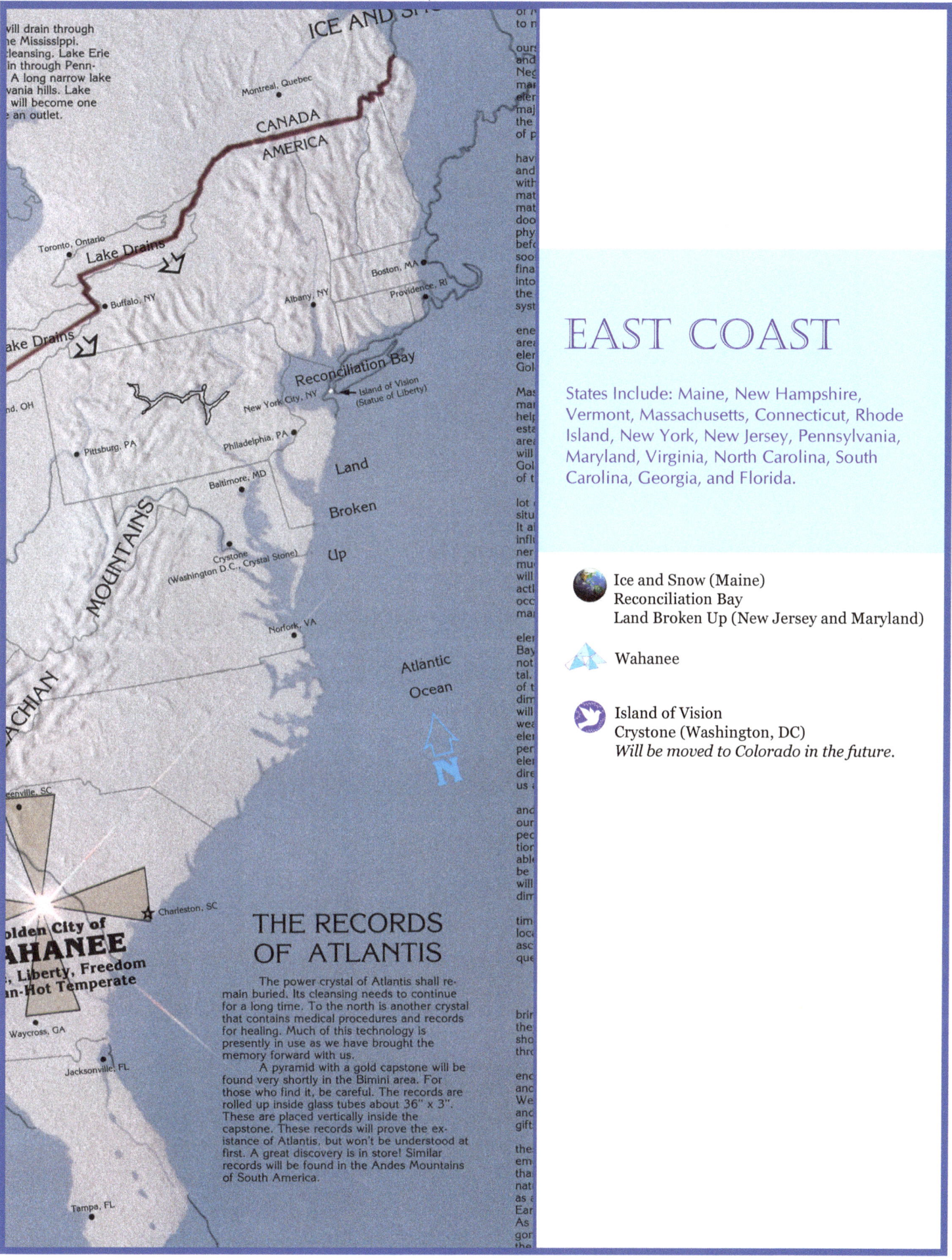

EAST COAST

States Include: Maine, New Hampshire, Vermont, Massachusetts, Connecticut, Rhode Island, New York, New Jersey, Pennsylvania, Maryland, Virginia, North Carolina, South Carolina, Georgia, and Florida.

- 🌎 Ice and Snow (Maine)
  Reconciliation Bay
  Land Broken Up (New Jersey and Maryland)

- 🔺 Wahanee

- 🕊 Island of Vision
  Crystone (Washington, DC)
  Will be moved to Colorado in the future.

THE RECORDS OF ATLANTIS

The power crystal of Atlantis shall remain buried. Its cleansing needs to continue for a long time. To the north is another crystal that contains medical procedures and records for healing. Much of this technology is presently in use as we have brought the memory forward with us.

A pyramid with a gold capstone will be found very shortly in the Bimini area. For those who find it, be careful. The records are rolled up inside glass tubes about 36" x 3". These are placed vertically inside the capstone. These records will prove the existance of Atlantis, but won't be understood at first. A great discovery is in store! Similar records will be found in the Andes Mountains of South America.

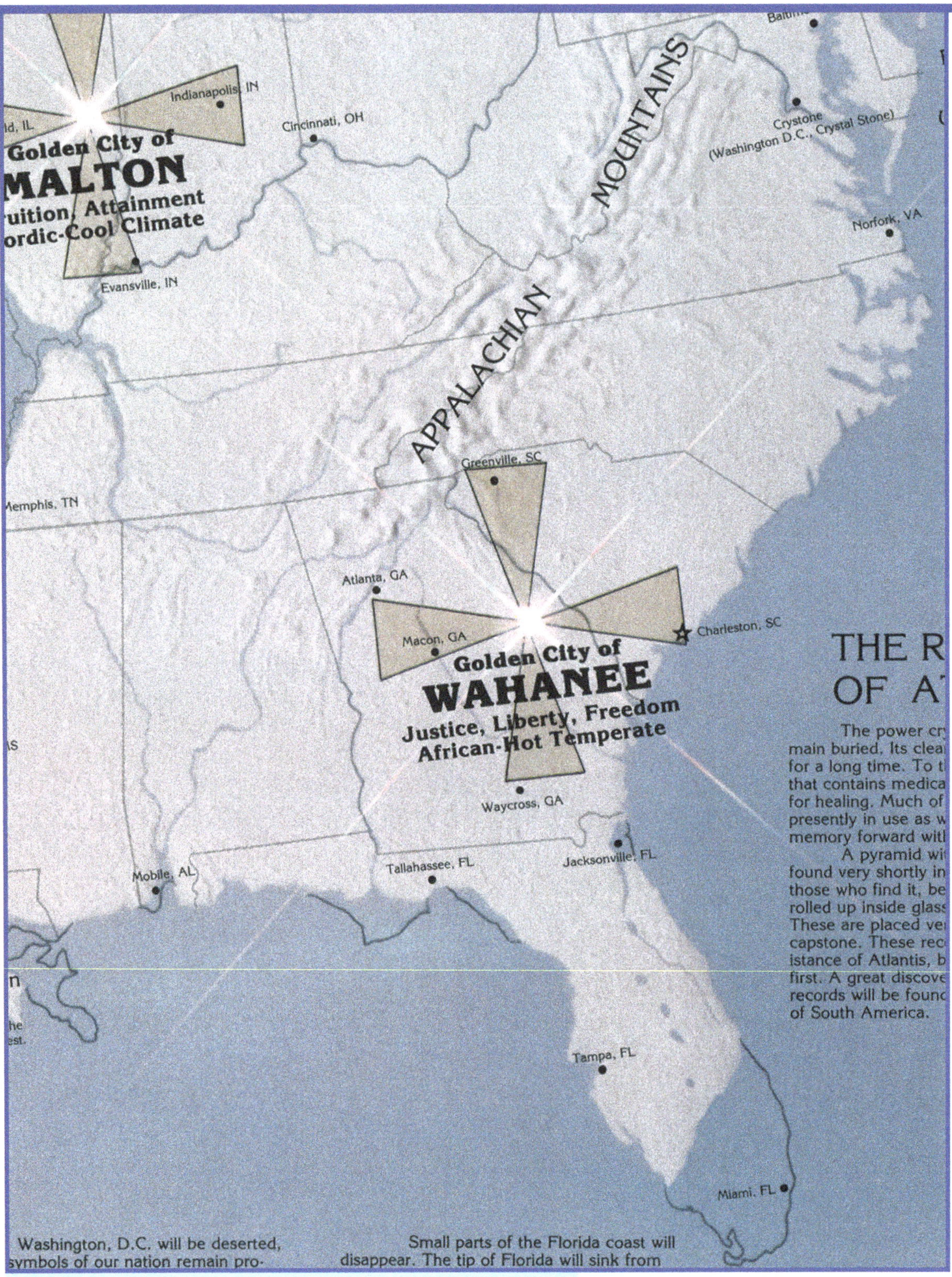

SOUTHEAST STATES

States Include: Kentucky, West Virginia, Virginia, Maryland, Tennessee, North Carolina, Mississippi, Alabama, Georgia, and Florida.

 Florida (Southern Florida under water.)

 Wahanee
Malton

 Crystone (Washington, DC)
Appalachian Mountains: *Endure the changes.*
Celebration Island
Records of Atlantis: *Off Florida East Coast.*

From the Bay of Harmony, a river passage opens to Denver, Colorado. Denver's proximity to this river passage and the new ocean coastline help it to prosper as a seaport city in the New Times. A new ocean bay will be formed west of Denver, Colorado. Denver will not be affected much by the Earth Changes; however it will feel tremendous earthquakes. Most of Utah will eventually be under water. The range of mountains—the Wasatch Range—becomes a series of islands that will be renamed "The Tablet Islands."

The lands in eastern Montana as well as North and South Dakota experience very few changes. A new Continental Divide forms. Starting in central Canada, this range of mountains follows the flow of the River of Cooperation (new Mississippi River), extends into Kansas, as far south to present New Mexico. At the beginning of the mouth of the River of Cooperation, it is almost two miles wide. The Missouri and Mississippi Rivers eventually merge and become one large river, known as the "River of Cooperation."

The Mississippi and Missouri Rivers flood. The Mississippi River will almost cut the nation in two. The Mississippi River forms a large bay covering large portions of Texas. Houston and Corpus Christi are under ocean waters. The newly widened banks of the Mississippi River cause the river to be named "The River of Cooperation." Because this becomes one of the major sources of fresh water in the nation, this large river becomes a major source of irrigation water in the United States. Areas along the River of Cooperation become the new agricultural areas of the nation. Most of the state of Louisiana becomes a salt-water bay. Baton Rouge is under water, along with New Orleans. Eventually a small island appears near Lafayette, Louisiana, becoming a delta area.

Lake Michigan drains near Chicago, Illinois, further creating a bay in Texas. Lake Michigan drains, and the remaining Great Lakes change and form one large lake—Unity Lake. Chicago will experience tremendous flooding during the changes, due to the drainage of Lake Michigan, but it will survive the changes.

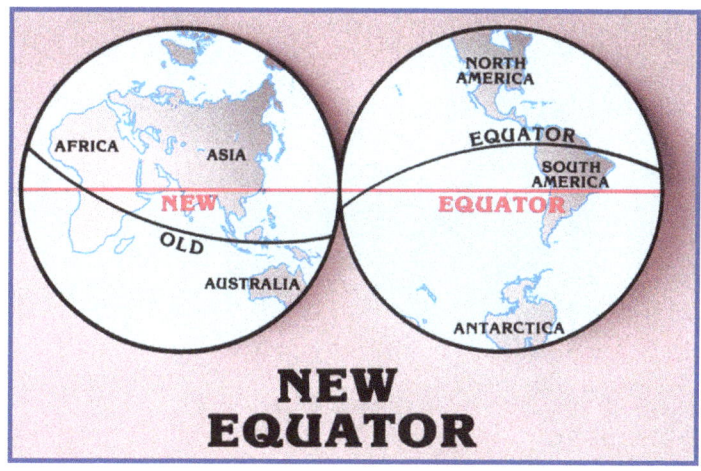

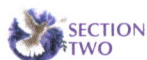

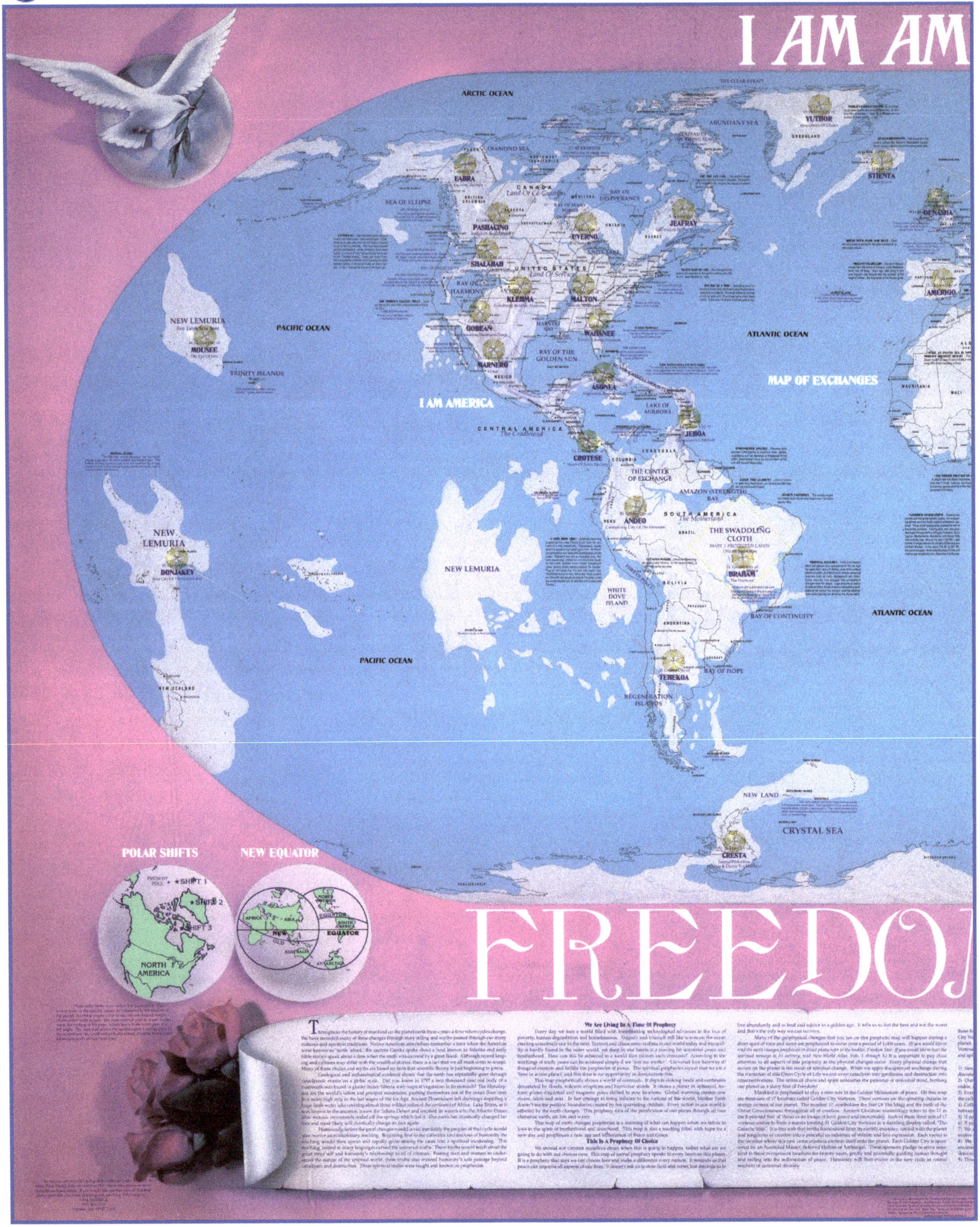
I AM AM
FREEDO
ARCTIC OCEAN
PACIFIC OCEAN
ATLANTIC OCEAN
MAP OF EXCHANGES
I AM AMERICA
NEW LEMURIA
MOUSEE
TRINITY ISLANDS
DONJAKEY
NEW ZEALAND
CANADA
UNITED STATES
CENTRAL AMERICA
SOUTH AMERICA
THE SWADDLING CLOTH
WHITE DOVE ISLAND
BAY OF CONTINUITY
BAY OF HOPE
REGENERATION ISLANDS
NEW LAND
CRYSTAL SEA
GRESTA
YUTHOR
STIENTA
FABRA
PASHACINO
SHALAHAH
KLEHMA
GOBEAN
MARNERO
WAHANEE
MALTON
JEAFRAY
UVERNO
ASONEA
JEHOA
CROTESE
ANDEO
BRAHAM
TEHEKOA
AMERIGO
ABUNDANT SEA
SEA OF ELLIPSE
BAY OF THE GOLDEN SUN
LAKE OF MIRRORS
THE CENTER OF EXCHANGE
AMAZON (STRENGTH) BAY
POLAR SHIFTS
NEW EQUATOR
PRESENT POLE
SHIFT 1
SHIFT 2
SHIFT 3
NORTH AMERICA
EQUATOR
AFRICA
ASIA
NEW
OLD
AUSTRALIA
ANTARCTICA

CANADA

Provinces and Territories: Yukon, British Columbia, Alberta, Saskatchewan, Manitoba, Northwest Territories, Nunavut, Ontario, Quebec, Newfoundland and Labrador, Nova Scotia, Prince Edward Island, and New Brunswick.

- Diamond Sea
- Vancouver Island
- Bay of Many Forms
- Bay of Deliverence
- Plateau of the Rising Sun
- Abundant Sea
- Great River
- Unity Lake

- Eabra
- Pashacino
- Uverno
- Jeafray

- Thirteen Star seeds

On the east coast of the United States, there will be high winds. Northern portions of Maine will be covered by ice. During the changes, Washington, D.C., will experience strong, cold, frigid winds. A large energy Vortex currently covers New York City, extending into Connecticut, New Jersey, and Pennsylvania. During the Times of Changes, the energy of this Vortex—not a Golden City Vortex—becomes "misplaced." (During the changes many Vortices and lei-lines move and shift, along with "Earth Changes." However, this word from the trance-scripts indicates a misuse of energy. Could it be a nuclear disaster?) This causes a constant wind to blow throughout this area, which will become covered by water, and nothing will live there for some time after the major Earth Changes. Also, no islands will form. This bay will be named, "Reconciliation Bay."

After the changes, Washington, D.C., will cease to be the capital and political center for the United States. However, for many centuries into the New Times, the symbols that are contained there (i.e., Washington Monument, the Capitol Building, etc.) will be preserved. In the future, many will travel to view the symbols and their historical significance.

In Maine and parts of New England, because of constant thawing and freezing, much of the land erodes. The land and the climate become unstable. There will be an earthquake in either Lake Erie or Lake Ontario.

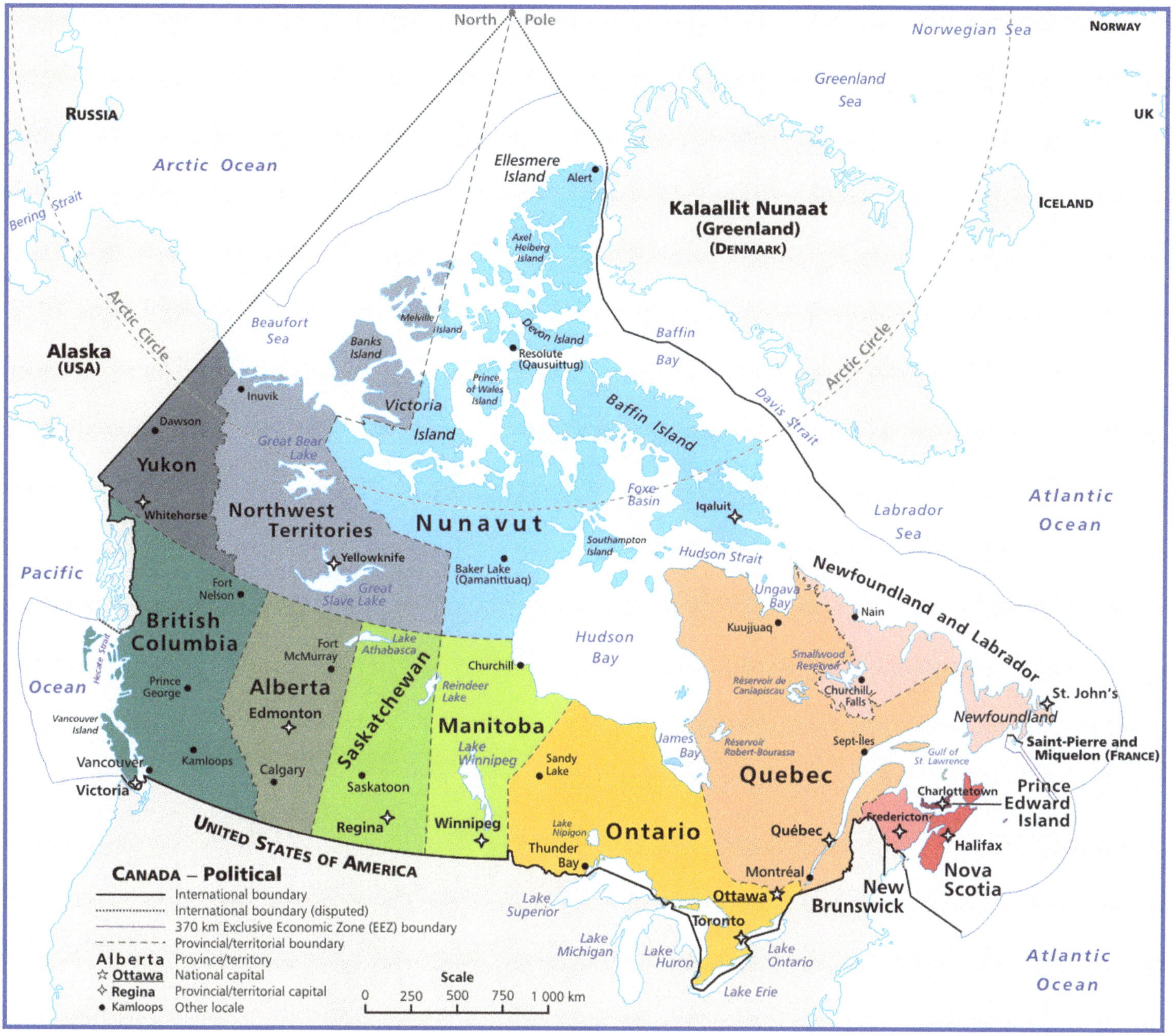

[Above: *Canada Map.*[1]]

This massive quake will inevitably lead to the sinking of land around Washington, D. C.

The east coast of the United States does not have major earthquakes; however, much of the land breaks up into small islands due to flooding and high winds. In the New Times, the east coast will be peppered with many small islands.

Due to global warming and climate change, the United States will experience the "see-sawing" of the four seasons. Winter can become summer, and spring can immediately become fall. Hurricanes and tornadoes will become common weather anomalies during the Time of Change. ⚜

Prophecies for the I AM America Map

Compiled from New World Wisdom, Book One

Alaska and Canada

In Alaska, the North Slope melts due to rising seas and global warming. Alaska will also be hit by several tsunamis. Overall, the climate gets warmer in Alaska. When the ice melts, there will be remnants of ancient civilizations that underwent

I AM AMERICA ATLAS 35

GREENLAND

- Abundant Sea
  The Clear Strait
- Yuthor

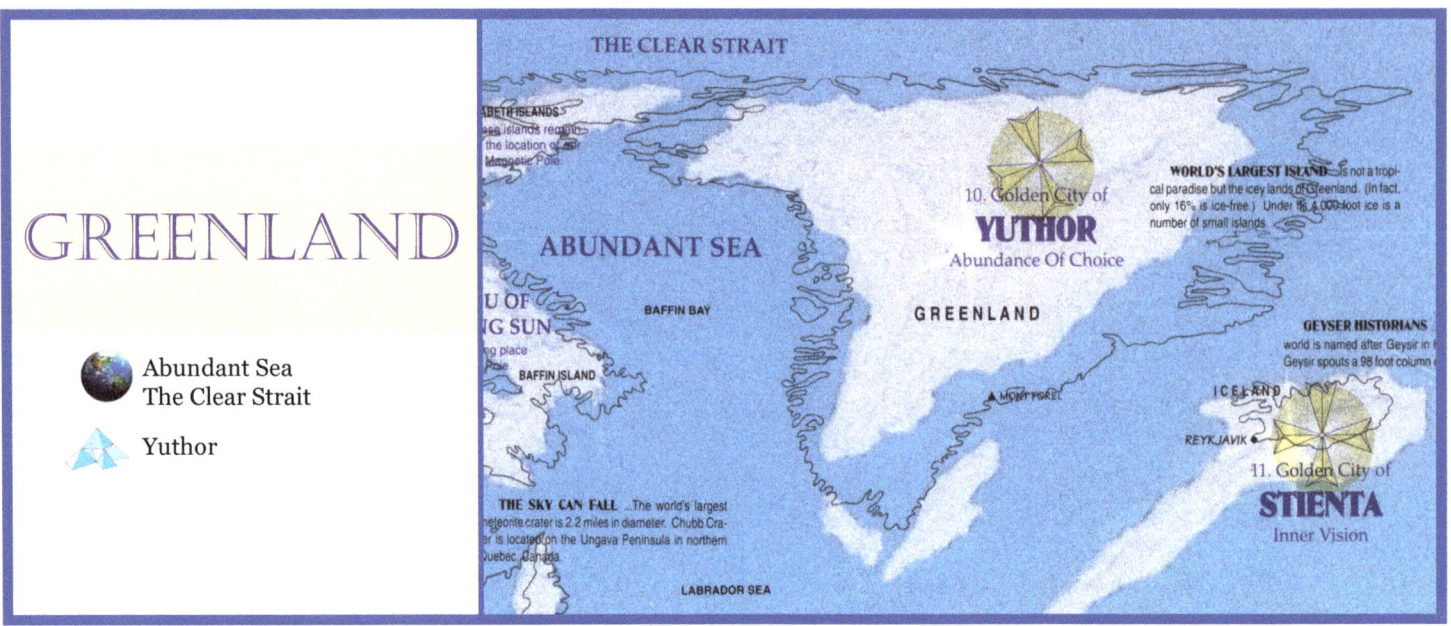

massive Earth Changes in the past. The western coastline of Canada will change. In the future, this change will allow for better transportation routes to Alaska. The Canadian territories of the Northwest Territories and Nunavut, and the two Canadian islands of Victoria Island and Baffin Island are prophesied to break into many islands. The western coast of the Canadian province of British Columbia is prophesied to sink, and the Rocky Mountains define its new coastline following the present-day Coast Mountains. Southern Alaska and the city Juneau are also prophesied to sink in this Earth Change. The Kenai Peninsula meets a similar fate; however, the Alaskan city of Anchorage remains. The Aleutian Islands are prophesied to disappear into the Pacific Ocean. The Yukon Territory loses land on its northern coastline due to global warming. A new bay forms in Alaska and the Yukon Territory and floods the Yukon Flats, leaving the Alaskan town of Fairbanks a seaport town in the New Times. The Province of Alberta remains unscathed during the Earth Changes.

The Saint Lawrence River and gulf are prophesied to widen significantly during the Time of Change leaving the cities of Ottawa, Montréal, and Quebec under water. It is also prophesied that Northern Quebec (Ungava Peninsula) breaks into small islands. Labrador becomes an island. Newfoundland has few changes; however, global warming raises ocean waters, leaving many of its southeast coastal land and towns under water.

Greenland

During the Time of Change and due to global warming, it is prophesied that Earth's oceans will contain little or no fish; however, the oceans near Greenland will retain remnants of this precious sea life. The lands of Greenland are prophesied to thaw, sizably reducing the island's size and coastlines.

Prophecies for the I AM America Map

Compiled from New World Wisdom, Book One
Mexico, Central America, and South America

Massive earthquakes are prophesied to break Mexico's Baja Peninsula into a series of islands. These same earth movements are prophesied to ripple the entire west coast of South America, causing enormous earth slides of coastal lands into the Pacific Ocean and submerging the Yucatan Peninsula. Several hundred years later, movements of tectonic plates form the Cooperation Mountains. This new range of mountains is prophesied to exist from the United States, through Central America, and extend into South America. Another mountain range is prophesied to rise during the Time of Change, comprising the Yucatan Peninsula, the West Indies, Cuba, Puerto Rico, and the Virgin Islands. This mountainous chain—the Silver Crystal Mountains—will connect Cuba and Venezuela and enclose the Caribbean Sea.

[Right: *Mexico Map.*[2]]

MEXICO
CENTRAL AMERICA

Countries: Mexico, Belize, Costa Rica, El Salvador, Guatemala, Honduras, Nicaragua, Panama, Cuba, Haiti, Dominican Republic, Puerto Rico, Jamaica, Trinidad and Tobago, Bahamas, Barbados, Virgin Islands, and Grenada.

 Diamond Islands
Bay of the Golden Sun
Silver Crystal Mountains
Lake of Mirrors

 Marnero
Asonea
Crotese
Jehoa

I AM AMERICA ATLAS 37

[Above: *Central America and the Caribbean*.³]

The ocean waters of the Caribbean Sea are prophesied to become one of the world's largest fresh-water seas in the future, and it is surrounded on all sides by this new ring of mountains.

Much of the west coast of South America is prophesied to change through volcanic, earthquake, and tsunami activity. Most of Chile is underwater, and Bolivia and Argentina comprise the new western coastline. Lima, Peru, becomes a coastline city. The lands of Patagonia and Argentina become a free-floating island as the southern tip of South America breaks into islands, with a larger island forming to the north of the Falkland Islands.

The Amazon River basin widens into a large bay, and Colombia has both a west coast that touches the Pacific Ocean and a small east coast, where the waters of the Atlantic Ocean lap. A large bay forms near Rio de Janeiro; however, several small islands form near this Brazilian city, known as the Islands of Southern Brazil.

I AM AMERICA ATLAS 39

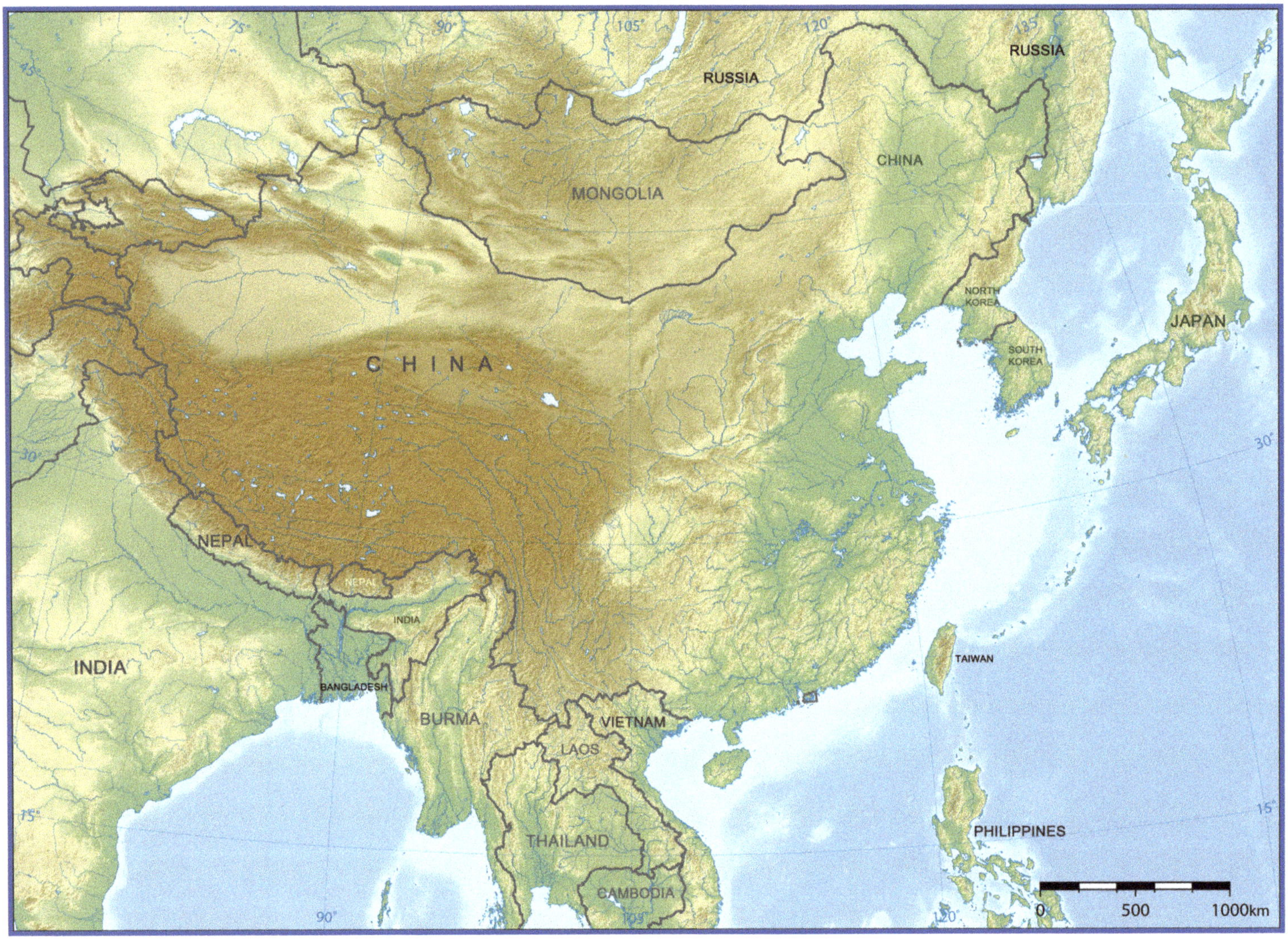

[Above: *East Asia Topographic Map*.4]

Prophecies for the Freedom Star World Map
Compiled from New World Wisdom, Book Two

Japan, Korea, China, Australia, and India are known by the Spiritual Teachers as "The Greening Map."

A large peninsula of land rises in the Sea of Okhotsk, and Sapporo, Japan, is located on its most southern coastline. This greatly reduces the size of the Kamchatka Peninsula, on both sides—to the west and the present-day Sea of Okhotsk, and to the east is the Bering Sea.

Due to planetary global warming, most of northern Russia is under water and breaks up into islands and peninsulas. The Stanovoy Mountain Range forms part of the new northern coastline in Russia and China. Beijing, China, is underwater.

Japan breaks into three smaller islands and suffers many tsunamis and earthquakes. Osaka and Tokyo are under the Pacific Ocean.

Both North and South Korea break into islands; however, the Golden City of Presching manifests over North Korea—which is a Golden City of the Angels.

Bangladesh and lands that border Bhutan and Nepal flood and eventually create a large bay—the Bay of Scented Flowers. Kanpur, India, is located on the coastline of this new bay. Ocean waters cover the Great Indian Desert. Pakistan is also deluged, and India now resembles a free-floating island, with a singular umbilical peninsula connecting it to mainland

EAST ASIA

Countries: China, Japan, Mongolia, North Korea, South Korea, and Taiwan.

- Land of Light
  Sea of Great Mercy
  Regeneration Bay
  Blazing Bay
  Lake of Deep Truth

- Presching
  Nomaking
  Arctura
  Gobi
  Zaskar

- Heavenly Islands
  Fertile Plain

Asia. Delhi and New Delhi are located on this unique peninsula of land.

The Himalayan Mountains rise to even higher elevations in the New Times.

A large river, almost like an ocean bay, forms in the center of India, between the Western Ghats and the Eastern Ghats. This becomes a sacred river for India, and its waters flow from the north, near the Golden City of Prana, to the south, and empty into the ocean. Bangalore becomes a coastal city on the west side of this large, river-like bay.

Large earth rifts open central China, forming the Great China Peninsula. Wuhan, China, is located on the northeast side of this large peninsula, and Chengdu, China, is under the waters of a new ocean bay to the west of this peninsula. Lanzhou, China, becomes a seaport city. The waters of what will be known as "The Blazing Bay" will cover Hanoi and most of Laos, including Da Nang. A large ridge of new mountains rises in the center of Laos and extends into China; this is known as "The Rim of Eternal Balance." Most of Thailand and Cambodia, which are to the west of this new chain of mountains, are underwater in the New Times, and parts of southern Myanmar (Burma) are also prophesied to be under the present-day Bay of Bengal.

Australia breaks into two halves, and Alice Springs becomes a seaport city. New lands rise in the Coral Reef and in the Coral Sea and connect to the eastern half of Australia. The central and southeastern coast-

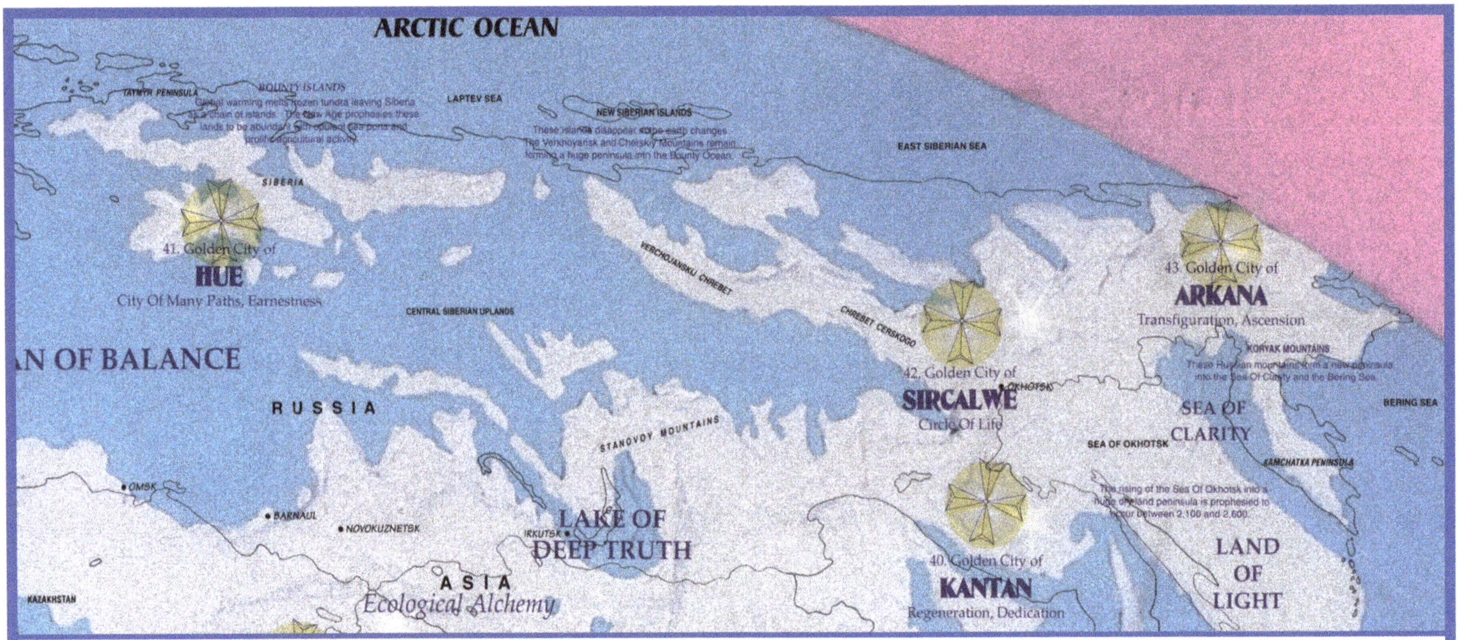

NORTH ASIA

Countries: Russia and Siberia.

- Land of Light
- Sea of Clarity
- Lake of Deep Truth
- Ocean of Balance

- Kantan
- Sircalwe
- Arkana
- Hue

[Right: *North Asia.*[5]]

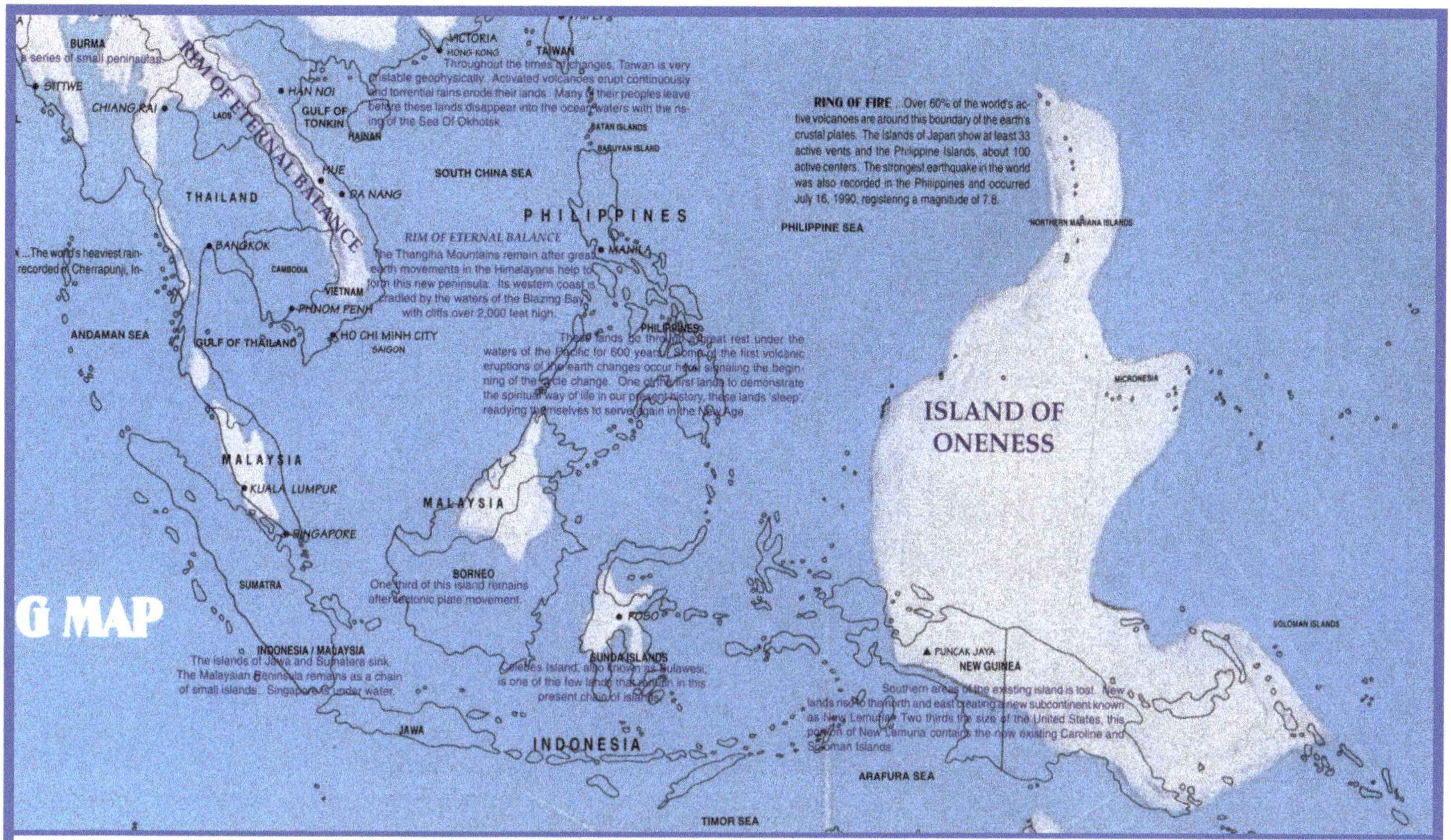

SOUTHEAST ASIA

Glory Ocean
Bay of Scented Flowers
Island of Oneness

Countries: Indonesia, East Malaysia, Singapore, Philippines, Cambodia, Laos, Myanmar (Burma), Thailand, West Malaysia, and Vietnam.

[Left: *Southeast Asia*.[6]]

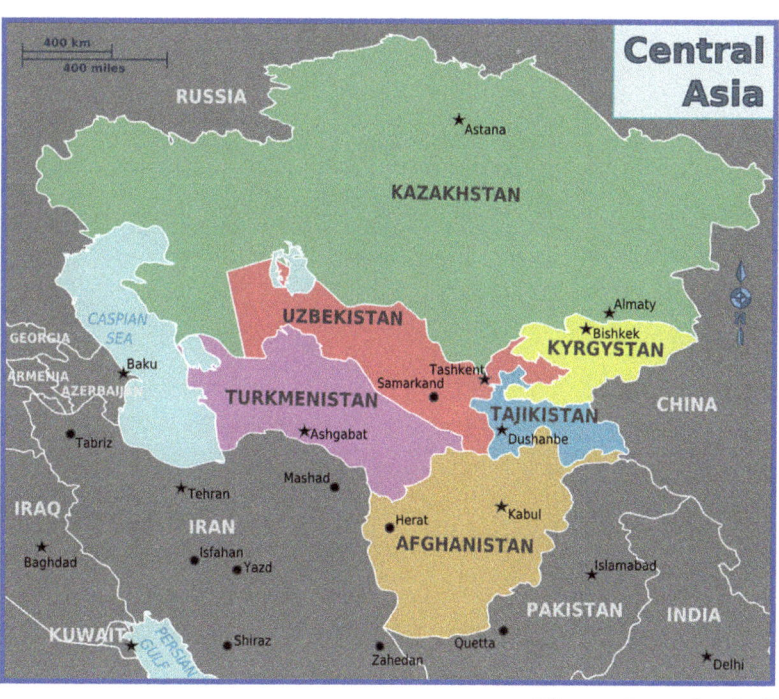

[Above: *Central Asia*.[7]]

I AM AMERICA ATLAS 43

CENTRAL ASIA

Countries: Afghanistan, Tajikistan, Kyrgystan, Uzbekistan, Kazakhstan, Russia, Mongolia, China, and Tibet (region).

Serenity Bay
Awakening Mountains
Ocean of Balance
Fertile Plain
Lake of Deep Truth
Sea of Calm

Adjatal
Purensk
Hue
Zaskar
Gobi

[Above: *The Region of Tibet.*[8]]

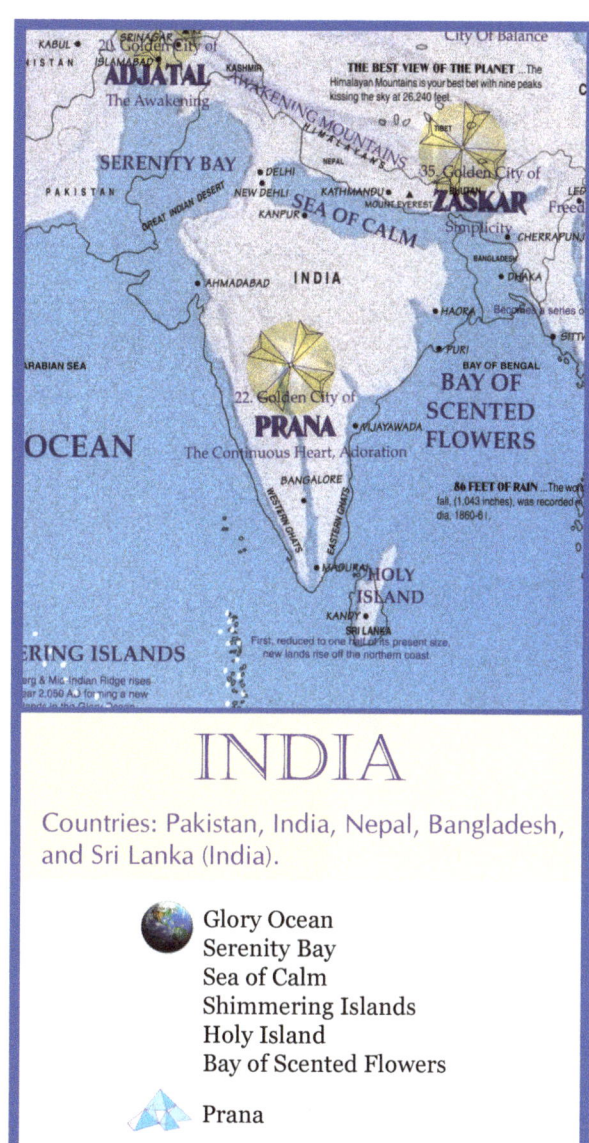

INDIA

Countries: Pakistan, India, Nepal, Bangladesh, and Sri Lanka (India).

- Glory Ocean
  Serenity Bay
  Sea of Calm
  Shimmering Islands
  Holy Island
  Bay of Scented Flowers

- Prana

lines of Australia remain unscathed during the Time of Change, however Melbourne and Adelaide suffer many changes and are nearly covered with the ocean waters with many tsunamis. Tasmania Island pivots to the northeast in a severe shift of tectonic plates. Hobart becomes the center of the new island.

This same tectonic shift literally reveals a new continent, prophesied to appear near New Zealand, and these new lands are four times the size of this present-day southwestern Pacific Ocean country. ⚜

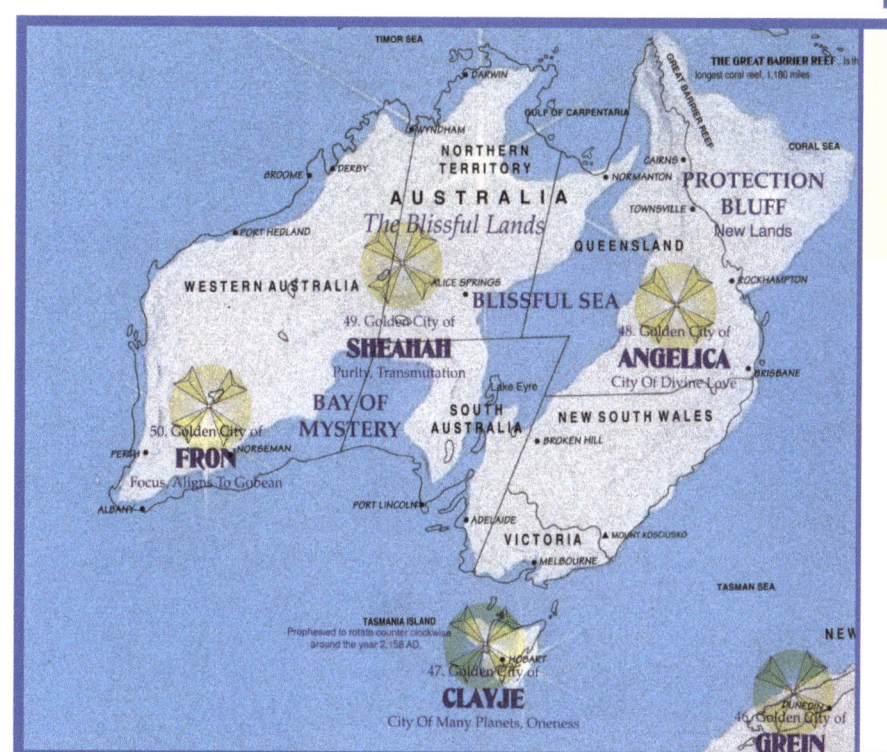

AUSTRALIA

Countries: Australia, New Zealand, and Tasmania (Island).

- Blissful Sea
  Bay of Mystery
  Protection Bluff

- Angelica
  Sheahah
  Fron
  Clayje
  Grein

I AM AMERICA ATLAS **45**

EUROPE

Countries: Austria, Belarus, Belgium, Bulgaria, Czech Republic, Denmark, Estonia, Finland, France, Germany, Greece, Hungary, Ireland, Italy, Latvia, Lithuania, Moldova, Netherlands, Norway, Poland, Portugal, Romania, Russia, Slovakia, Spain, Sweden, Switzerland, Turkey, and Ukraine.

Ocean of Balance
Sea of Grace

Gruecha
Denasha
Amerigo
Braun
Afrom
Ganakra

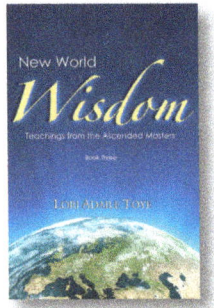

Prophecies for the Freedom Star World Map

Compiled from New World Wisdom, Book Three: Map of Exchanges

The Earth Changes Prophecies for Europe and Africa are perhaps the most alarming. As the Earth Changes close in the islands of Japan, Europe chimes in with riddling earthquakes and volcanic explosions, and the dawn of the new world is near.

In the prophecies, harmony is born as the perception of separation dissolves. As Earth accepts Fourth-Dimensional consciousness, alignment shifts the layers of the atmosphere and great tears occur in the

46   I AM AMERICA ATLAS

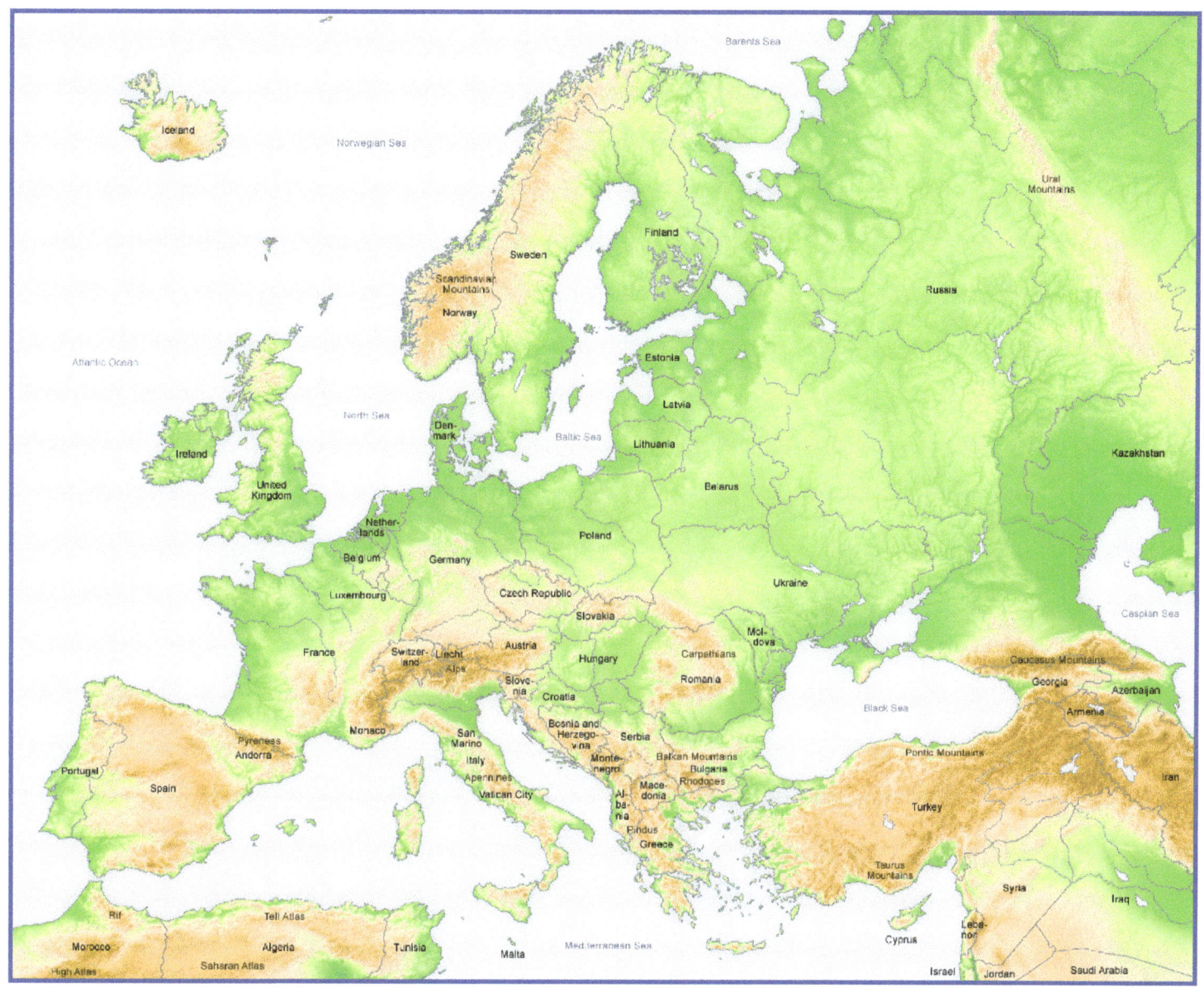

[Above: *Europe Topography*.9]

first three layers of the atmosphere. The phenomenon of ice sheeting occurs, as huge layers of ice (some as large as one mile thick) cover areas throughout Europe and Western Asia; some regions are ten square miles in diameter.

Europe and Africa develop into conscious lands of spiritual exchange, and a bridge of conscious collective thought extends a creative wave onward to reach the cosmos. Through this expansion and assimilation, the Earth and humanity receive Rays of universal healing. It is prophesied that two of the most focused Ascended Masters of healing assist: Lady Nada, Europe; Master Kuthumi, Africa.

The first event for Europe is prophesied to begin roughly after the sinking of the upper portion of Vancouver Island (Canada). The original reference point was around the year 2000—so this timeline has morphed into the future. Tectonic plates in the Atlantic Ocean grind, and a series of earthquakes strike northern Europe. Especially affected are Norway, Sweden, Finland, and Eastern Europe, with this earth movement felt far east into Moscow, Russia. Soon, torrential rains and windstorms are prophesied to hit the coast of England, France, and Spain. During the second shift of the pole, lands in England, France, and Germany are engulfed by the newly formed Ocean of Balance. Cities engulfed in this Earth Change are: Helsinki, Stockholm, Oslo, Copenhagen, London, Dublin, Hamburg, Berlin, Warsaw, Krakow, Amsterdam, Brussels, Paris, and Bordeaux.

Global warming shifts ice and glaciers. Combined with rising waters and erosion, the breakup of land forms many new islands in upper Ukraine, Sweden, Germany, and France. These cities become New Age

seaports for the Ocean of Balance: Glasgow, Sherffield, Manchester, Essen, Prague, Berdichev, and Galati. The lands of Iceland rise, with the Reykjanes Ridge raising in a tail-like shape on the southwestern portion of the island.

Tears in the ozone layer create sheets of ice crashing onto Eastern Europe and remaining parts of Poland and Germany. The thermohaline current of the Atlantic Ocean changes direction and temperature. This occurs for several years.

The next event for the Map of Exchanges is the formation of the Sea of Grace. This corresponds to the rising of the Himalayan Mountains into the Awakening Mountains. As this massive Earth Change occurs,

[Below: *Middle East*.[10]]

the Black Sea, the Azov Sea, the Caspian Sea, and the Aral Sea all form one large body of water—the Sea of Grace. Lands lost in this Earth Change are: sections of northern Turkey, parts of Iran and Afghanistan, Ukraine, eastern coastlines of Romania and Bulgaria and extending north to the Ural Mountains. Newly created seaport cities are: Zonguldak, Tehran (approximately 100 miles from the new coastline), Samarkan, Turkistan, Baikonur.

The Ural Mountains form into a large island, named the Shiny Pearl. This island becomes a trade center for the Ocean of Balance with seaport cities covering her coastline. Several of these present-day cities are: Kuybyshev, Ockenburg, Aktobe, and Sterlitamak. During the Earth Changes, many people will migrate to this island and it evolves into one of the most prosperous lands in the New Times.

At the close of the period of worldwide cataclysmic Earth Changes, many scientific experiments evolve into a major nuclear detonation. Through this man-made change, (which enlarges the Mediterranean and Red Seas), the Sea of Eternal Change is born. Her waters cover the lands of Libya, Egypt, Sudan, Israel, Jordan, and western Syria, the western coastline of Saudi Arabia, northern Ethiopia, and Tunisia. Much of Italy, Yugoslavia, Albania, all of Greece, and southern Turkey are covered by ocean waters. Cities lost in this change are: Rome, Venice, Naples, Barj, Tirana, Athens, Izmir, Thessaloniki, Tripoli, Tunis, Benghazi, Alexandria, Cairo, Yafo, Beirut, Tel Aviv, and Jerusalem. New Age seaports for the Sea of Eternal Change are: Ghat, Omdurman, Khartoum, Addis Ababa, and Asmera. On the eastern coast of the Sea of Change:

I AM AMERICA ATLAS *49*

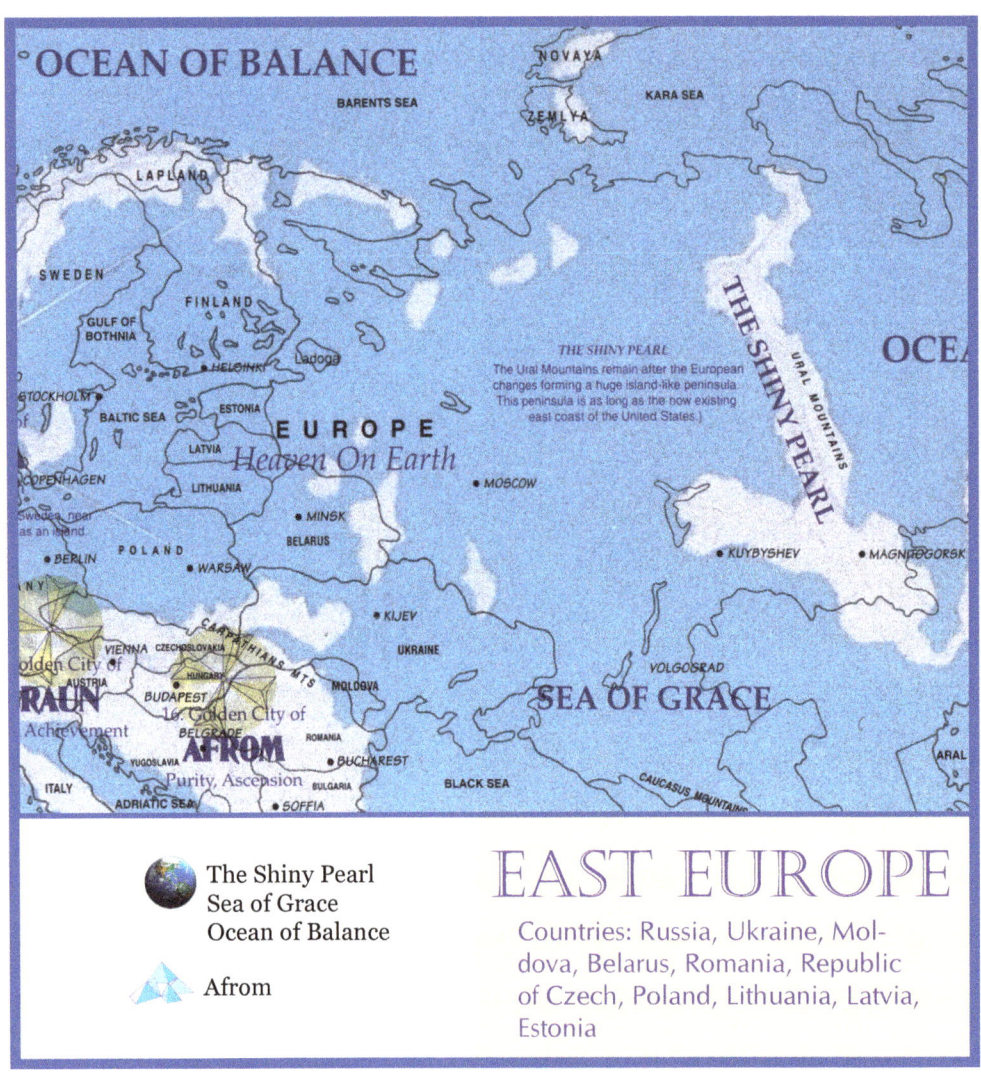

The Shiny Pearl
Sea of Grace
Ocean of Balance

Afrom

EAST EUROPE

Countries: Russia, Ukraine, Moldova, Belarus, Romania, Republic of Czech, Poland, Lithuania, Latvia, Estonia

Mecca, Medina, and Tobruk. More cities surrounding this new sea: Damascus, Aleppo, Sofia, Milan, and Turin.

Within the next twenty to thirty years, the Persian Gulf, (now renamed Bay of Holy Prayer), widens through more shifting of tectonic plates, forming another large bay into the Glory (Indian) Ocean. Lands lost are the western coastlines of Oman, Saudi Arabia, and Iraq. New Age coastline cities are: Riyadh and An Najaf. The Euphrates and Tigris River basin is covered with this new sea and the western coastline of Iran is buffered by the Zagros Mountains.

The final land movements for the Map of Exchanges begin when new lands enlarge the countries of Portugal and Spain. This original reference point was around 2100 AD, but is likely hundreds of years into the future. Lands enlarge the southern tip of Africa and the countries of Namibia and South Africa, and the Island of

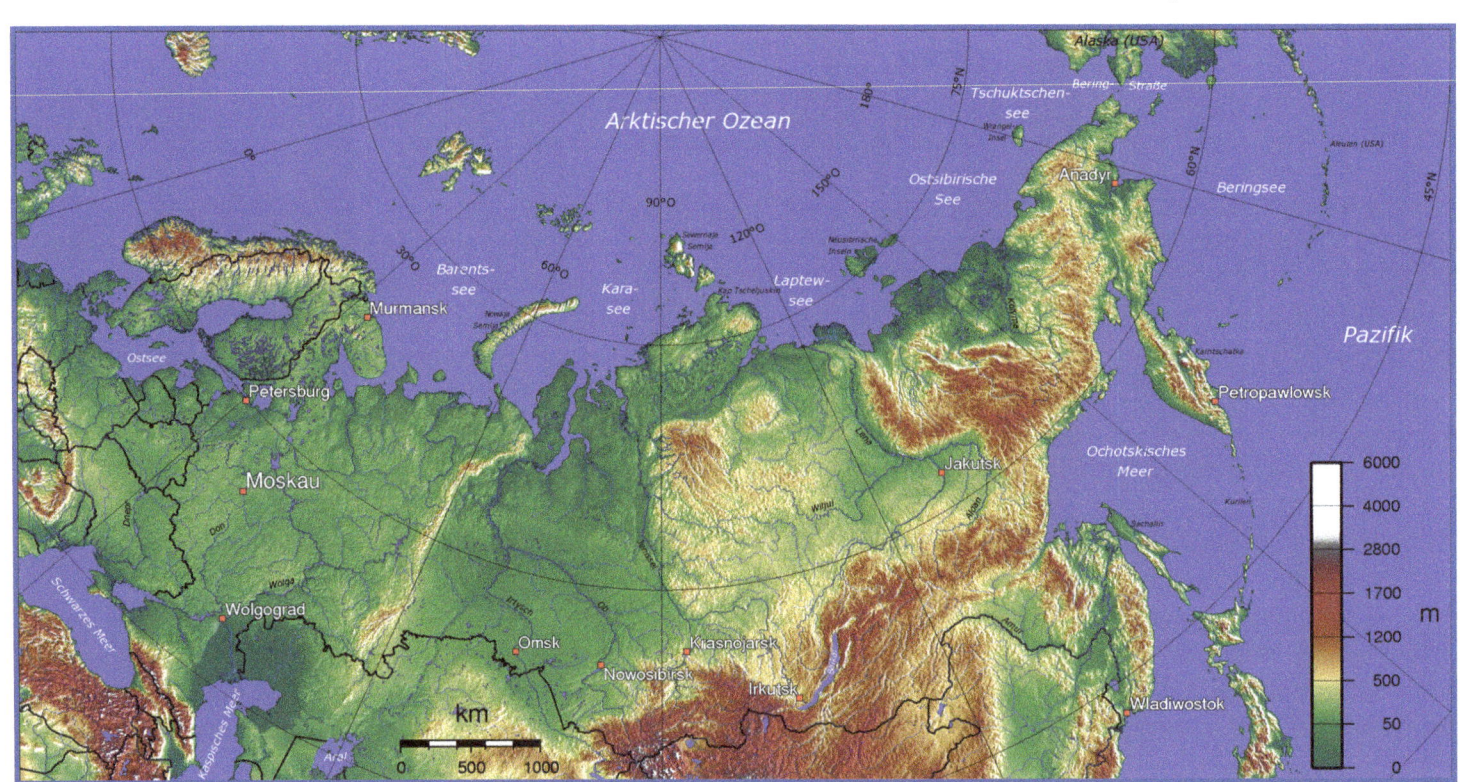

[Above: *Russia Topography*.[11]]

Madagascar doubles in size. With this movement, the western coastline of Africa falls into the Atlantic Ocean, creating new coastlines in the countries of Algeria, Morocco, submerging all of Western Sahara, Mauritania, and Senegal. A new coastal bay, the Bay of Protection, enlarges the Gulf of Guinea, cutting into central Africa's Nigeria and Cameroon. Central African Republic and the country of Chad now have coastlines on the Atlantic Ocean.

The southern coastlines of the African countries of Guinea, Ivory Coast, and Ghana drop into the Atlantic Ocean/Guinea Basin. The countries of Sierra Leone and Liberia are submerged in this Earth Change as well as most of Togo. Gone are the cities of Freetown, Monrovia, Abidjan, Accra, Lome, Porto Novo, Lagos, and Bioka. A 400-mile swath cuts into the western coast of southern Congo and Angola, sinking all of Cabinda. The eastern coastline of Africa breaks into a series of tiny islands, creating a large coastal bay near Lake Victoria and the Rift Valley. This Earth Change destroys all of Somalia and Ethiopia becomes a seaport country to Glory Ocean. Kenya, Tanzania, and Zimbabwe also touch Glory's waters, and Mozambique is broken into many small islands.

South Africa splits apart and the inland country of Botswana becomes a seaport country. Cities gone in this Earth Change event are: Muqdisho, Dar es Salaam, Maputo, and Durban.

After these changes, more Earth Changes ensue for over 200 years and new lands emerge. The rising of the ancient lands of Lemuria complete Earth's entry into the millennium of peace and grace. The first new lands of Lemuria are seen northwest of the Hawaiian Islands, around the

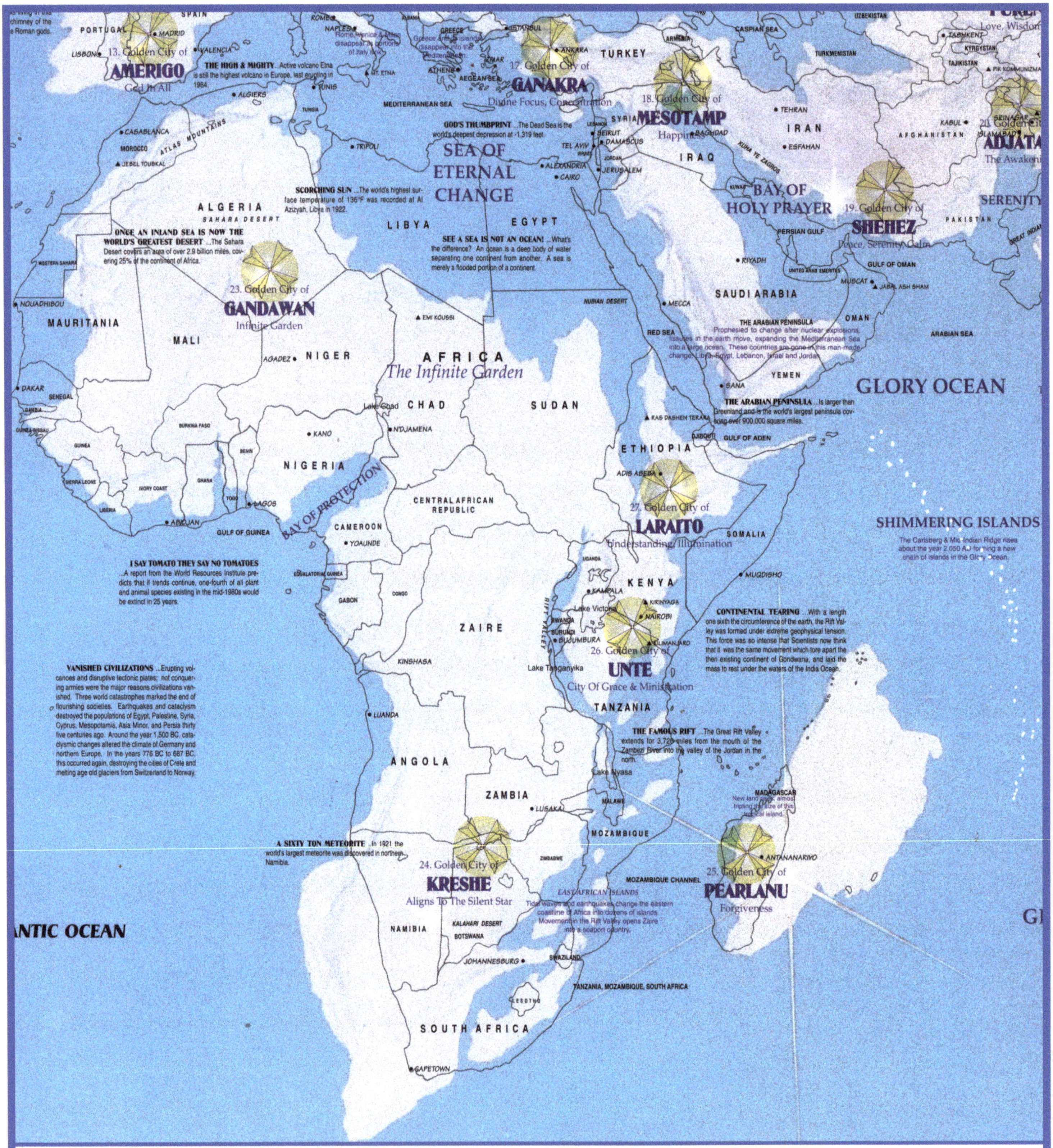

13. Golden City of
AMERIGO
God In All
THE HIGH & MIGHTY ...Active volcano Etna is still the highest volcano in Europe, last erupting in 1984.
17. Golden City of
GANAKRA
Divine Focus, Concentration
18. Golden City of
MESOTAMP
Happiness
GOD'S THUMBPRINT ...The Dead Sea is the world's deepest depression at -1,319 feet.
SEA OF ETERNAL CHANGE
SCORCHING SUN ...The world's highest surface temperature of 136°F was recorded at Al Azizyah, Libya in 1922.
ONCE AN INLAND SEA IS NOW THE WORLD'S GREATEST DESERT ...The Sahara Desert covers an area of over 2.9 billion miles, covering 25% of the continent of Africa.
SEE A SEA IS NOT AN OCEAN! ...What's the difference? An ocean is a deep body of water separating one continent from another. A sea is merely a flooded portion of a continent.
BAY OF HOLY PRAYER
19. Golden City of
SHEHEZ
Peace, Serenity, Calm
ADJATA
The Awakening
SERENITY
23. Golden City of
GANDAWAN
Infinite Garden
AFRICA
The Infinite Garden
THE ARABIAN PENINSULA
Prophesied to change after nuclear explosions, fissures in the earth move, expanding the Mediterranean Sea into a large ocean. These countries are gone in this man-made change: Libya, Egypt, Lebanon, Israel and Jordan.
THE ARABIAN PENINSULA ...Is larger than Greenland and is the world's largest peninsula covering over 900,000 square miles.
GLORY OCEAN
BAY OF PROTECTION
27. Golden City of
LARAITO
Understanding, Illumination
SHIMMERING ISLANDS
The Carlsberg & Mid-Indian Ridge rises about the year 2,050 AD forming a new chain of islands in the Glory Ocean.
I SAY TOMATO THEY SAY NO TOMATOES ...A report from the World Resources Institute predicts that if trends continue, one-fourth of all plant and animal species existing in the mid-1980s would be extinct in 25 years.
CONTINENTAL TEARING ...With a length one sixth the circumference of the earth, the Rift Valley was formed under extreme geophysical tension. This force was so intense that Scientists now think that it was the same movement which tore apart the then existing continent of Gondwana, and laid the mass to rest under the waters of the India Ocean.
26. Golden City of
UNTE
City Of Grace & Ministration
VANISHED CIVILIZATIONS ...Erupting volcanoes and disruptive tectonic plates; not conquering armies were the major reasons civilizations vanished. Three world catastrophes marked the end of flourishing societies. Earthquakes and cataclysm destroyed the populations of Egypt, Palestine, Syria, Cyprus, Mesopotamia, Asia Minor, and Persia thirty five centuries ago. Around the year 1,500 BC, cataclysmic changes altered the climate of Germany and northern Europe. In the years 776 BC to 687 BC, this occurred again, destroying the cities of Crete and melting age old glaciers from Switzerland to Norway.
THE FAMOUS RIFT ...The Great Rift Valley extends for 3,720 miles from the mouth of the Zambezi River into the valley of the Jordan in the north.
MADAGASCAR
New land rises, almost tripling the size of this tropical island.
A SIXTY TON METEORITE ...In 1921 the world's largest meteorite was discovered in northern Namibia.
24. Golden City of
KRESHE
Aligns To The Silent Star
25. Golden City of
PEARLANU
Forgiveness
EAST AFRICAN ISLANDS
Tidal waves and earthquakes change the eastern coastline of Africa into dozens of islands. Movement in the Rift Valley opens Zaire into a seaport country.
TANZANIA, MOZAMBIQUE, SOUTH AFRICA
PORTUGAL
SPAIN
LISBON
MADRID
VALENCIA
ROME
NAPLES
GREECE
ATHENS
ISTANBUL
ANKARA
TURKEY
MT. ETNA
AEGEAN SEA
MEDITERRANEAN SEA
ALGIERS
TUNIS
TUNISIA
TRIPOLI
CASABLANCA
MOROCCO
ATLAS MOUNTAINS
JEBEL TOUBKAL
ALGERIA
SAHARA DESERT
LIBYA
EGYPT
ALEXANDRIA
CAIRO
SYRIA
LEBANON
BEIRUT
DAMASCUS
TEL AVIV
ISRAEL
JORDAN
JERUSALEM
BAGHDAD
IRAQ
IRAN
TEHRAN
ESFAHAN
KUHA YE ZAGROS
ARMENIA
CASPIAN SEA
TURKMENISTAN
UZBEKISTAN
TASHKENT
KYRGYSTAN
TAJIKISTAN
PIK KOMMUNIZMA
AFGHANISTAN
KABUL
ISLAMABAD
SRINAGAR
PAKISTAN
KUWAIT
PERSIAN GULF
RIYADH
SAUDI ARABIA
UNITED ARAB EMERITES
GULF OF OMAN
MUSCAT
JABAL ASH SHAM
OMAN
ARABIAN SEA
MECCA
NUBIAN DESERT
RED SEA
YEMEN
SANA
GULF OF ADEN
DJIBOUTI
RAS DASHEN TERARA
WESTERN SAHARA
NOUADHIBOU
MAURITANIA
MALI
AGADEZ
NIGER
EMI KOUSSI
DAKAR
SENEGAL
GAMBIA
GUINEA BISSAU
GUINEA
BURKINA FASO
SIERRA LEONE
LIBERIA
IVORY COAST
GHANA
TOGO
BENIN
KANO
NIGERIA
LAGOS
ABIDJAN
GULF OF GUINEA
CHAD
Lake Chad
N'DJAMENA
SUDAN
ETHIOPIA
ADIS ABEBA
SOMALIA
MUQDISHO
CENTRAL AFRICAN REPUBLIC
CAMEROON
YOAUNDE
EQUALATORIAL GUINEA
GABON
CONGO
ZAIRE
KINSHASA
UGANDA
KAMPALA
KENYA
Lake Victoria
KIRINYAGA
NAIROBI
KILIMANJARO
RWANDA
BURUNDI
BUJUMBURA
RIFT VALLEY
Lake Tanganyika
TANZANIA
LUANDA
ANGOLA
ZAMBIA
LUSAKA
Lake Nyasa
MALAWI
MOZAMBIQUE
ZIMBABWE
MOZAMBIQUE CHANNEL
ANTANANARIVO
NAMIBIA
KALAHARI DESERT
BOTSWANA
JOHANNESBURG
SWAZILAND
LESOTHO
SOUTH AFRICA
CAPETOWN
NTIC OCEAN

AFRICA

Countries: Nigeria, Ethiopia, Egypt, Democratic Republic of Congo, South Africa, Tanzania, Kenya, Algeria, Sudan, Uganda, Morocco, Ghana, Mozambique, Angola, Ivory Coast, Madagascar, Cameroon, Niger, Burkina Faso, Mali, Malawi, Zambia, Senegal, Chad, Zimbabwe, South Sudan, Rwanda, Tunisia, Somalia, Guinea, Benin, Burundi, Togo, Eritea, Sierra Leone, Libya, Central African Republic, Republic of the Congo, Liberia, Mauritania, Namibia, Botswana, Gambia, Equalatorial Guinea, Lesotho, Gabon, Guinea-Bissau, Swaziland, Djibouti, Comoros, and Cape Verde.

Sea of Eternal Change
Glory Ocean

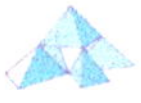

Gandawan
Laraito
Unte
Kreshe
Pearlanu

[Above: *Africa Topography with Borders.*[12]]

30° latitude and 170° longitude. Another large continent reveals itself that enlarges the lands of New Zealand from approximately the 55° latitude south to the 5° latitude. This new continent, larger than Australia, also includes the Fiji and Samoan Islands. The birth of this new land appears with the rising of the Tonga and Kermadec Ridge and the Austral Seamount Chain.

As the ice caps melt in global warming, new lands are revealed at the South Pole. The final earth movement begins hundreds of years into the Earth Changes and new lands form a peninsula on the South Pole region with the raising of the Scotia Ridge. ⚜

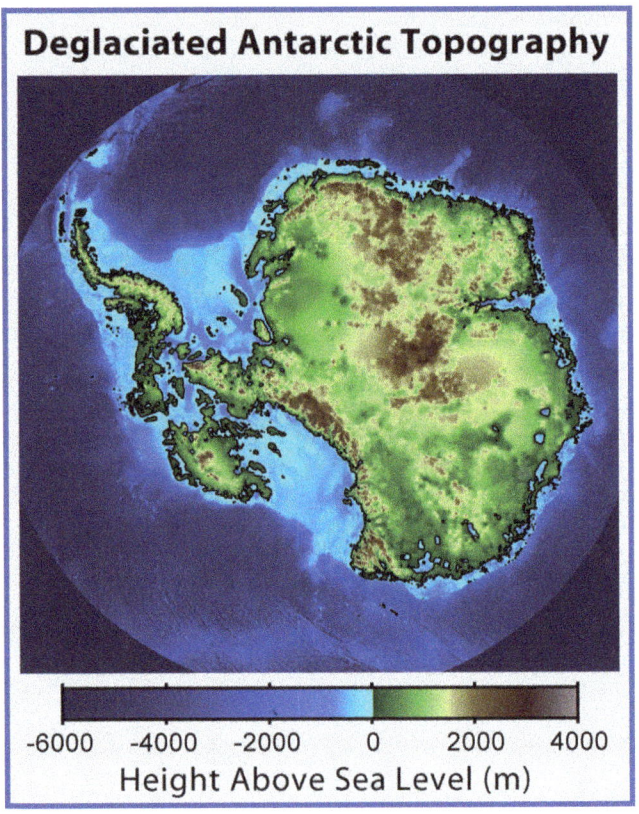

[Right: *Deglaciated Antarctic Topography Map*. "This is a topographic map of Antarctica after removing the ice sheet and accounting for both isostatic rebound and sea level rise. Hence this map suggests what Antarctica may have looked like 35 million years ago, when the Earth was warm enough to prevent the formation of large-scale ice sheets in Antarctica. Isostatic rebound is the result of the weight of the ice sheet depressing the land under it. After the ice is removed, the land will rise over a period of thousands of years by an amount approximately 1/3 as high as the ice sheet that was removed (because rock is 3 times as dense as ice). Approximately half the uplift occurs during the first two thousand years. If the ice sheet is removed over more than a few thousand years, then it is possible that a majority of the uplift will occur before the ice sheet fully disappears."[13]]

ANTARCTICA

Countries and Regions: Anarctica, Falkland Islands, South Georgia Island, South Orkney Islands, South Shetland Islands, and Capehorn.

 New Land
Crystal Sea

 Cresta

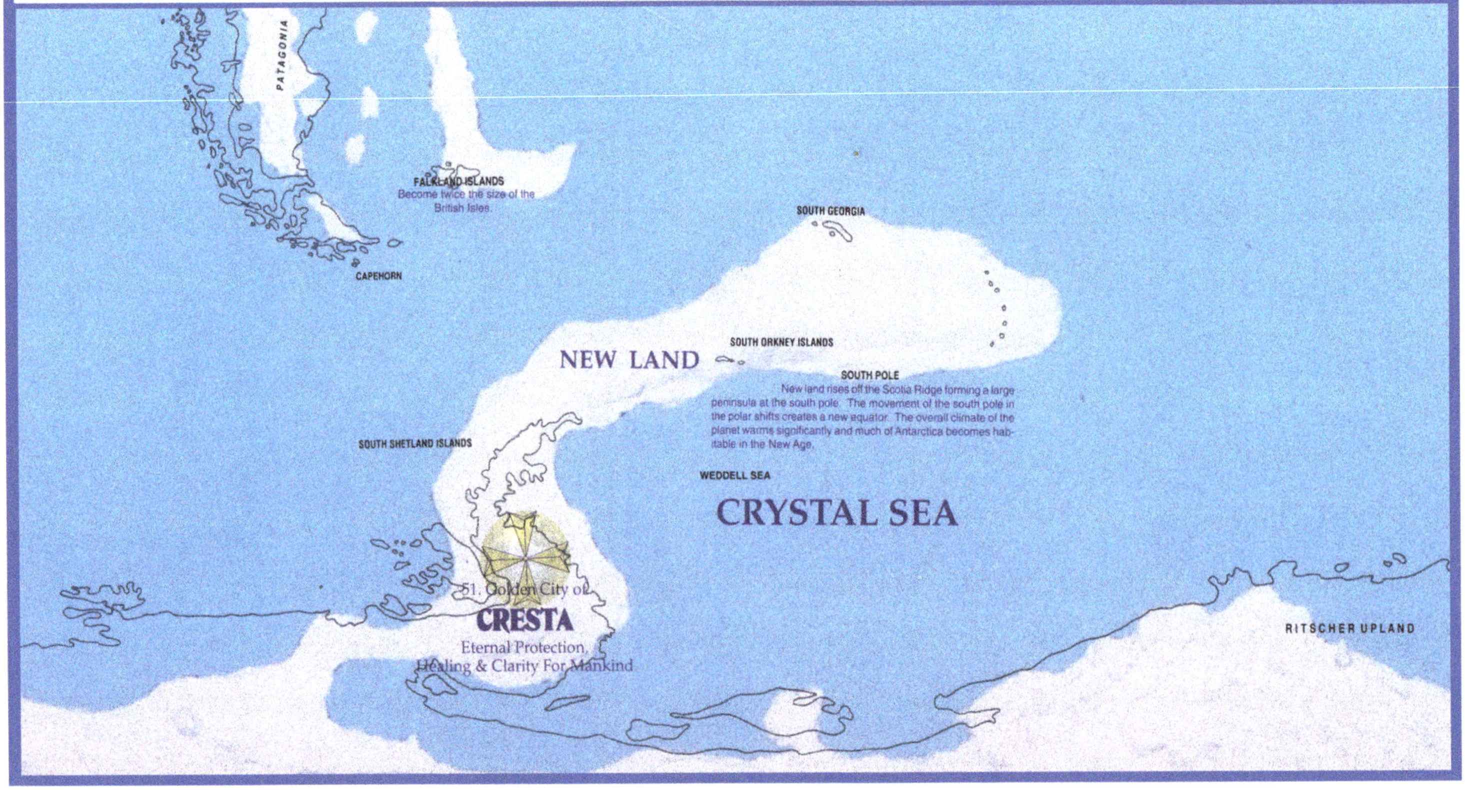

54 I AM AMERICA ATLAS

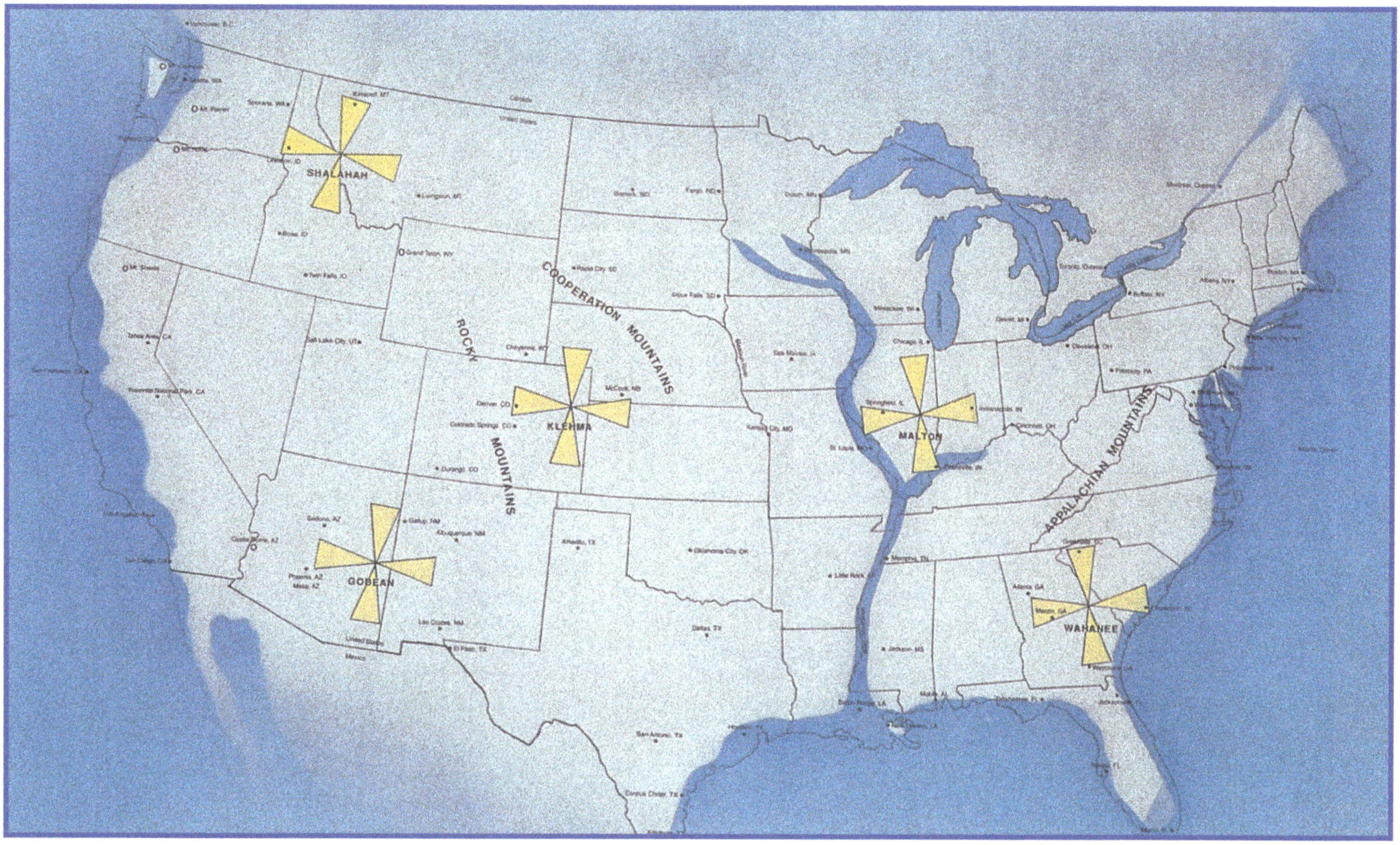

[Above: *Map Number One: Six-Map Scenario*]

SECTION THREE

Six-map Scenario

This series of maps is additional, detailed material to be used with the *I AM America Map* – an Earth Changes prophecy map of the United States. In 1983 the *I AM America Map* was first revealed in a dream to a young mother of three children. In this dream Lori Toye met four white-robed beings (the Master Teachers: Saint Germain, Sananda, El Morya and Kuthumi) and they unrolled huge maps of the United States, showing changes on Earth. (See New Wisdom Series.) Five years later, seeking to recapture the image of the map in meditation, the four spiritual Masters appeared again and expressed willingness to relay the important prophecies of change. After eighty recorded sessions over a six-month period, the I AM America material was born. The material contained spiritual teachings that would allow humanity to enter into a new time of peace and prosperity, if they were applied. Alongside the spiritual teachings were prophecies of Earth Changes which may or may not happen. There was a clear message that what transpires is contingent on humanity's choice. As the Earth Changes prophecies were very important and this portion of the material seemed to be the easiest for most people to understand, the United States Earth Changes map was the first information released. In 1989, the first full-color *I AM America Map* rolled off the presses.

Since that time, Lori and her husband, Lenard Toye, spent seven years receiving, researching and presenting the original information and eventually, they included new information and prophecies for the entire world as the Masters made them available. Having received continuous requests for additional information regarding the United States *I AM America Map*, the long period of silence regarding this material was finally broken on May 1, 1995 with a series of transmissions from three Master Teachers: "The focus of prophecy is to heal this planet; to heal your hearts and heal your minds. It is the focus of our three energies coming together that you will feel throughout this work, this *Update*. Many of you will see these as new prophecies, however, we would like to see it as a continuation of a work . . . as a seed planted, grows into a tree, soon, its branches unfold. Dilute not, that

I AM AMERICA ATLAS 55

first work, and consider this to be an important time as well. Share this work with many. Send this message to the Earth with love."

In the following weeks, the Master Teachers, Saint Germain, El Morya, Kuan Yin, Mother Mary, Serapis Bey, Lady Nada, Sananda and Kuthumi joined forces to relay a series of six Earth Changes maps and accompanying spiritual teachings and prophecies. This information includes five of those Maps.

This information is organized to show the changes as they could progress. According to the Master Teachers, the changes may be ameliorated, lessened, or averted altogether. This is dependent on the choices we make every day. In order to best understand our choices, it is important to observe the prophecies in sequential order.

"These probabilities are based on, experiences happening one at a time. Not one of these is laid in stone. However, each of these maps we present, allow for possibilities that will not only change the Earth, but change humanity's heart and mind."

Since this material was received some of the prophecies presented in the first map have already occurred and some have just occurred. "Note that if these events happen in sequential order, or begin to accelerate, you will then move to the second probability." Hence, the concept that choice activates the changes results in the various depictions of Earth's possible realities - six scenarios. Each of the maps contains excerpts from the original prophecies and points out solutions that can heal and transform our lives during these Time of Change. If we are to avert nuclear destruction and global ecological breakdown, we must make careful choices, now. It begins with each of us, now. The Time is Now. A Change of Heart Can Change the World!

The Midwest

Severe winters occur with temperatures dropping as low as 60° E below zero. Severe cold is sustained through mid-June. According to the prophecies, the seasons are out of kilter as the planet experiences the full range of the Greenhouse Effect. In the summers, watch for high winds and tornadoes accompanied by devastating floods that will threaten or destroy crops and agriculture.

Great Lakes

Extreme temperatures of hot and cold are prophesied, as the forces of nature are out of balance.

Texas

A moderate earthquake is prophesied to occur in Texas (somewhere in the 6.0 to 6.5 range). According to the prophecies, this will be another sign that we are living in Map One. There will also be severe hurricane storms in the Gulf of Mexico with heavy rains and winds prophesied to hit Houston.

The Galactic Web

According to the prophecies the Earth is covered by a huge web. Similar to the Creation Grid of the Native American Sioux, this web is created through and by consciousness. This consciousness is comprised of all things on the Earth – humans, animals, trees and rocks. At each intersection of this global web, a magnetic Vortex appears. In the prophecies these Vortices are called Golden Cities.

This is a work that cannot be used to create fear. It is a work that has been brought forward to create harmony and a sense of well-being between the nations, the genders, the races and the people of this planet."

Cosmic Wave Belts

The prophecies explain that Cosmic Wave Belts are much like an oceanic tidal system existing in the universe. The movement originates from the Galactic Sun and then moves to a certain point in the universe and then reverses. This reverse motion encounters other forward motion waves and soon the waves (forward and reverse) weave an infinite pattern that covers the universe. According to the prophecies, the movement of the waves and their influences on planets controls time and subsequently, evolution. During the Time of Change on Earth, the jumbling and tumbling of Cosmic Wave Belts causes time to go very slowly or causes time to speed up into *time compaction*. Two planets, Saturn and Neptune, are prophesied to help adjust these waves as they impact Earth and her inhabitants. This wave motion is at once disruptive and evolutionary, causing great disruption in human and animal nervous systems. The waves also cause an evolution of consciousness. It is prophesied humanity will move towards a greater understanding of unity, and through the understanding of unity, develop mercy and compassion for one another. "As I have always given that teaching along with beloved Kuan Yin, that it is forgiveness and compassion that can change *any* situation at *any* time."

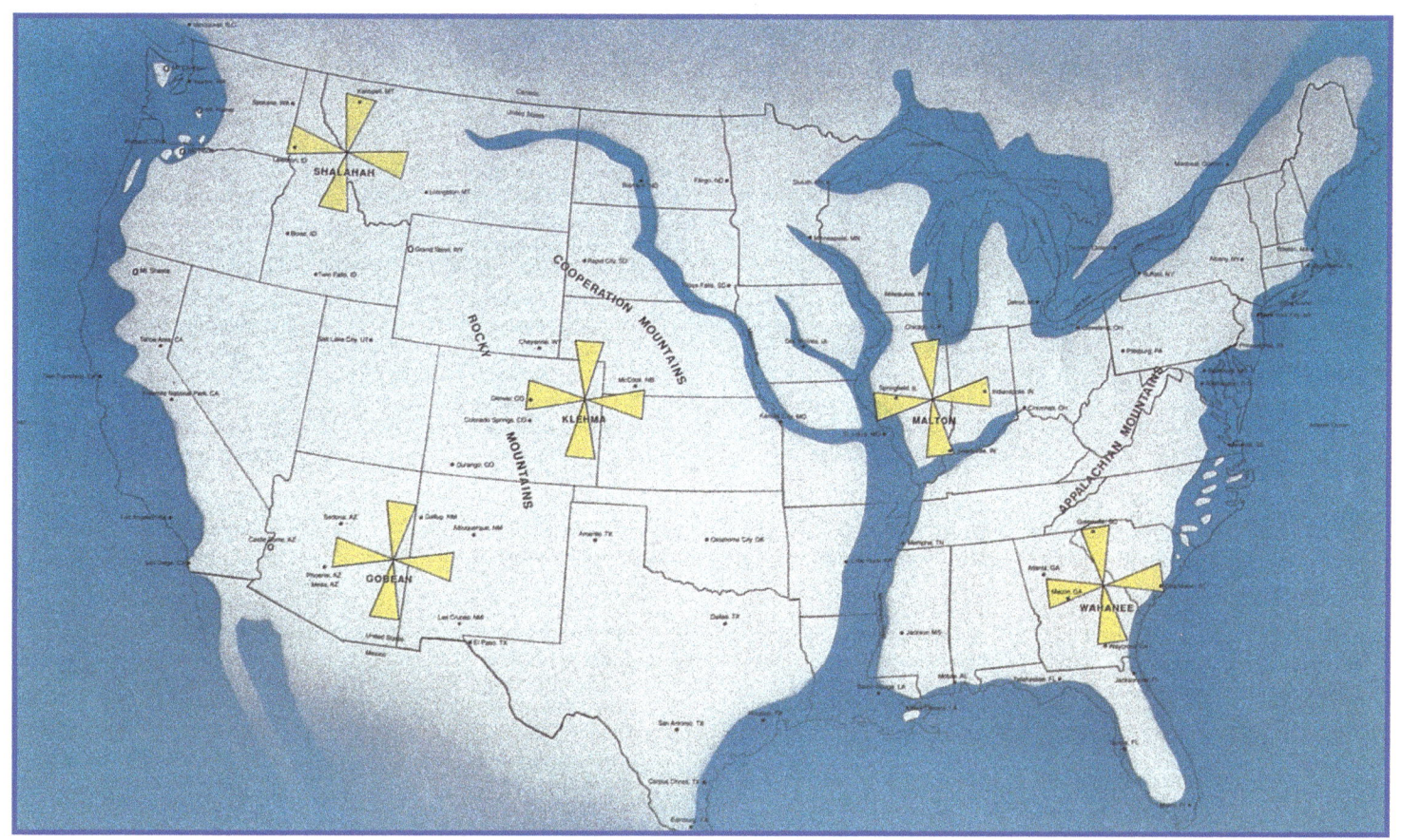

[Above: *Map Number Two: Six-Map Scenario*]

The Protective Field

The cosmic tidal motion is prophesied to affect the Galactic Web. As these two energy fields interact with one another, a magnetic and protective field emerges. This protective field is strongly detected at the apex of each Golden City Vortex. This field beneficially charges water and air in these locations. Because of the nature of this magnetic field, it is prophesied that the protective field will steadily adjust the environment of the Earth during high winds and tectonic plate movements. "It is important that we begin to understand the science of creation and the science of Earth as she travels through time. Then we can understand without fear."

Pacific Northwest

Global warming causes a depletion of coastlines in Washington State; several hundred and up to one thousand feet of water covers and or floods the city of Seattle. Two volcanoes, Mount Rainier and Mount Baker, are prophesied to erupt, covering the entire Pacific Northwest with ash. These eruptions cause crop failures in the area. The Pacific Ocean is prophesied to deplete Oregon's coastline 1,000 to 1,500 feet, flooding portions of the city of Portland. The Columbia River is also prophesied to flood extensively during the Time of Change.

California

A mild earthquake is prophesied to occur near Mount Shasta, and continuous earthquake activity will prevail between San Francisco and Los Angeles with more than twenty-five earthquakes in a seven-year period. However, the prophecies state that in this Earth Changes map, California will not entirely sink by tectonic plate movement, but also through continuous, torrential rains that flood the coastline. In the summers, fires and high winds will assault much of southern California causing tremendous economic breakdowns. During the Time of Change water supplies become severely depleted and polluted.

The Virginias and the Carolinas

Extensive flooding and hurricane activity are prophesied and the summers become tropical. This climatic summer trend will spread as far north as Boston. "Energy cannot be destroyed. Once energy is created, it is always in the process of taking new form."

Northeast United States

Extremely cold winters last until the end of April and then seesaw into hot and humid summers which last until the end of October. Unusual high tides and global warming cause ocean waters to cover areas of Long Island and New Jersey, depleting the Atlantic coastline there by 500-700 feet. This will pollute the water systems of New York City and Philadelphia. High tides will also flood Baltimore, forming a new swamp area. There is a possibility of a small earthquake striking New York City.

Florida

The Everglade area of Florida will flood again and again and residents can expect rising ocean waters to deplete the coastlines by 100 to 600 feet along the eastern seaboard.

Mystic Message: Map Number One
Divinity is in all things.

"It is as simple as understanding the divinity of the heart. But that call is not heard by ears long plugged; eyes, blinded. It is important at this time that we extend this message in a hope that universal fellowship and love will bring a balance to the time of suffering and darkness that has covered this planet. It is important that as we enter into this new age, a Golden Age, and that peace be held as our first goal."

Map Number Two

Pacific Northwest

Global warming raises ocean waters 200 feet and leaves the Olympic Peninsula of Washington State as a freestanding island. The subsequent eruptions of Mount Baker and Mount Rainier produce tectonic plate movement that shift portions of Washington's western coast and form several small islands near the town of Aberdeen, Washington.

In British Columbia rising ocean waters deplete the Pacific coastlines by 1,500 to 2,000 feet.

Ocean waters wash over and flood many of the San Juan Islands, but after the waters recede, the islands are reclaimed and habitated. Seattle and Tacoma are under water and the ocean waters begin to lap into the Cascade Range of mountains as several ocean water inlets move east as far as Leavenworth, Wenatchee and Ellensburg, Washington.

The Columbia River floods, and rushing waters form small islands between Portland and The Dalles, Oregon. An earthquake – 7.8 to 8.6 point magnitude – is prophesied to strike the Oregon coast which will severely alter artesian activity and fresh water supplies in the area. Ocean waters deplete the Oregon coastline and the Pacific Ocean breaks across the coastal ranges up to 1,000 to 1,500 feet elevation. Ocean waters lap the shores of Salem, Eugene and Corvallis in the Willamette Valley.

California

Mount Shasta remains during this Time of Changes, however, the large earthquake that strikes the Oregon coastal area signals a series of earthquakes in California. This earthquake area extends southward from San Francisco to Los Angeles, and eventually forms a huge bay on the Pacific with inlets close to the Sierra Nevada Mountains. During this time California suffers economic bankruptcy and eventually San Francisco is completely covered by the Pacific Ocean.

Central United States

The Mississippi and Missouri rivers flood, as do the tributary rivers extending into Montana, North and South Dakota. An Earth-shattering earthquake strikes Colorado and Wyoming (7.5 to 9.3), extending north to the Grand Tetons. "This earthquake changes many minds. Those who fled to the interior lands seeking safe lands . . . now understand a (spiritual) change in the heart and mind."

Texas

Earthquake activity continues in Texas. One earthquake helps to sculpt Texas land into a huge bay that empties into the Gulf of Mexico. This bay extends past New Orleans, LA and enters into Arkansas. Texas will be severely affected according to the prophecies embodied in Map Number Two. Houston and Galveston are left completely under ocean water and many other cities and towns are flooded.

Great Lakes

Flooding and global warming waters deplete the shorelines of the Great Lakes by 100 to 125 feet. The prophecies state that during the Time of Change the Saint Lawrence River will widen.

Maine

An ocean floating glacier land-locks to the tip of Maine and winter weather is extremely cold and very high winds hit the coast of Maine.

Northeast

Boston, sections of New York, and Philadelphia become islands. Washington D. C. and Baltimore, MD are now completely under water due to flooding and global warming. The small earthquake prophesied to strike New York City (see Map Number One) extends to upper New York State.

The Appalachian Mountains stop the rising waters, however, lands to the east of this mountain chain are severely affected with high winds and flooding. "This area is part of an ancient remnant of that continent of

Atlantis... everything that lies to the eastern side will be a belt of uncertainty... filled with pollutants and man's lack of harmony with the environment."

Carolinas

North and South Carolina break apart into dozens of small islands. This is caused through high winds, flooding and global warming.

Florida

Massive storms and hurricanes hit Florida. Cuba is prophesied to be completely covered with ocean waters, that later recede, during the Time of Change of Map Number Two.

Spiritual Change

"Many are moving beyond structured and organized religion... to a unity of the heart and a spirituality that speaks to the ONE."

Golden Cities of Other Times

As prophesied in the first *I AM America Map*, five Golden City Vortices appear to "serve the spiritual and healing needs of humanity." During the Time of Change, many of the present day energy Vortices change locations. For instance, an ancient Vortex exists over New York City and Philadelphia.

Destiny of the United States

The United States is prophesied to become the first country to experience devastating Earth Changes. Later, it recovers to give aid and support to other nations of the world.
"It (the United States) is said to hold a cup of freedom for the entire world. But freedom is as it chooses. If you continue to make choices that enslave you further, there will be other countries of the world that will take up this mantel of freedom and carry it forward for the Earth and her peoples."

The Heart of the Dove

In the original *I AM America Map* prophecies, a spiritual center exists over Kansas City, MO. It is prophesied that a spiritual center for universal fellowship and peace will be developed there. "In the center of the United States is a great spiritual focus for the entire Earth. I ask all members of humanity to travel to the heart of the dove. That is where world peace can be greatly affected, where the heart of humanity can be affected, where wars and social injustice can be altered."

Community Gardens

"Community Gardens to be planted in all areas of the United States are symbols of cooperation. Bring forward a garden that flourishes and flowers from the inside out... understand that all change starts from the inside, first. Plant these gardens in cities of rubble. Plant these gardens in countrysides. Plant gardens wherever there are those who will tend, weed, and keep them. The seed that is planted in each external gardens, is a seed planted in the heart, internal. These are gardens that can change the heart of the United States."

The Mystic Message: Map Number Two
Cooperation
"This is an age of cooperation, not an age of competition. You are brothers and sisters of one great family."

Map Number Three

The Lost White Brother

Shortly after their emergence into the Third World, Ancient Hopi prophecies speak about Bahana (Pahanna) the lost white brother, a part of their family who becomes lost. The I AM America prophecies identify Bahana as the Europeans who, upon their return to America (Turtle Island), greet their NativeAmerican brother with a consciousness completely bereft of the memory of their loving unity with all peoples. The prophecies state that through this consciousness the pattern of the European civilization in the United States (which began in the Rio Grande Valley in present-day New Mexico around 1520 A.D.) with its inherent exploitation and destruction, will repeat itself through Earth Changes: "For then, many will understand why the changes will occur on the western side, and then make their movement over to the eastern seaboard." After the Earth Changes, the prophecies state that the peoples of the United States, of all cultures and races, will live in unity and harmony.

Ancient Cultures

The prophecies speak about the first colonization of America originating from the Ancient peoples of Lemuria, Mu, and present day India. "These are lands (the Pacific Northwest of the United States) that were first visited by those of Hindu extraction, known from those lands of Lemuria and the Indus Valley (Rama). Many have wondered why it is that Native American traditions are so similar to those of eastern origin. They come from ONE. Birthed long ago in the lands of Mu and brought across by ancestors of the native Eskimo and coastal Indians who now share this information in song, dance and ritual."

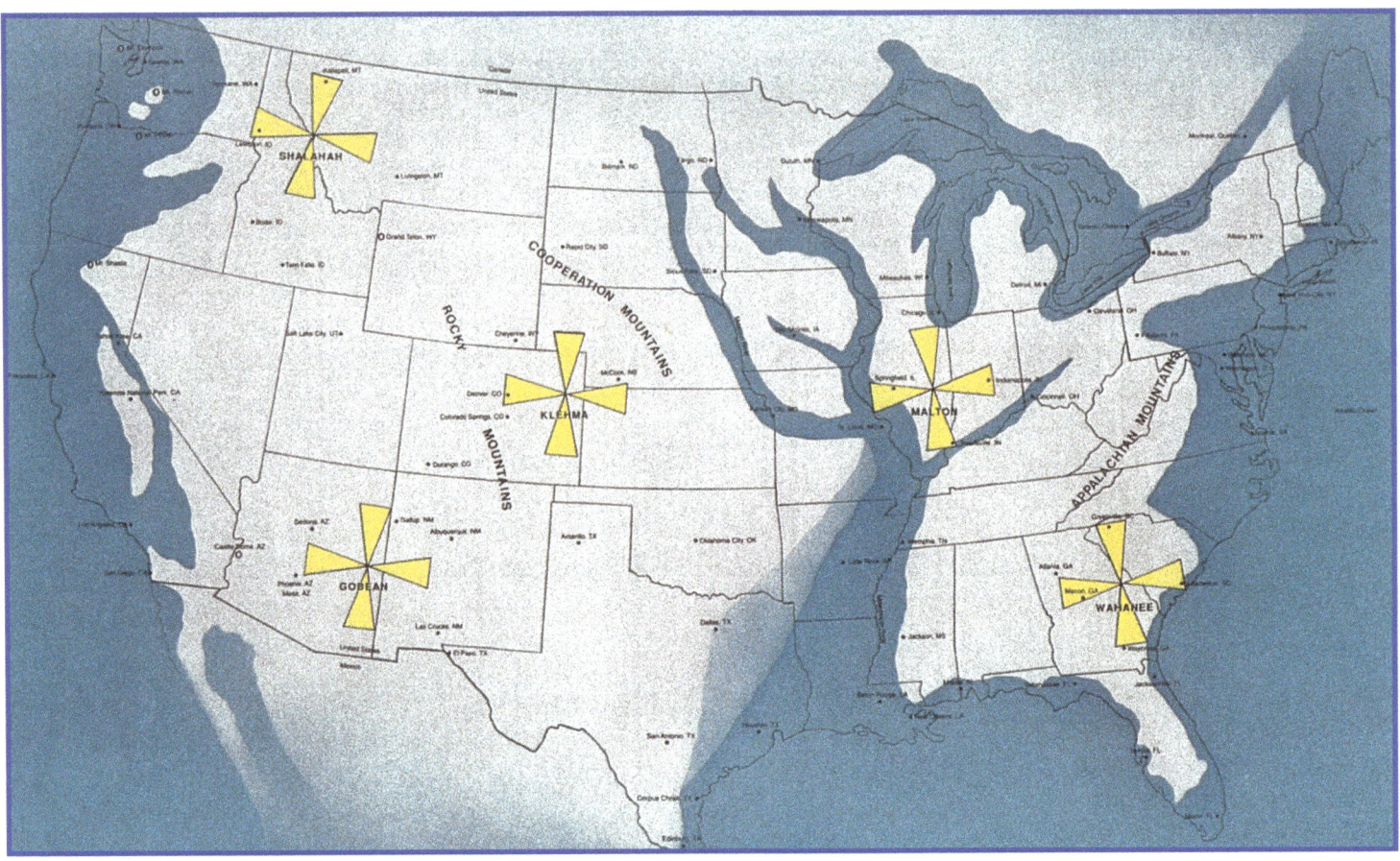

[Above: *Map Number Three: Six-Map Scenario*]

Pacific Northwest

The volcanic eruptions of Mount Baker and Mount Rainier, constant rains, and tectonic activity turn the Cascade Mountains into a chain of very erosive islands. An Earth movement shatters and fractures plates that exist under southern Washington State and northern and eastern Oregon. It is prophesied that this fragile land will transform from Bend, Oregon to La Grande and Baker, Oregon. In this map it is prophesied that portions of Oregon's new coastline will exist as far east as Baker, Oregon.

The Inland, Underground Sea

The prophecies explain that a sea exists underneath much of the interior lands of Oregon State. "Once you see that earthquake, as prophesied in Map Number Two, then, this next event . . . the cracking of the basalt flows and into the inland sea." This underground, inland sea is prophesied to have many underground caverns that extend all the way into the state of Montana. "Many caverns which run as far inland as Missoula, Montana."

California

The Sierra Nevada (Madres) Mountains erode into one large island with a small strip of land between Los Angeles and San Diego. The prophecies speak about the state of California: "This purification of Earth through fire is tremendous for her (California). It is also a time of purification for her people and the social structures. For this is an area asked to turn its competitive and conquering nature into that nature of cooperation, love and harmony . . . the unity of consciousness of ALL. Move into Unana, the Oneness, and the beingness of ONE."

Midwest United States

An earthquake is prophesied to open Arkansas and the Mississippi River into a huge ocean bay. The epicenter of this earthquake is prophesied to be in Missouri,
"Springfield, Missouri and that area therein will become as an island in the middle of the delta or bay area."

Lopsided temperatures are prophesied to cause extreme temperatures in the Midwestern states with temperatures as high as 120° in the summer and wind-chill factors which drive the temperatures 60° to 80° below in the winter. "This is due to the lopsidedness of the cycles, the tilting of the poles and the volcanic ash in the atmosphere."

Global Warming and Climate Change

"We will experience an overall global warming and tremendous rains. We will also experience tremendous humidity and high temperatures in spring and summer. This will throw many of the seasons off by two to three months, extending summers into December and winters beginning as late as February."

Flooding of the Mississippi and Missouri Rivers

"Many years of rain and flooding, waters moving throughout the entire valley created through the Mississippi and Missouri rivers . . . earthquake activity in Texas, Arkansas and the Mississippi (River) opening up the bay."

Great Lakes

Flooding is prophesied to continue in the Great Lakes areas, depleting another 50 feet of the coastlines. Many rivers carry her flooding waters, including the Missouri, Mississippi and the Ohio rivers.

Changes in Government

The prophecies state that the Earth Changes will cause many upheavals and changes in our government. Five governmental regions will be developed around each Golden City Vortex area. Each of these regions will function as a sovereign area during the Time of Change. "Democracy evolves into the Law of the Golden Rule."

Northeast United States

Landlocked glaciers transform the state of Maine into a giant ice cap. Much of this area becomes uninhabitable. High winds and rains constantly pelt the eastern seaboard, leaving Philadelphia, New York City, Baltimore and the state of Delaware under water. The new coastline extends to upper New York State south to Pittsburgh. "We see many new bays forming of salt water . . . many become marsh-like during the Time of Change."

North Carolina

Many new islands form during the Time of Change on the new mid-Atlantic coastline and waters lap the mainland cities of Winston-Salem and Charlotte, North Carolina. It is prophesied that winds of up to 200 m.p.h. may hit this area. "Compassion is the only law that can rule the peoples in these lands. And as we are separated through geophysical changes, we are unified in the consciousness of the ONE,.."

Florida

An earthquake, with its epicenter located somewhere in the West Indies, sinks the lower tip of Florida. Several bays are formed in the upper portion of Florida and new inlets form on the peninsula.

Texas

Ocean waters completely cover the city of Houston and are prophesied to continue to rise, transforming Dallas into a seaport city. Later, it is prophesied that these waters will recede, 175-200 miles east of Dallas. "Many of these areas will be covered with water and then later, the lands will rise up as the waters recede. This is the purifying motion of water."

Transportation during the Time of Change

Since the country may be literally broken apart during the Time of Change, the prophecies speak about the isolation of many small towns and cities. This will cause the formation of travel units (groups), each guided by their respective governmental region, to transport needed food and supplies: "Many groups of people will now band together in travel units. They will establish five governments across the United States . . . each of them selecting the best law to serve them during the tumultuous times."

During this time, the prophecies state that it will be difficult to move food supplies and fresh water will become a rare commodity. "It is important to understand that the breaking apart of our nation, breaks us into smaller groups so all things can be scrutinized and reorganized. We must look closely to the intent and motives that we hold, not only for our families and loved ones, but for our governments and communities."

A Time of Choice

"It is a Time of Change, Dear Ones; a time where many will be called to understand their hearts. It will be a time, yes, of suffering and purification; however, it is a time of choice."

Pole Shift

Three distinct shifts of the poles are prophesied to occur. (Please see the original *I AM America Map* and *Freedom Star Map* for more information on pole shifts.) The first shift of the pole magnetically activates the Galactic Web (as discussed in Map Number One). "This shifting of the poles could cause severe winds upon the planet for a three-hour period, with winds exceeding 900 miles per hour. Since very few could survive such torrential winds, let us see a shift in consciousness versus a shift of the poles."

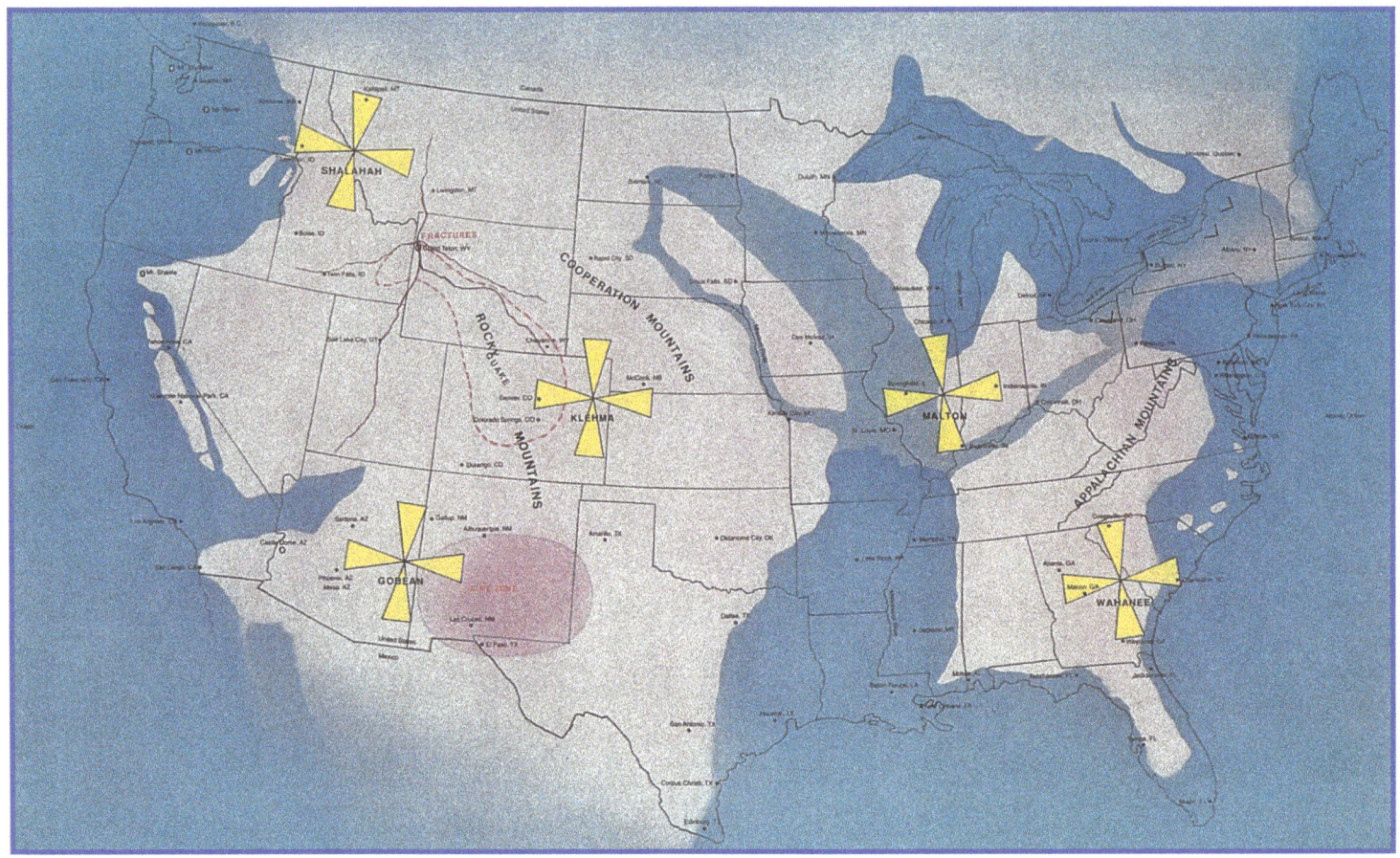

[Above: *Map Number Four: Six-Map Scenario*]

The Mystic Message: Map Number Three
Purify Your Intentions
"Scrutinize your intent and the true motives of your heart. Examine the purpose of all of your actions. Remember the divine plan of the best and the highest good."

Map Number Four

Pacific Northwest and British Columbia
Continuous rains begin to erode many lands that are now on the new Pacific Ocean coastline and this crumbling effect continues into British Columbia. The earthquake that was prophesied to register 7.8 to 8.6 in Map Number Two registers above 10. Extreme devastation results in the sinking of the lower portions of British Columbia and the upper portion of Vancouver Island, B.C. This creates fractures to the Canadian city of Penticton, B.C. and further tectonic movement leaves Spokane, Washington a coastal city. This new coastline extends south to Lewiston, ID, following the Snake River Canyon. Many small islands are formed near the small Washington state communities of Colfax, Pomeroy, Clarkston, and Asotin. This series of small islands extend south to Ontario, Oregon.

The state of Oregon continues to crumble under the pressure and force of tectonic movement and Baker, Oregon become a Pacific coastline city. The Wallowa Mountain Range remains as one large island during the Time of Change as depicted in Map Number Four.

Hurricane Force Winds in the Pacific Northwest
During tectonic movement, the Pacific Ocean covers much of Washington and Oregon and hurricane-force winds are prophesied to hit the new coastlines. These winds affect the communities of Spokane, Washington as well as Moscow and Lewiston, Idaho.
"It is important for those who seek a preparation in those areas to prepare for gale forces of 200 to 250 miles-per-hour."

California
Mount Shasta becomes uninhabitable for several years due to volcanic activity. Eventually the mountain becomes a peninsula that later erodes into a series of small islands (See Map Number Five). The Sierra-Nevada Mountains are prophesied to become a free-floating island. Due to the explosion of the Ring of Fire, what was formerly the California coast and its many cities is now entirely under ocean water. "Gone are the cities of coastal California as far south as San

Diego. And that last portion of land that had existed as a safety portal between Los Angeles and San Diego (See Map Number Three) is now worn away through lapping oceans and continuous rainfall brought through the explosion of the Ring of Fire . . . not only now in the United States, but extending to South America and throughout the eastern portion of this Ring into Micronesia and Japan."

A New Grand Canyon in California and Arizona

The forceful earthquake that strikes the Pacific Northwest in Map Number Four forever changes southern California and the state of Arizona: ". . . opens a new canyon as deep as the gorge in the upper portion of North Arizona (the Grand Canyon) and exists between San Diego and the lands of Arizona."

Nevada, Utah, Wyoming, and Montana

It is prophesied that the same movement that births the new canyon also creates new fault lines, and stimulates old ones, which extend into Nevada and Utah. Utah is also affected by tectonic plate movement and fault lines whose center is near Grand Teton, Wyoming. These fault lines extend to the north, past Livingston, Montana, southeast to Cheyenne, Wyoming, hundreds of miles south to Saint George, Utah and west to the Columbia Plateau, past Twin Falls, Idaho,

The Southwest

Underground caverns, filled with natural gas, in the state of New Mexico are prophesied to explode, creating a fire zone in the southwest. Map Number Four prophesies fires extending for the western border of Texas, north to Gallup, New Mexico and as far west as the White Mountains of Arizona. "It is important for those individuals located in the southwest to consider reserves of fresh water, for there will be pollution of aquifers."

The Earthquake Belt in Colorado

"(The) earthquake belt extends over to Colorado . . . for we shall see continued earthquake activity. Again, many fractures will open in the Rockies, and waters will rush into these areas, forming deep oceans and quite narrow (canyons)."

The Asteroid

The prophecies speak about an asteroid (or large meteor) that appears in the Earth's skies. The asteroid is attracted through the sound vibration of grinding tectonic plates.

"These small fractures severely affect the stability of plate movement and a grinding noise carries a sound vibration throughout the atmosphere of the planet. The sound vibration attracts an asteroid close, within range, dangerously close. It is as if Beloved Babajeran (the Earth Mother) cries a moan of birth to the entire cosmos. This asteroid comes as a witness of this great birth."

It is prophesied that the asteroid is carried for some time in the Earth's gravitational field and it appears as if the Earth has two moons. This causes many Earth Changes, primarily extremely high tides.

High Tides

Since many new coastal bays have been formed due to the Earth Changes, the prophecies outline new tidal regions. "Bays open up and (there are) tremendous tidal pulls. Water (moves) north to Bismarck (North Dakota) through this asteroid that has entered into the atmosphere. Gravitational pulls of tides in Harvest Bay cover parts of Mississippi, Arkansas and far north into the Dakotas."

Global Warming

"Spring and Fall no longer exist. One day is hot, the next day is cold. The melting of many glaciers and snowcapped poles create weather patterns that are unpredictable. This situation causes floods in the Midwest."

Maine to Boston

Maine remains uninhabitable during the Map Number Four Time of Change, as pockets of arctic air stabilize over the state. The city of Boston is prophesied to experience the same fate: "Boston is frozen in such a manner. The waters that cover her, carrying glaciers that have broken free from the global warming of the North Pole."

Northeast United States

Global warming begins to thaw the island of Greenland, rushing waters into the Great Lakes, depleting coastlines another 100 feet. Lake Erie and Lake Ontario spill over into upper state New York and flood western Pennsylvania. Pittsburgh is now a coastal city.

Virginia

"High tides seriously affect areas of Richmond, Virginia. Many coastal areas of Virginia are now under water . . . Virginia Beach is broken up into small islands. Many of them uninhabitable at this time due to cold and rushing winds of hurricane force."

Georgia

The state of Georgia is also prophesied to be hit with hurricane-force winds. "It is important to stay located as close to the apex of Wahanee (Golden City Vortex) as possible. As you see, it is a Time of Change. A time where the Earth forces are unleashed to help cleanse humanity."

On Nuclear Energy

"At this time, it is important for man to walk a simple path. Live a simple life. When he (man) reaches for anything out of his grasp, he looses his sense of discipline and throws systems off. For instance, man does not yet have within his capacity (in his soul) to grasp nuclear energy. He does not yet understand how to clean up radioactive waste! It is like a bird building a nest with bricks! The poor bird cannot even carry mortar! It is out of his grasp."

Meditation, Prayer, Solitude

The prophecies of Map Number Four share simple solutions that show how we can cope with tumultuous change and find healing and serenity. "Take one hour each day and touch God, the Source. Do this through meditation, prayer and time alone. Spend time with the Earth mother. Take walks in forests. Take walks along lakes . . . for these are healing to the soul. Find the simplicity and the solace that rests within."

Mystic Message: Map Number Four
Simplicity

"It is important to take a simple approach to life. Do not complicate it unnecessarily. Find ways to uncomplicate your life. Stay on a strict diet of simplicity. See things emotionally simple and do not read more into events then is necessary. It is important to live simple lives. For in simplicity, we see truth."

"In understanding the self through the path of simplicity, the soul is naturally lead to love. Love that generates from the center of the heart cannot be extinguished. There, find the unity of all people."

Map Number Five

Changes in Flora, Fauna, and Humanity

According to the prophecies, the physical changes are only one aspect of many changes that are happening. The Galactic Web that covers the entire Earth (see Map Number One) is changing location and this movement changes many of the energies filtered through it. The change of the energies on the Earth not only alters the face of our Earth through Earth Changes, but alters all life on the planet. It is prophesied that the changes will produce new strains of grasses, flowers, birds, and mammals. Most importantly, humanity will change: "The whole Creation Grid, that which is known as the Galactic Web, is shifting its location at this time. Earth and her evolution will go forward. Humanity will be changed. New lifestreams will come to the planet."

"It is simply an acceleration of the evolutionary process affecting you at the cellular, emotional and mental levels. You will become aware of other dimensions that are also filled with life."

New Dimensions

"Life expresses itself somewhat differently in the new dimensions. You will learn how energy moves in these dimensions and how you can access them." The prophecies of Map Number Five explain that our human energy bodies (aura) are changing during this time. This will allow us to understand many things that, in the past, have remained hidden and unknown. A new science will evolve from this knowledge, primarily spiritual knowledge about physical death. All fear of death will be removed as it is understood that life continues and only changes form as it moves into new dimensions. "(Humanity will) Experience the other dimensions without the experience of (physical) death."

Earth's Grid and Planetary Ascension

The changes and fluctuations in the Earth's grid are prophesied to assist in mass ascension. The prophecies explain that this has happened before in Earth's history (the disappearance of the Mayans, for instance) and that the electromagnetic centers of the Earth's grid play an important role. "The fluctuations in the Earth's grid will allow a mass ascension. There are points on this grid where this is possible. As stated in earlier prophecies, these locations will cover the entire planet. It is our hope to reveal as many of these locations as possible. This is an opportunity for cellular assistance and acceleration." During the times of Earth Changes, the fluctuation of the Earth's electromagnetic grid will open and close these magnetic centers. The Golden City Vortices are very large electromagnetic centers which are prophesied to remain open during the time of great change. (If you would like to know more about the specific locations of these five centers, please see the original *I AM America Map*.) "The ascensions at this time will be nationwide. There will be locations every 400 to 600 miles. However, for simplicity's sake, the apex of each Golden City Vortex is considered an ascension point. That is why the Golden City locations have been established.

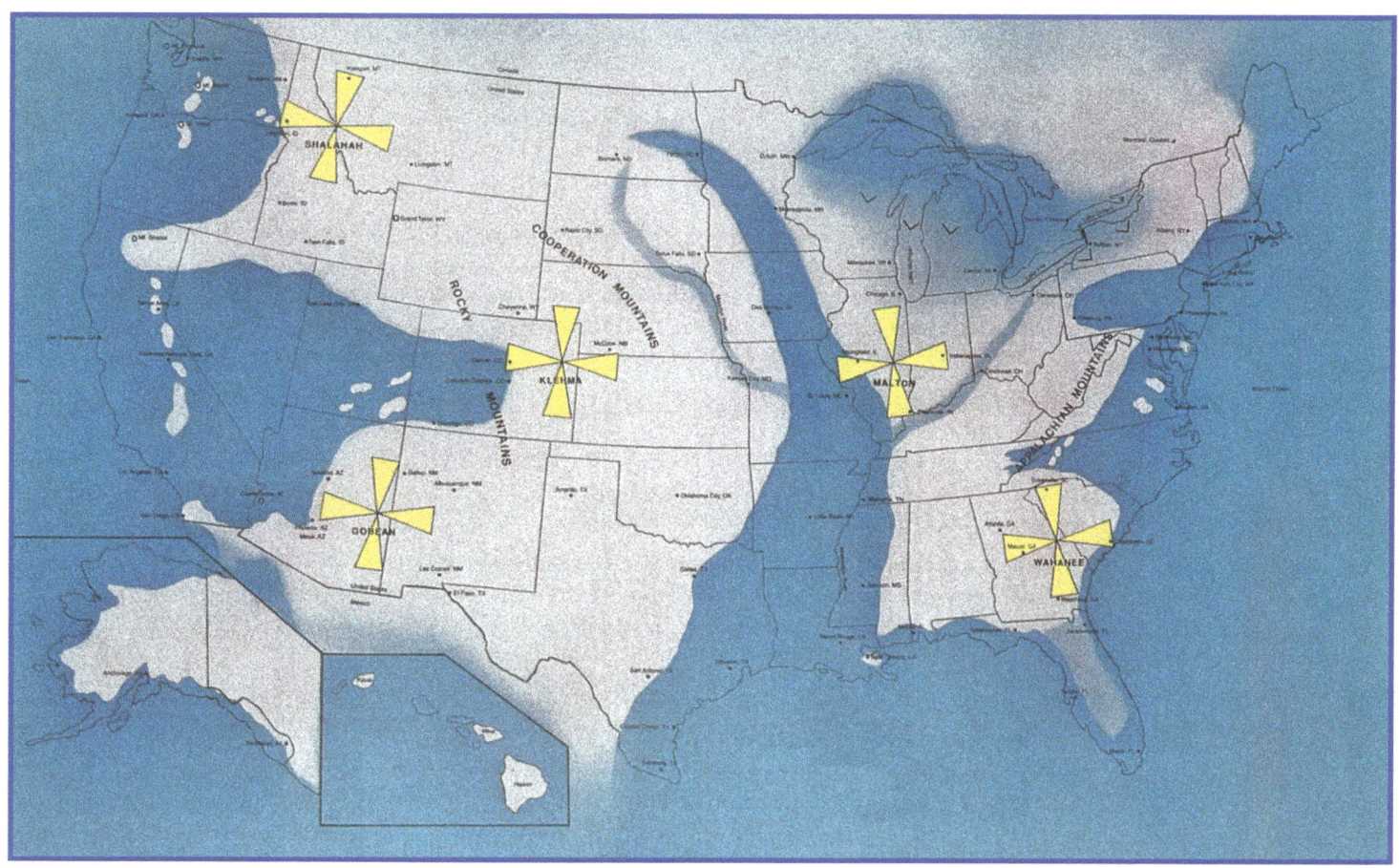

[Above: *Map Number Five, Six-Map Scenario*]

These are places where these grid centers, or portals, are constantly opened."

Pacific Northwest

The new coastline is prophesied to begin in British Columbia and extends south through Spokane, WA, Lewiston, ID, and Ontario, OR. A chain of islands are all that remain of the Cascade Mountains. "Many of them are 700 to 800 feet in elevation, their mountain tops now lap with ocean water – the Pacific Ocean."

The New West Coast

"We see what remains of Salt Lake City is just a series of islands. The coastline extends to what we know as Denver, Colorado . . . parts of southern Colorado and central Colorado left under water." It is prophesied that the Rocky Mountains in Colorado will be left as a series of islands, protecting Denver, Colorado, now renamed the *Golden Port*. The new western coastline extends south above New Mexico and cuts through central Arizona, leaving Sedona and Prescott under water. The earthquakes that result from the asteroid impact and the Teton earthquake create fractures in the coastline that are prophesied to be very severe. "The quake is so extensive; it will be felt from the Island of Gibraltar (the Sierra-Nevada Mountains) to the midlands of Illinois. Its shaking shall be so loud, it will be felt from pole to pole."

Pollution during the Time of Change

During the Time of Change (Map Number Five) many toxic waste sites will be disturbed and chemical spills will pollute water supplies. The prophecies state: "There are southern portions of Utah that will remain as islands for 500 years. However, eventually, many of them become uninhabitable due to the pollutants and toxins that will float above what is known as the Bay of Harmony. Over a period of time, however, these pollutants and toxins move from the water and are cleansed through the release of volcanic ash." On the eastern seaboard of the United States it is prophesied that during the Time of Change the water will no longer be drinkable. However, new technology will be developed after the great Earth Changes that will clean up the polluted waters, air, and environment. "For 150 to 250 years many of the waters are polluted. Much of it filled with petro-chemicals and is unfit for drink. Through new technology and the use of what is known as *free energy* water is processed and made to be drinkable again. The air is cleaned up within 75 years. The pollution and the ash that once filled these areas are no longer."

Phoenix, Arizona

Map Number Five gives detailed prophecies for the city of Phoenix: "Many lands now under water to a resting place not to raise up again for several more ages to come. The new coastline will extend to the west side of Phoenix. However, locations such as Glendale and what is known as west Phoenix will all be under water. Phoenix will be largely uninhabitable during this period of change."

Harvest Bay

Due to the prophesied breaking of Lake Michigan, a huge bay is formed in the middle of the United States. The prophecies compare the breaking of Lake Michigan to the breaking of the ice age lakes of Lake Bonneville and Glacial Lake Missoula that once existed in present day Utah, Nevada, and Idaho. "This forms some of the most bountiful farmland that the worlds have ever seen. After some time, the water recedes from all of these areas, and then is reclaimed for agricultural purposes. Many new grains and plants now flourish on the Earth in this new time...from the planet Venus."

Mount Shasta

"We see the peninsula of land as it extends out to Mount Shasta, however, within 200 to 300 years that peninsula will erode. That series of islands will lead their way to the Vortex of Shalahah."

California and Migrations

"San Diego remains as an island attached to the Baja peninsula." Eventually, it is prophesied that San Diego erodes away from the Baja peninsula and becomes a free-standing island. California becomes a series of very small islands and one large island made up of the Sierra Nevada mountain range (Gibraltar Island) is the remnant of the great state. "And islands of California, as they shall be known by, are what are left of that once great state that led this country into a time of gold rush and fever for all that is tangible (material). Now it is time for us to seek into the heart to find a Law of Opposite, that which is intangible, that which is untouched, that which is spiritual in nature and finds the unity of all things written within it." It is prophesied that many people will leave California for the inland western states: "Migrations of people from the islands of California, finding their way to what they consider the stable lands of Arizona, New Mexico, and Colorado."

The Great Lakes

When the large earthquake impacts the fractures in the Tetons Mountains, it is prophesied that lower end of Lake Michigan will drain, sending a tidal wave of water over the Midwest. "The tectonic plate moves across the land, rippling like a wave and affects another fracture that exists in the center of that lake (Michigan). Opening its mouth wide, (its) waters rush down into the Bay of Harmony. Many Midwestern towns are flooded over with 80 feet of water. They will become habitable again after several decades during the times of great change."

The New Capital of the United States

"Washington, D.C., the capital city, must be moved." Due to the rising waters of the Atlantic Ocean, the nation's capital is prophesied to be moved to the state of Colorado. "There will be some debate as to where to move this capital city. But its final resting place will be in the Golden City of Klehma. There, in this center part (central United States), the new nation is rebirthed into the glory of the New Age."

Maine

"The state of Maine is still covered in rock, glacier and ice activity. There will come a time, 1,000 to 1,200 years after this time of ice and glacier activity, at which time these lands will thaw again." After this time, it is prophesied in Map Number Five that Maine will become habitable and restored to a natural beauty. "Many new people will come to inhabit this land. The cultures will be much like the ancient Celtics . . . ancient rites will be re-observed and the sacredness of this land celebrated."

Florida, Louisiana, Texas

Florida is prophesied to be covered entirely by water at one point during the Time of Change. After the waters recede, it becomes, again, a tropical paradise. New Orleans, LA, remains under water for some time, but it is prophesied that after 250 years we will see the appearance of a small island named *Harvest Island*. The ocean waters eventually recede from Dallas, Texas, however, it is prophesied that the coastline of Texas forever stays under water after the Time of Change.

Nevada

In Map Number Five, the asteroid that has circled the Earth (see Map Number Four) crashes into the Nevada desert. This causes a series of events that alters the western United States forever. "When you look into the skies and see the asteroid moon, a day shall come that it crashes into the Nevada area. It is the impact of this that sets off the fracture in the Tetons. In less than three months a series of convulsive earthquakes grasp the lands of Nevada and much of Utah under the Pacific waters for many, many years."

The Northeast and the New Islands of the Eastern Seaboard

Western Pennsylvania is prophesied to become a flood land after Lake Erie ruptures (See Map Number Four). Pittsburgh becomes a coastal city on the Atlantic Ocean. "Many cities are under water with free floating glaciers surfacing the top. Gone are cities such as New York City, Long Island . . . long gone . . . Pennsylvania, much of it as swamp land and under frigid waters. Philadelphia and Baltimore, long gone."

After the Time of Change of Map Number Five, many islands are prophesied to exist, forming the new eastern United States seaboard. After 600 to 700 years, these islands become a beautiful paradise. "The coastline is moved as far west as Tennessee. Little bays, much like the fjords of Norway, fill the east coast in the Appalachian Mountains. Many people are quite surprised at the stunning beauty that these Earth Changes have left the eastern seaboard of the United States. It becomes a new vacation land for many . . . much like a park setting. Within 600 to 700 years new plants and animals begin to populate the lush forests that now cover the eastern United States. It becomes a garden that it once was (again). The pollution of industrialization is too, cleaned up, as Mother Earth makes her great birth transition into the New Age."

The Mystic Message: Map Number Five
See the Unity of All Things

"This Map is based on the unity of all things. For the unity of all things does not see a separateness (separation) in the pairs of opposites. There is hot and there is cold. There is left and there is right. There is up and there is down . . . and so on and so forth. Are these not opposites? But, in the law of correspondence, these things are related to one another. They are *part of* one another. Together, they represent the whole, the sum . . . this is called unity. The sum of all parts equals unity. Open your eyes and see the unity of all things! This is how love and harmony is achieved. See harmony and unity in all things, then you can begin to see the love that binds us all."

Map Number Six

"This outcome lies in your hands . . lies in the responsibility of your choice."

According to the prophecies, the Sixth Map will never be shown to humanity.
"It is important for you to understand the choices you have created from. This map that sits on this table, rolled so tightly, its result lies in the power of humanity's choice. For this reason, we as members of this lodge, refuse to unroll this map . . . for this is a prophecy that is undetermined at this moment. It is a prophecy that will be determined by your own power and your ability to act responsibly."

Clearly, our future and the future of the Earth is up to us. The prophecies of the Sixth Map teach, "The outcome of the future is left in your hands. The outcome for future generations is left in your choice. The outcome of the times to come, is not inevitable. It is changeable. It is mutable. It is created through your choices. We cannot unroll this map for humanity, for it is a map that must be unrolled by humanity (itself). Humanity must now create this Sixth Map."

If you would like to read the transcript for the sixth map of prophecy, please see *New World Wisdom, Book Two.* ✺

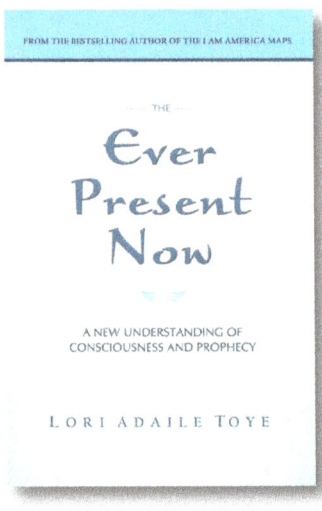

The Ever Present Now:
A Genuine Prophet - Always Wrong!

By now you are likely in shock, disbelief, or completely overwhelmed after reading these literal prophecies. Please indulge me for a minute. Closely examine your "feeling" and allow that emotion to move you internally into metaphoric thinking. Now, re-consider the information. At this stage everyone is a bit different. Some rapidly flow into the images of Prophecy and their inherent allegories, while others do not.

As mentioned earlier, when Westerners hear the words "prophet" or "Prophecy," their likely response will be, "Oh yeah, Armageddon." And since the Book of Revelations is the only significant body of Prophecy that the Western world has yet to experience, this inclination makes perfect sense. Traditional cultures of the East are often referred to as "descending cultures" that protect customs and beliefs based on literally thousands of years of individual practice and knowledge. Through this time-worn, ancestral wisdom, descending cultures innately understand the heart of Prophecy and know that this spiritual teaching is an important signal to personally purify and seek redemption and healing. The Master Teachers present the I AM America Prophecies to illustrate how individual balance and harmony are created through our daily choices.

The common difficulty and subsequent confusion of Westerners who confront Prophecy is due to the fact that their ears are not trained to hear metaphor. This makes the truest comprehension of the meaning of Prophecy—written in the language of the superconscious—almost impossible. Joseph Campbell said, "The Metaphor is the Mask of God through which eternity is experienced." The spiritual teachings that are conveyed by most prophecies are designed to open your ears to a richer understanding of meaning.

Traditional biblical Armageddon destroys the old world, rewarding the gift of paradise to the deserving: again, another age-old battle arguing the ethics of good and evil. But the path of Prophecy is experiential. The visions of Prophecy are spiritual teachings containing warnings which—if experienced and heeded—are designed to heal and renew our experience of our lives. So please don't ask, "When is this going to happen?" Honestly, we don't know. We can only share the messages with you and leave it up to you to interpret. However, we might point you to the Twelve Jurisdictions (Spiritual Teachings that are given in *New World Wisdom*). Or address the Golden Cities and how Earth and Human energy fields are ideally ONE.

There is a saying that a prophet's work is truly complete when the events that are prophesied never occur. If they do not occur, then those who had the "eyes to see" and the "ears to hear" made the choice to heal and transform their lives. Catastrophe and destruction may be averted or avoided altogether. So inevitably, a genuine prophet is always wrong.

Spiritual Insights on Earth Changes

1. Since our planet and humans share the same physical composition, we are virtually ONE. You cannot disconnect the two.

2. Our world is a thought, feeling, and action hologram created by many kingdoms, (mineral, vegetable, animal, human, etc.), that inhabit Earth. The Earth and our bodies have many systems—these systems are interrelated.

3. Every individual thought, desire, and action is recorded, and subsequently influences and creates a "Collective Consciousness."

4. Collective Consciousness plays a major role in the outcome of events. It can make the difference between a cataclysmic hurricane and a gentle summer rain.

5. If you live fear, you will create fear.

6. If you live love, you will create love.

7. We are all creating and experiencing World Earth Changes as an opportunity to develop personal Mastery and evolve spiritually.

8. We must change ourselves enough that this change reflects in our societies, governments, and environments. We have a conscious choice in the upcoming Earth Changes, and that choice will help determine the outcome.

9. This is an urgent time—the time is now! ✦

SECTION FOUR

Golden Cities

What Exactly Is a Golden City Vortex?
Golden City Vortices—based on the Ascended Masters' I AM America material—are prophesied areas of safety and spiritual energies during the Times of Changes. Covering an expanse of land and air space, these sacred energy sites span more than 400 kilometers (270 miles) in diameter, with a vertical height of 400 kilometers (250 miles). More importantly, Golden City Vortices reach beyond terrestrial significance and into the ethereal realm. This system of safe harbors acts as a group or universal mind within our galaxy, connecting information seamlessly and instantly with other beings. The Master Teachers call this phenomenon the Galactic Web.

As mentioned earlier, fifty-one Golden City Vortices are stationed throughout the world, and each carries a different meaning, a combination of Ray Forces, and a Divine Purpose. Some are older than others; some Vortices are new; and some shift locations. The activation of Golden City Vortices occurs in patterns—that's the crux of the numbering system. The Master Teachers call Earth "Beloved Babajeran."

Although the Masters, as a group, oversee all Golden Cities, each Master stewards his or her own Vortex. A Golden City Vortex works on the principles of electromagnetism and geology. Vortices tend to appear near fault lines, possibly serving as conduits of inner-earth movement to terra firma. The Gobean Vortex near the fissure-filled Mogollon Rim of Arizona; the Malton Vortex of the Midwest, adjacent to the New Madrid fault line; and the Shalahah Vortex of Idaho, an ancient cleft near the Snake River and Hells Canyon, lend credibility to this theory.

Geology has a profound effect on the potency of a Vortex. Not surprising, the five Golden City Vortices rest on areas of highly magnetic geologic formations. The iron-rich content of basalt pillars and ancient-lava deposit serve as natural conductors of electromagnetic energy; igneous rocks, according to geologic data, create more magnetic pull than sedimentary rocks. That's why Gobean exudes so much energy. Landmarks—such as Mount Baldy in Arizona, the apex of the Southwestern Vortex, and the Golden City Vortex of Shalahah—are filled with basalt and iron-rich rocks.

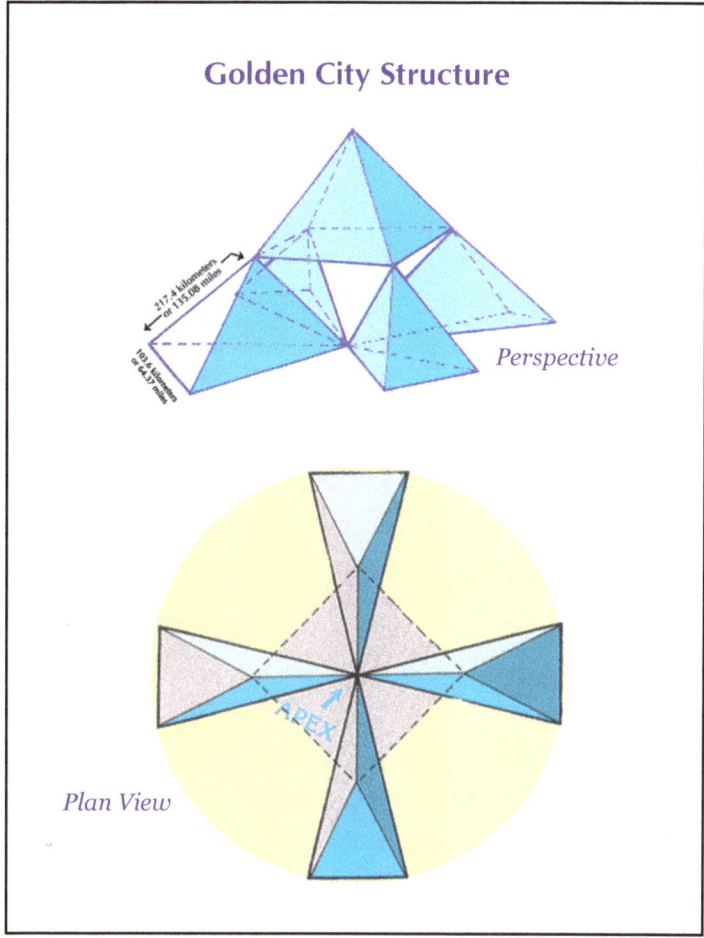

[(Top) *Golden City Structure:* Perspective
(Bottom) Plan View]

Water also drives the disbursement of Vortex energies. The Gobean Vortex sits atop the largest aquifer in the Southwest. Shalahah, too, surrounded by three, huge freshwater lakes near Coeur d'Alene and Pend'Oreille, Idaho, and Flathead Lake in Montana draws power from water.

Visitors to Golden Cities experience spiritual and psychic development—they feel a heightened sense of balance, harmony, and peace. The Golden Cites are natural places of meditation, connection with spirit guides, and contact with past-life experiences. Vortices can instantly align the human energy field (aura). During your first stay in a Vortex, you may sleep more while your body adjusts to powerful energies. As you acclimate, you'll undergo a rejuvenation of the body and the spirit. After the shock subsides, many Vortex-seeking pilgrims will engage in prayer and group ceremonies with friends and spiritual mentors, awakening deep connections among fellow humans. ✤

[*Ray Forces and Golden Cities:* (Right) Rays originate from the Galactic Center. (Below) Ray enters Golden City.]

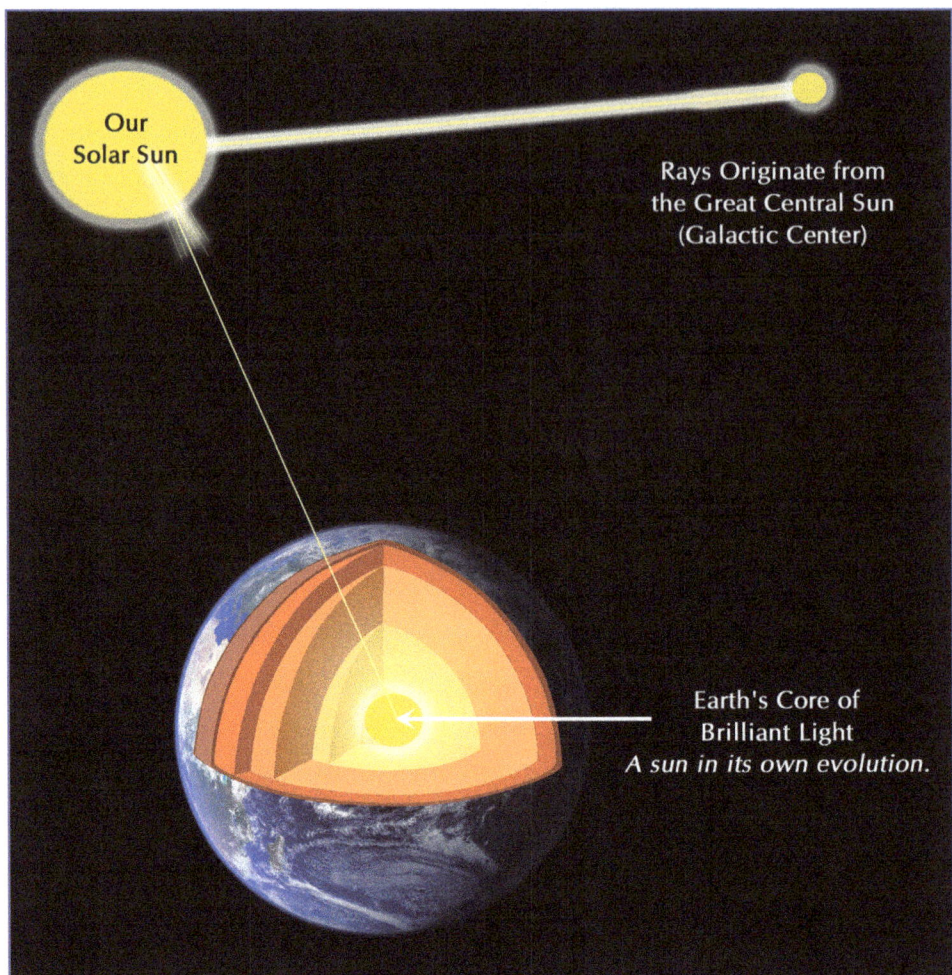

Divine Destiny: **Arcing of Ray Forces to Golden City Vortices**

The Seven Rays of Light and Sound originate from the Great Central Sun—or Galactic Center—as it is known in Hindu and Mayan cultures. Ray Forces are an unseen type of energy that are said to function like a non-visible, quasar–type of light. Since Ray Forces control many human evolutionary aspects, they distribute their energies by arcing through the planets of the Fire Triplicity of our Solar System to Earth: Mars (Aries, the spiritual pioneer); Sun (Leo, the spiritual leader); and Jupiter (Sagittarius, the spiritual teacher). Vedic Rishis and Master Teachers concur that the amount of galactic light streaming to Earth as the Seven Rays controls lifespans, memory function, ability to absorb and respect spiritual knowledge, and access to the Akashic Records. Golden City Rays arch primarily through our solar sun and enter the earth's core. The movement of Golden City Vortices draws the Ray Force through, to the center of the Vortex—the Star. Energies of the Ray are disbursed from the Star throughout the entire Vortex. ⚜

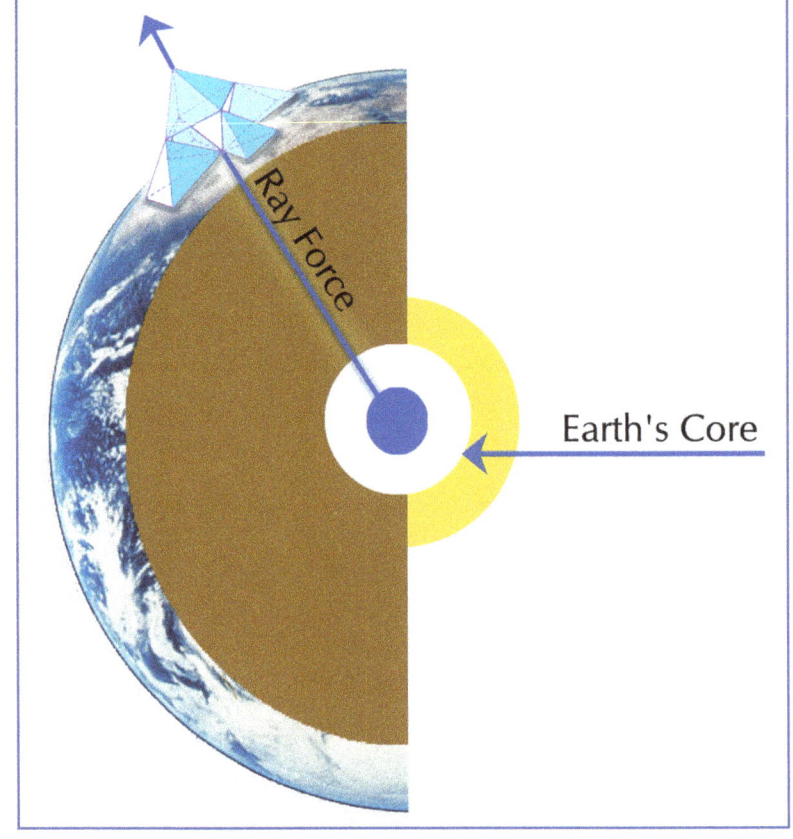

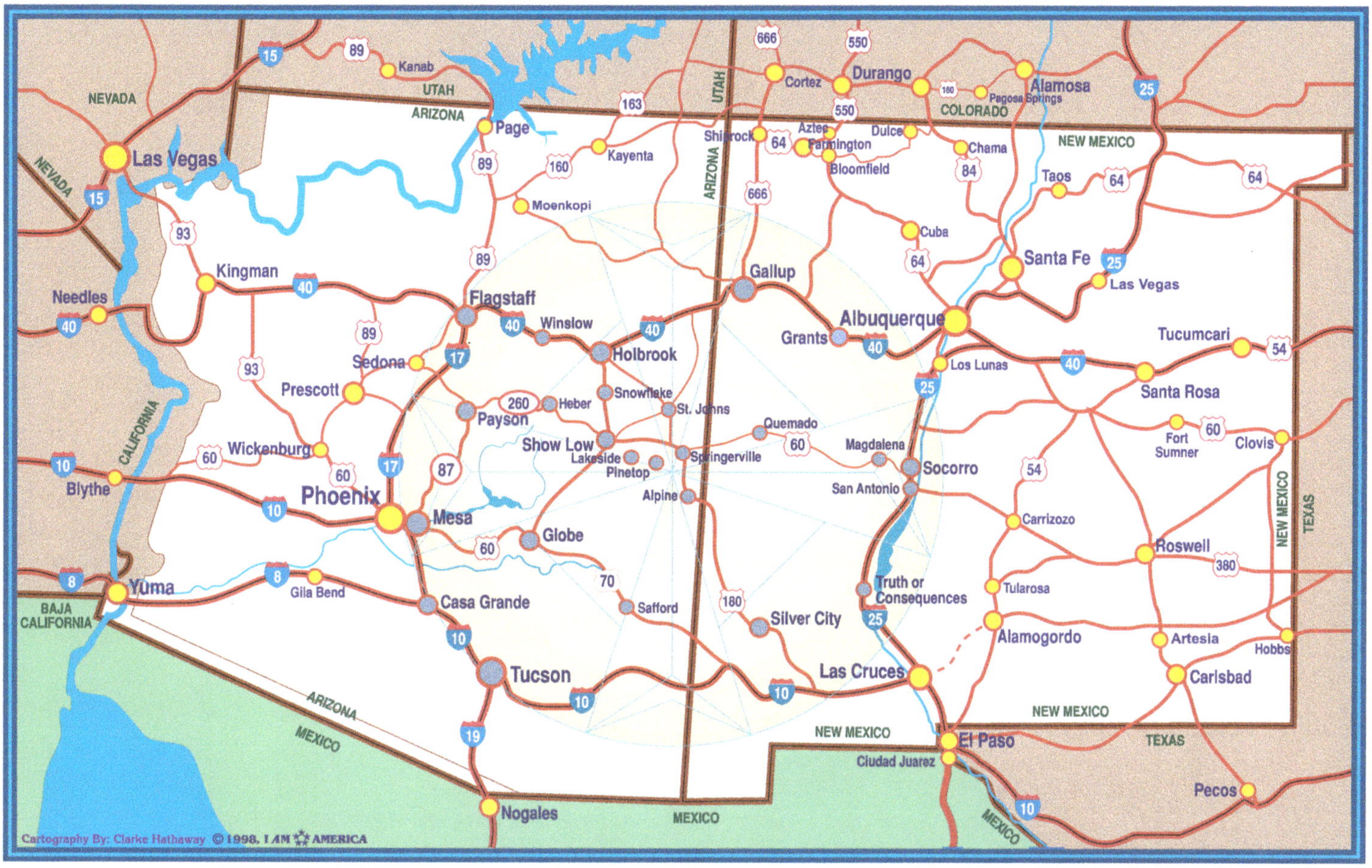

[Above: *Golden City of Gobean*.]

The Five Golden Cities of the United States

The first Vortex to manifest in the United States during the Times of Changes is the Golden City of Gobean (pronounced Go'bee un) and is located in Arizona and New Mexico. The Master Teacher prophesied to teach in this area is Master El Morya (*pictured left*). The spiritual qualities and teachings that are identified with Gobean are Transformation, Harmony, and Peace. Gobean plays a critical role in the Spiritual Awakening as it was the first city to manifest the new energies of the New Times, which occurred in the early 80's. It is also prophesied that the energies of Gobean align the Will to the Divine Will.

The Ray Force, which is a Golden City's spiritual light, radiates as the color blue. Michael is the Archangel of the Blue Ray. Each Ray of a Golden City enters at the apex and originates from the Great Central Sun. The apex of Gobean is Mount Baldy, Arizona. The energies of Gobean hold the wisdom of Ancient Egypt and align with the Golden City of Gobi (which is near Shamballa). The spiritual sound of Gobean is OM SHANTI and produces peace and harmony when repeated in prayer.

Vortices seem to appear at intersections of the Earth's grid, or bio-magnetic field of the Earth. These intersecting strands of Earth's energy are also known as lei-lines. The ancient symbol for a Vortex is a cross in a circle. In the I AM America Prophecies, each Golden City Vortex is marked by a Maltese Cross within a circle.

What are the benefits of visiting or living in a Golden City Vortex? The most obvious is that in the I AM America Earth Changes Prophecies, Golden City Vortices are safe places to live. The Ascended Masters refer to them as protected areas. Many people notice an increased psychic ability and telepathic awareness in a Vortex. This is due to the fact that two dimensions are overlapping and etheric realities become more perceptible. Thus, Golden City Vortices are natural places for meditation, meeting spirit guides, and triggering past and future life information. Because strong Vortex energies have the ability to instantly align the human energy field (aura), you may feel more balanced, harmonious and peaceful in a Golden City Vortex. In your first visits, this realignment may cause you to sleep

[Above: *Golden City of Malton*.]

a great deal. After your body makes the adjustment, Vortex energies energize and rejuvenate the body. Most importantly, each Golden City Vortex is connected to an even larger web of creation. The Master Teachers call this 'The Galactic Web' – and it acts like a group or universal mind within our galaxy to connect information seamlessly and timelessly with others. Intentional desires, prayers, and ceremonies with groups of friends in Golden Cities can demonstrate measurable results. With this in mind, many people have moved to Golden City Vortices to hold a focus for a peaceful Golden Age.

Malton (pronounced Mal tone') is the second Golden City to manifest in the United States, which occurred in 1994. Malton's role during the Times of Changes will help to purify and protect the Elemental and Deva kingdoms. It is prophesied that Malton will be one of the first places after the changes that elemental life

(fairies and gnomes) will be seen and will openly interact with humanity. Fruition and attainment of desires are its spiritual qualities. The Master Teacher is Kuthumi (*pictured left*), the Archangel is Uriel, and the Ray Force is the Ruby Ray. The spiritual sound of Malton is OM EANDRA (pronounced E on' draw) and invokes a blessing to Mother Earth and all animals, plants, and minerals when said in this Vortex. Ancient Druid and Celtic cultures are said to be felt in Malton and this Golden City Vortex holds their ageless records. On the Earth's grid, Malton aligns with its sister Golden City of Denasha (located in Scotland and England). The apex of Malton is located near the city of Mattoon, Illinois.

[Above: *Golden City of Wahanee*.]

The I AM America prophecies describe the Golden Cities as large Vortices and their size is over 400 kilometers in diameter and over 200 miles high. Their sacred shape is built as a series of pyramids. This symbology reinforces how man's consciousness, at this time, is evolving from a Third Dimensional orientation to Fourth and Fifth Dimensional awareness. Saint Germain's introductory information about Golden Cities refers to these areas as protected and that they would serve as a focus for "interaction with spiritual energy."

Wahanee (pronounced Waa hah'nee) is the third Golden City to manifest in the United States and holds the energies of the Violet Ray. Saint Germain, (*pictured right*), is the Master Teacher of this Vortex that manifested its energies in early 1996; therefore, its spiritual qualities are Brotherhood and Sisterhood for all of humanity, and freedom and justice. Records of Ancient Africa are held ethereally throughout this Golden City Vortex and can be accessed and understood through meditating on Wahanee's subtle energies. Wahanee's Sister City is the Golden City of Eabra (located in Alaska and Yukon, Canada) and it is prophesied that the Violet Ray will arch between these two power points on the Earth's grid creating a sense of Brotherly Love for all of humanity in the New Times. Archangel Zadkiel is the Angel of the Violet Ray (known also as the Violet Flame). Ascended Master myths claim that it was this angel that brought the healing, transmuting flames of the Violet Ray from the Temples of Atlantis

I AM AMERICA ATLAS 73

to the United States before the continent's demise. The spiritual sound of Wahanee is OM HUE (pronounced *hu* as in *you*) and when repeated in prayer throughout this Vortex produces a sense of calm, peace, and the ability to perceive other dimensions. Wahanee is prophesied to play an important role in humanity's global healing in the New Times. The apex is located in Augusta, Georgia on the banks of the Savannah River.

Golden Cities of the I AM America prophecies represent the power of choice and its ability to overcome the adversity and catastrophe presented in the Earth Changes prophecies. Master K. H. clearly states, "Within your heart lies the gentle revolution which can redirect the course of such events." The four doors (four directions) of each Golden City are an integral part of the spiritual and alchemical teachings of I AM America and the Golden Cities.

[Above: *Golden City of Shalahah*.]

The Northern Door, also known as the black door, represents discipline and hard labor. Kuan Yin lends spiritual insight to this concept, "If you are to travel to the northern portion of the Vortex, you will find that you will be asked to transmute and forgive." However, as these Golden City energies are absorbed and integrated, worldly benefits can emerge. Northern Doors are said to manifest and fructify our desires and can manifest physical abundance. In the New Times it is prophesied that the energies of the Northern Doors will produce the most abundant and prolific food crops, and are the best locations for commercial and business endeavors.

Southern Doors, also known as the red door represent the Healing of the Nations through enlightened love, non-judgment, faith, and courage. Energies of this door are good for healing at any level – body, mind, and spirit. In the New Times it is prophesied that many miracle healings will be demonstrated in these areas, and because of the natural, benefic energy are good locations for hospitals, healing clinics, retreats, and spas. The energies of Southern Doors are alleged to assist in physical regeneration.

Shalahah (pronounced Shaw law' hah) is the fourth Golden City to manifest its energies, which occurred in 1998. Sananda, (*pictured right*), also known as Jesus, is sponsor of the Great Change, and is the Master Teacher of Shalahah, and aligns to the Green Ray. The apex is located near Lolo Pass on the Bitterroot Mountain Range on the Montana and Idaho border. Abundance, prosperity and healing are the spiritual qualities of Shalahah and it is said to align with the ancient cultures of Eastern India.

74 I AM AMERICA ATLAS

[Above: *Golden City of Klehma*.]

Present within the Shalahah Golden City Vortex are two unique energy anomalies: Ascension Valley and the Transportation Center. Ascension Valley, located between Potlatch and Saint Maries, Idaho, contains a very high spiritual energy that is prophesied to regenerate, restore, and prepare the body, mind, and spirit for Fourth and Fifth Dimensional awareness. The Transportation Center is a Vortex of energy that exists over Coeur d'Alene, Idaho and is prophesied to become a timeless and spontaneous travel portal to other locations throughout the world and when prop-

[Above: *Ascension Valley*.]

erly developed and utilized will become a very common form of travel in the Golden Age. It is prophesied that these two types of energy centers will become models for similar energy sites that will be discovered as the Earth progresses through the Golden Age.

Historical Hells Canyon (the deepest gorge in North America) is located on the west side of Shalahah and flowing through it, between present day Oregon and Idaho, is the Snake River. The Snake River flows to the north similar to the Nile River of Africa, and its waters originate near Grand Teton – said to be a retreat for the Ascended Masters. The waters of the Snake River are spiritually healing and many ancient petroglyphs are etched in the rocks along her banks.

Shalahah's sister city is the Golden City of Prana, which is physically located in the center of India. Archangel Raphael is the Angel of the Green Ray and the spiritual sound for Shalahah is OM SHEAHAH (pronounced Shee' aw hah) which means, "I AM as ONE." When chanted, sung, or meditated upon in prayer, this mantra can produce spiritual healing, a feeling of Oneness and Unity Consciousness which the Master Teachers call, Unana.

The Eastern Door is also known as the blue door. Its energies demand purification and sacrifice, but with the great reward of alchemy. Saint Germain refers to the path of the Eastern Door as, "the Elixir of Life." The blue door also signifies friends, family, and those who are helpful. The Master Teachers claim that any relationship or family problem can be solved through time spent in contemplation on or in this doorway. In the New Times, it is prophesied that the Eastern Doors of the Golden City Vortices are perfect locations for communities, group activities, residential homes, and schools for young children.

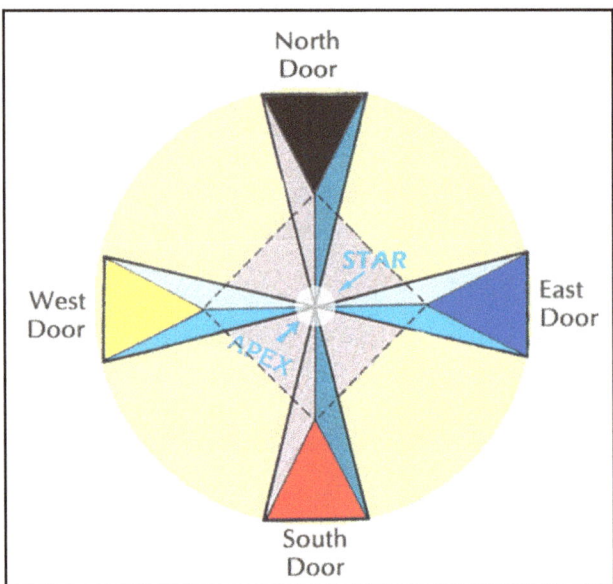

[Above: *Doorways and Star of Golden City*.]

In the I AM America teachings, the Western Door is also known as the Yellow door. It is the path of wisdom, and is sometimes referred to as the "Philosopher's Stone." It is also said to be the path of adeptship and perfection, and is the conclusion of the four initiatory pathways before entry into the "Star of Knowledge." Western doors are good locations for universities and schools of higher and spiritual knowledge. The Master Teachers claim that in the New Times governmental activities should be located within the energies of the Western Doors.

Klehma (pronounced Klee' maw) is the fifth Golden City in the United States and its energies were complete in 2,000 AD. The Master Teacher Serapis Bey, (*pictured left*), holds the spiritual focus of continuity, balance and harmony in this Vortex which is said to identify with Native American culture.

Klehma is derived from the word khem – a name for Egypt, used thousands of years ago. Klehma is also an ancient name for the Pleiades, the seven stars clustered in the Taurus constellation. The Seven Sisters and the Taurean Bull, known as Apis or Serapis, are famous in the sacred lore of Native Americans and early Egyptians.

Klehma is prophesied to become the capstone of the Golden Cities of America. The final of the five Golden City Vortices in the United States, Klehma is prophesied to hold the New Capital (moved from Washington D.C.) after the changes. It is also prophesied that many visionaries and leaders of the New Times will live in this area. Quetzalcoatl, the Mayan and Aztec God of Peace, is said to have educated his people in the arts of government. America is derived from the Peruvian name for Quetzalcoatl, Amaru. Amaruca means, "Land of the Plumed Serpent."

The Ray Force of Klehma is the White Ray of purity which is associated with the Archangel Gabriel. The spiritual sound for Klehma is the same as Malton's. OM EANDRA (pronounced E on' draw) and invokes a blessing to bring Mother Earth and all of her inhabitants into balance when said in this Vortex. The apex is located near Cope, Colorado.

The center (apex) of each Golden City Vortex is called the "Star." The path of the Star is ideally the Star of Self-Knowledge. Living in a Golden City Star area will produce self-knowledge and self-empowerment. The Star is by far one of the most powerful areas of a Golden City Vortex, and since all four energies of the doorways coalesce throughout, it is identified with the color white. Stars of Golden City Vortices are said to be forty miles in diameter, but the benefits of this radius can be felt for up to sixty miles. In the New Times, the Stars will be used as ceremonial grounds and their energies are good for self-renunciation, meditation, and spiritual liberation. It is also prophesied that during the Times of Changes that the energies of the Stars will become so purified and beneficially charged that this is where the Master Teachers will be able to manifest in physical form. It is then prophesied that much spiritual teaching and more miracle healing will occur. ✤

LAND OF CO-CREATION
Canada and Greenland

[Above: *The five Golden Cities of Canada and Greenland are pictured above. Not to scale.*]

Golden Cities of Canada and Greenland

EABRA: This Golden City became active in 2004, and the energies of its Star mature in 2021. The apex is located on or near Apex Mountain, in the mountainous Dawson Range. The Ray Force for this Golden City is the Violet Ray, and its steward is Portia. *(Portia, pictured above.)* Eabra is aligned with the United States Golden City Wahanee.

JEAFRAY: Archangel Zadkiel is the steward of this Golden City of the Violet Ray. The energies of this eastern Canadian Vortex activated in 2006, and its brilliant Star matures in 2023. Jeafray's apex is located southeast of Fermont, Quebec, with Vortex energies likely driven by plentiful iron deposits. Southern Adjutant points are the Groulx Mountains, east of Manicouagan Reservoir. It is theorized that this reservoir was created over two-hundred million years ago by a meteor strike. *(Archangel Zadkiel pictured right.)*

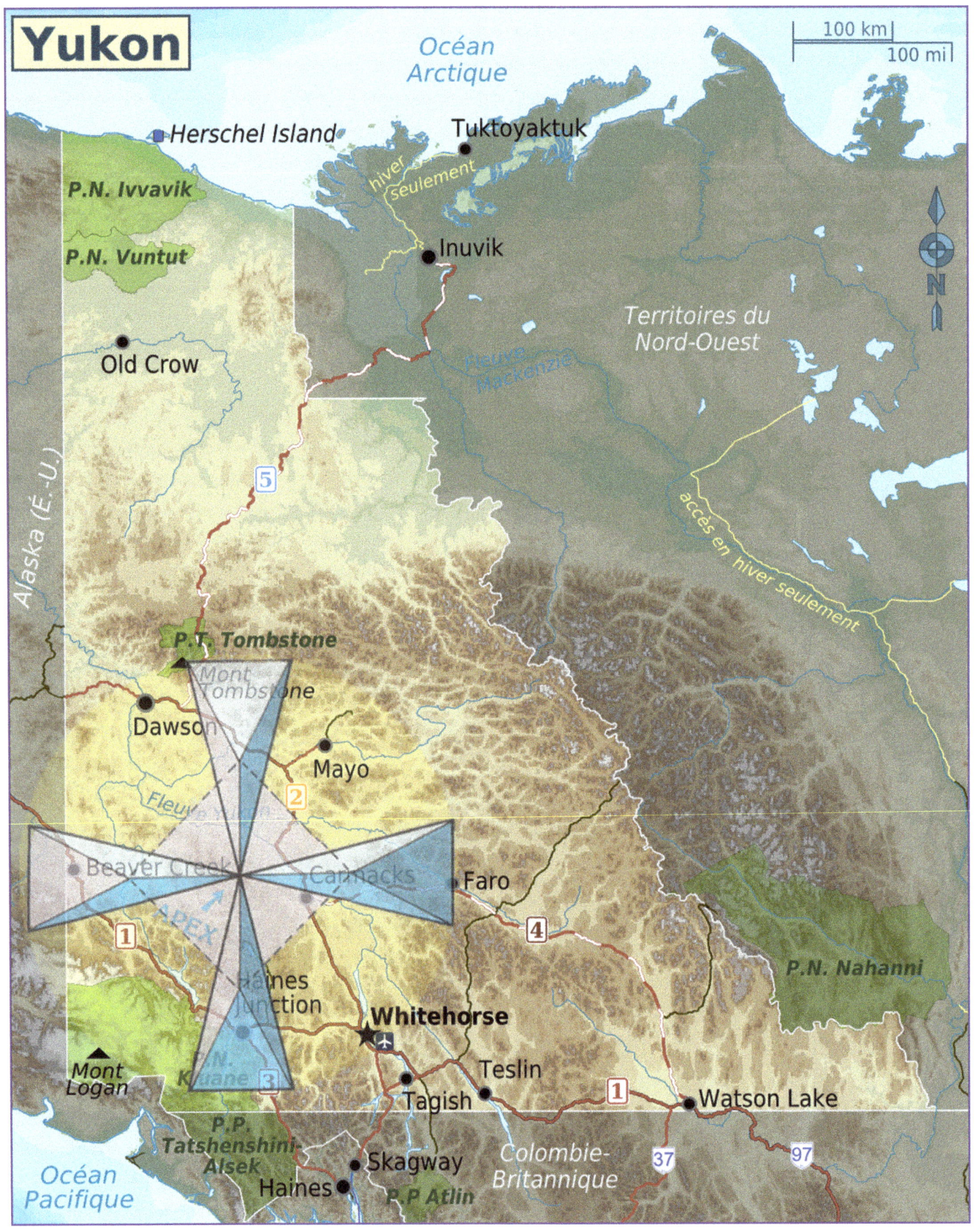

[Above: *The Golden City of Eabra, located primarily in the Yukon Province of Canada.*]

[Left: *The Golden City of Jeafray, located primarily in the Labrador and Quebec Provinces of Canada.*]

PASHACINO: The western Canadian Golden City of the Green Ray is stewarded by the Ascended Master Soltec. (*Soltec, pictured left.*) Its apex is located near Wabamun Lake, located in Provincial Park, Alberta. Calgary, Alberta lies in the flux of this great Vortex that became active in 2002. The energies of the Star activate in 2019. The city of Edmonton, Alberta is also located in Pashacino.

UVERNO: The Golden City of Uverno is stewarded by the Ascended Master Paul the Venetian. (*Paul the Venetian, pictured right.*) The energies of this Golden City activated in 2008, with the Star energies completing their growth in 2025. Its Ray Force is Pink. The Southern Door adjutant point is Lake Seul, and the

I AM AMERICA ATLAS 79

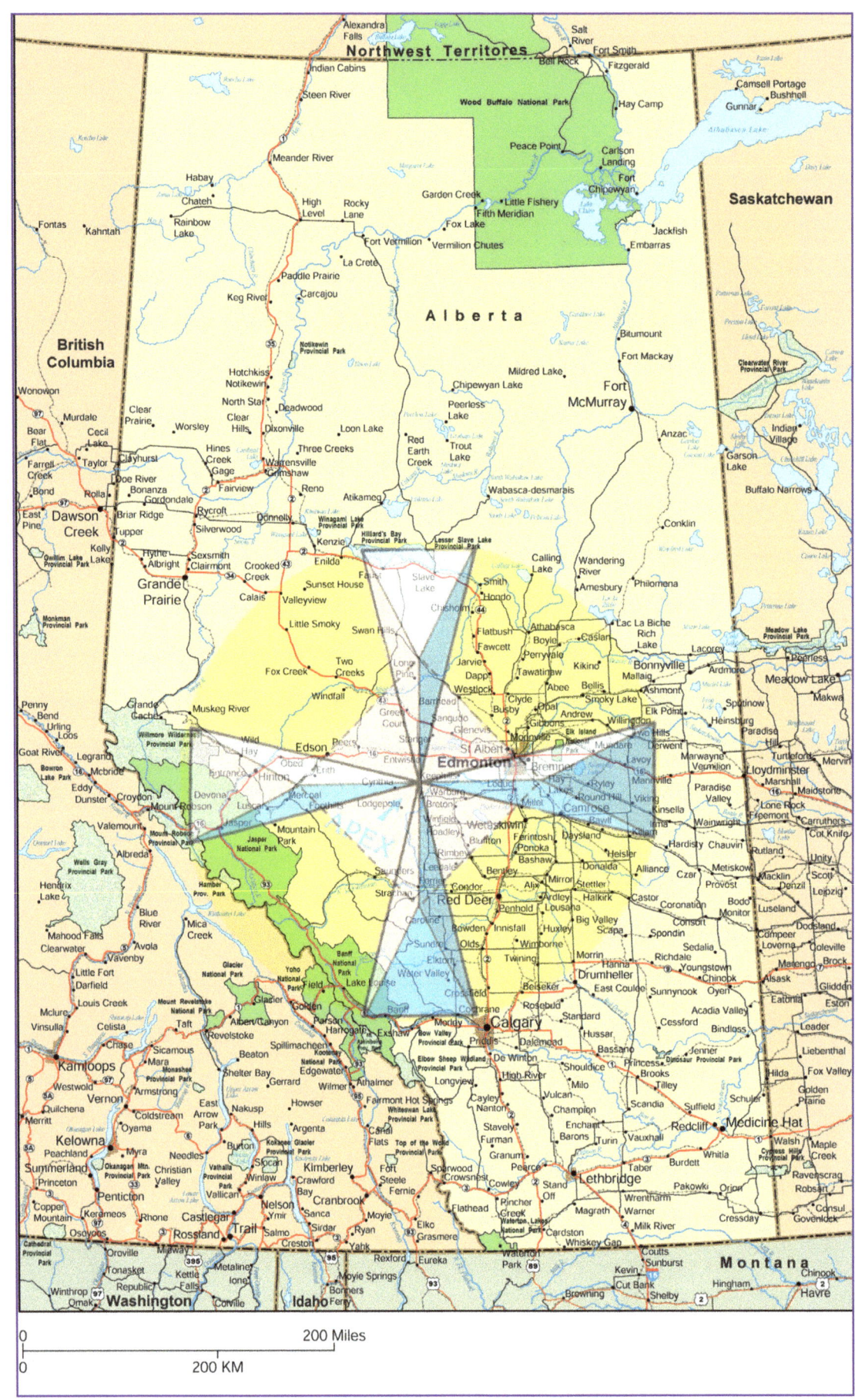

[Above: *The Golden City of Pashacino, located primarily in the Alberta Province of Canada.*]

[Left: *The Golden City of Uverno, located in the Province of Ontario, Canada.*]

apex is located near a series of five lakes in the Ojibway First Nation. Uverno contains one of the richest gold mines in the world.

YUTHOR: This Golden City is located over the glacial ice of Greenland that is prophesied to thaw and create a beautiful inland lake filled with new species of fish and aquatic life. Yuthor's steward is Master Hilarion of the Green Ray and the Vortex activated in 2010. Its Star energies fully establish in 2027. (*Hilarion, pictured above.*)

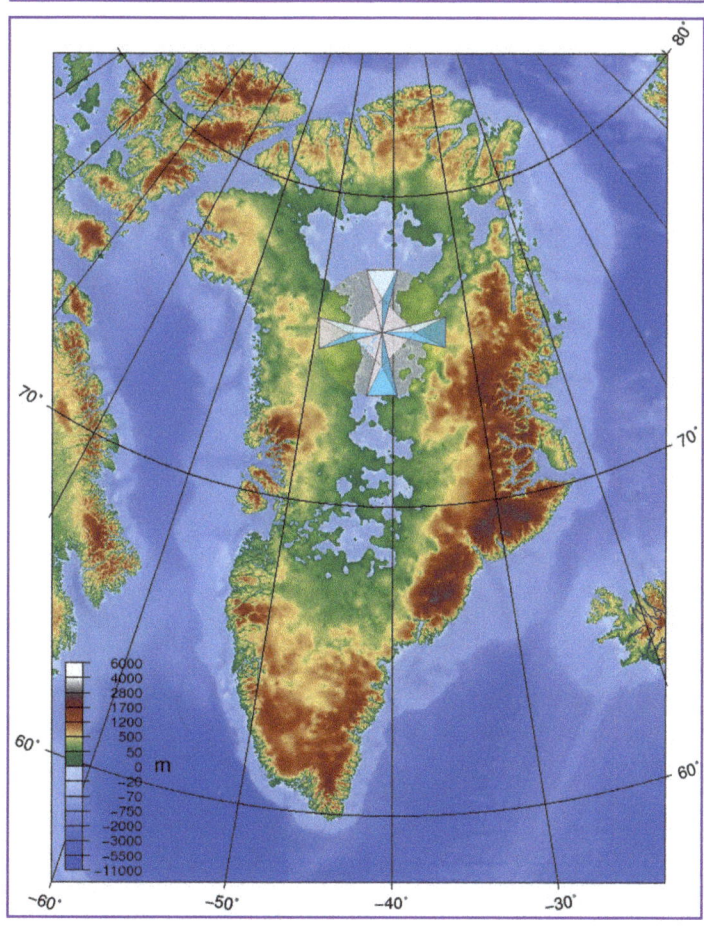

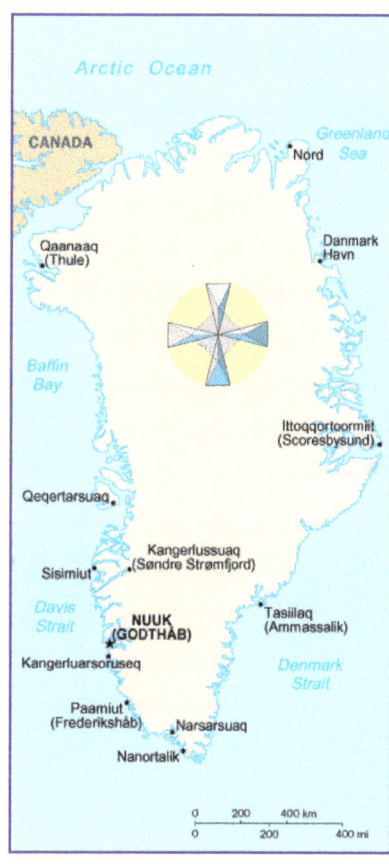

[Left: *As glacial ice melts, the Golden City of Yuthor protects large inland waters of Greenland and many new species of fish. The Golden City of Yuthor is located over the northern glacial ice of Greenland.*]

[Above: *The four Golden Cities located in the Cradleland: Mexico and Central America. Not to scale.*]

Golden Cities of Mexico and Central America

MARNERO: Mother Mary's Golden City of the healing Green Ray activates in 2046, and the energies of the Star complete in 2046. The apex of Marnero is located near the community of Santa Maria del Oro, in the state of Durango. *(Mother Mary, pictured left.)*

ASONEA: This Golden City of the Yellow Ray is stewarded by Ascended Master Peter the Everlasting. The apex is located near Santa Clara, on the island of Cuba. The Vortex activates in 2048, and the Star matures in 2065. *(Peter the Everlasting, pictured right.)*

[Right: *The Golden City of Marnero is located in Mexico.*]

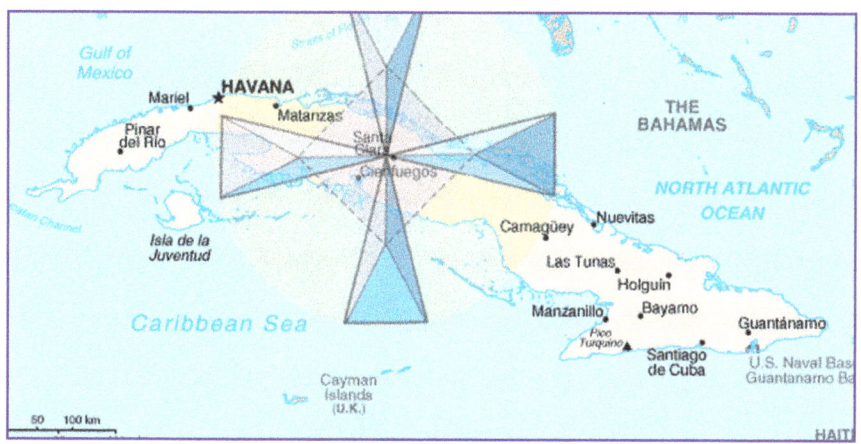

CROTESE: The energies of this Golden City of the Pink Ray activate in 2056 and fully mature in 2073. Crotese's sublime custodian is the Ascended Master Paul the Devoted. The apex is located near Volcan Irazu, Costa Rica. *(Paul the Devoted, pictured above.)*

JEHOA: Most of this Golden City is currently located west of the island chain of the Lesser Antilles, and the island of Saint Lucia is the eastern adjutant point of this Vortex of the Violet Ray. The islands of Grenada and Martinique are also held in the transformative energies of Kuan Yin, who is the steward of this Golden City. Jehoa anchors the qualities of compassion and gratitude over new lands that are prophesied to emerge in the Caribbean. This Golden City's energies activate in 2058, and the Star matures in 2075. *(Kuan Yin, pictured above.)*

[Above: (Top) *The Golden City of Asonea, located in Cuba.* (Next) *The Golden City of Crotese is located primarily in Costa Rica.*]

I AM AMERICA ATLAS *83*

[Right: *The Golden City of Jehoa is located in the Caribbean.*]

[Right: *Petit Piton is a volcanic spire located near Soufirere, Saint Lucia Island, in the Golden City of Jehoa.*]

SECTION SEVEN

MOTHERLAND
Golden Cities of South America

Golden City of
Andeo
Consistency, The Feminine

Golden City of
Braham
The Nurturer

Golden City of
Tehekoa
Devotion

[Above: *The three Golden Cities of South America. South America is known as the Motherland. Not to scale.*]

I AM AMERICA ATLAS 85

[*Above: The Golden City of Andeo, located primarily in Peru.*]

Golden Cities of South America
ANDEO: This is the first of three feminine Golden Cities that serve South America, also known as the Motherland. The city of Iquitos, Peru is located at the adjutant point of the Western Door of the Vortex. The half-million populated city has the distinction of being reached only by airplane or boat, and is home to the one of two world renown Amazon libraries

of Latin America. Andeo's stewards are Goddess Meru (also referred to as the First Sister) and the beloved Archeia Constance (*pictured right*). They assist the dual Ray Forces of both the Pink Ray and the Gold Ray in this Golden City primarily located in Peru. The Golden City's energies fully activate in 2050, and the Star matures in 2067. (*Lord Meru and the Goddess Meru, pictured to the left.*)

86 I AM AMERICA ATLAS

[Left: *The Golden City of Braham, located in Brazil. Note the four points of the Swaddling Cloth, delineating the protected lands of Mother Mary, dedicated to the New Children.*]

BRAHAM: The second Golden City of the Motherland (South America) is located within Mother Mary's Swaddling Cloth of protected lands. Braham's steward is the Second Sister, also known as the Goddess Yemanya. *(The Second Sister of the Motherland, Yemanya, pictured above.)* Braham's apex is located in the Veadeiros National Park, near Alto Paraiso de Goias. This Brazilian Golden City activates in 2052, and the energies of the Star fructify in 2069. Braham is affiliated with the Pink Ray.

TEHEKOA: Located in Argentina, the third Golden City of Tehekoa anchors the feminine energies of both the Pink and Violet Rays. Pachamama is also known as the Third Sister of the Motherland and this Golden City activates in 2054; the Star energies fully develop in 2071. Tehekoa's apex is located near Nahuel Mapa, a village located in central Argentina. *(Pachamama, the Third Sister, pictured above.)*

I AM AMERICA ATLAS

[Right: *The Golden City Tehekoa is located in central Argentina, west of Buenos Aires.*]

[Above: *Valle Grande near San Rafael, Argentina, in the Golden City of Tehekoa.*]

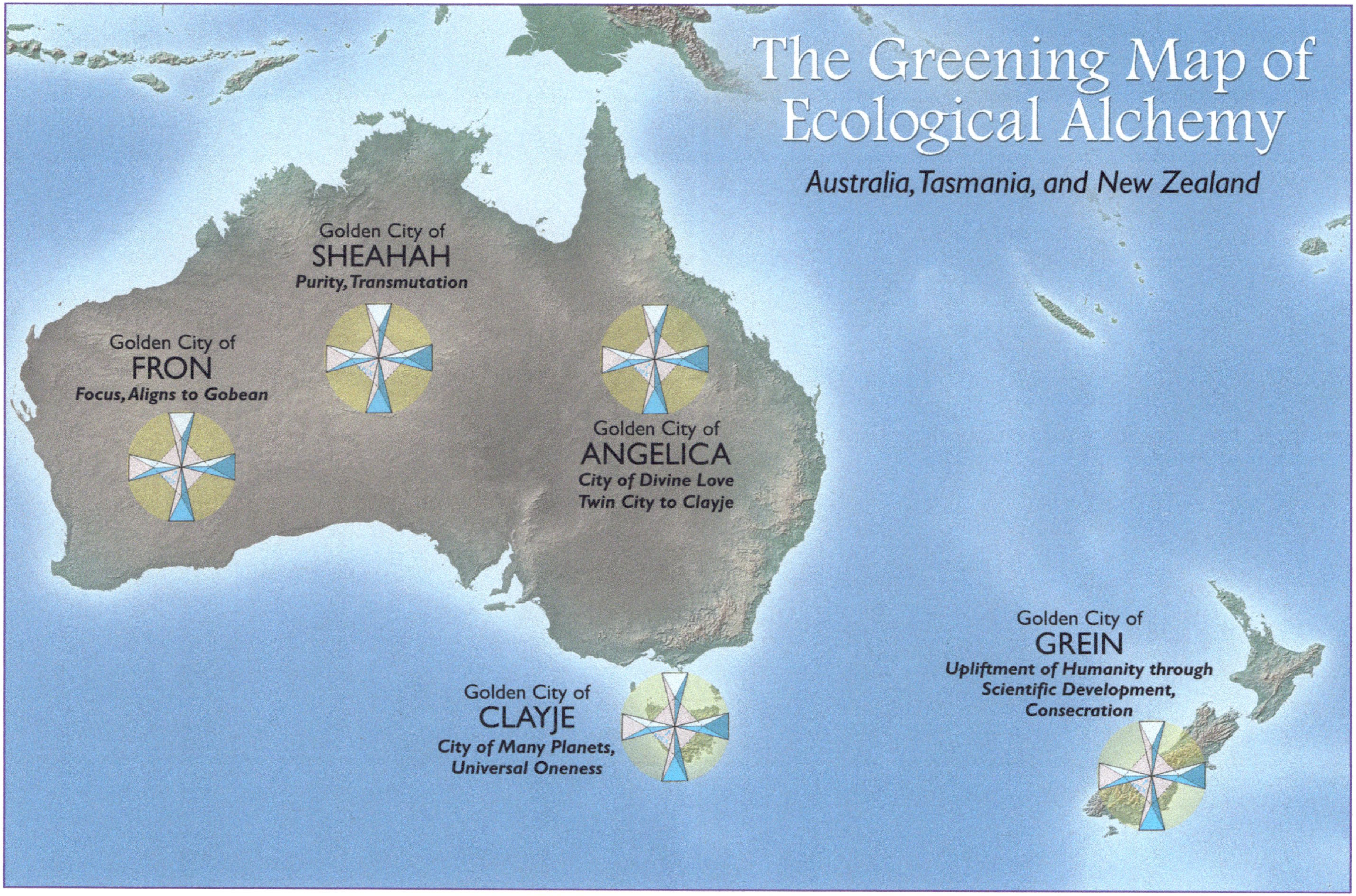

[Above: The five Golden Cities of Australia, Tasmania, and New Zealand. Australia and surrounding areas are known as the Greening Map, and contain prophecies of ecological alchemy.]

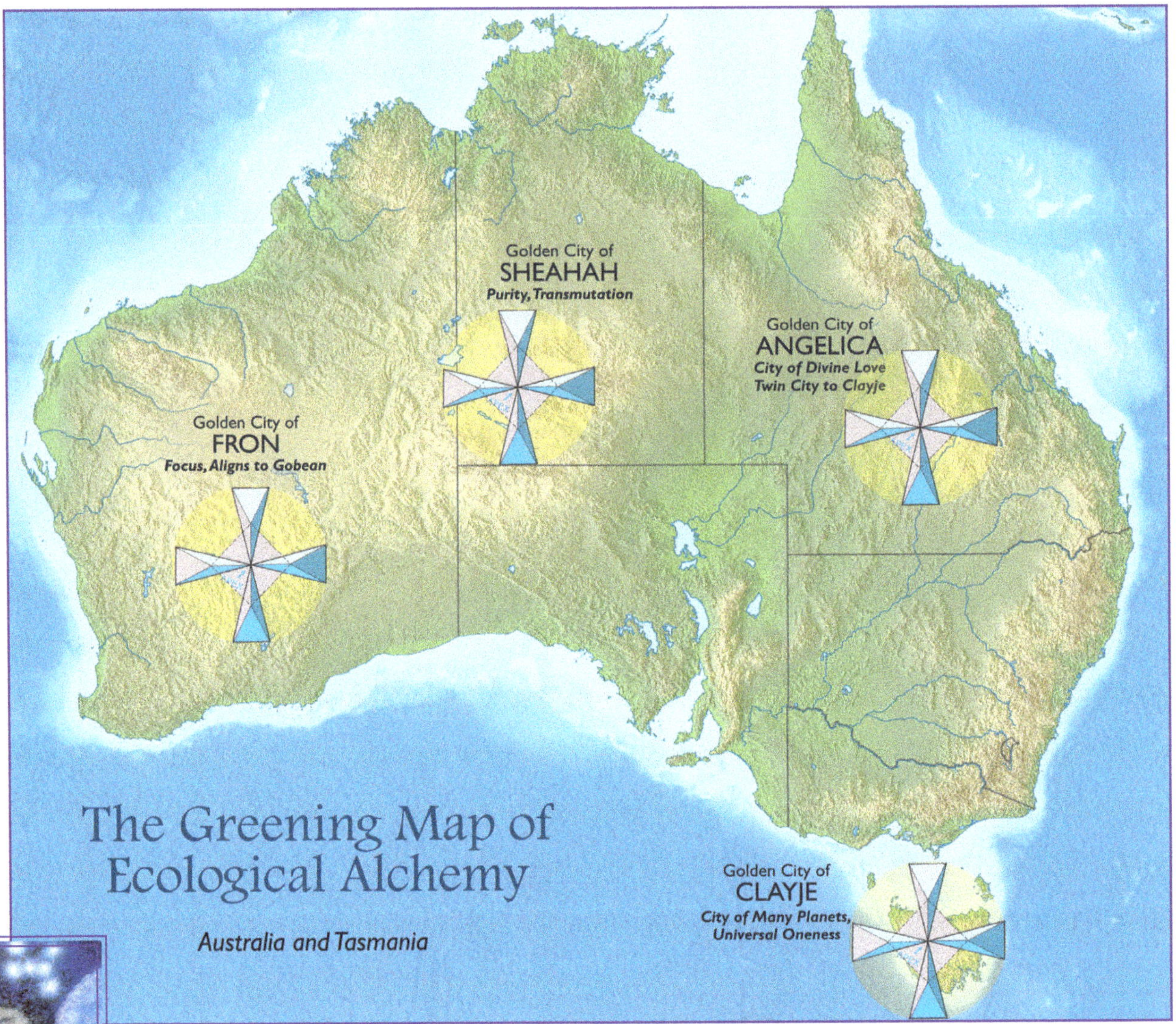

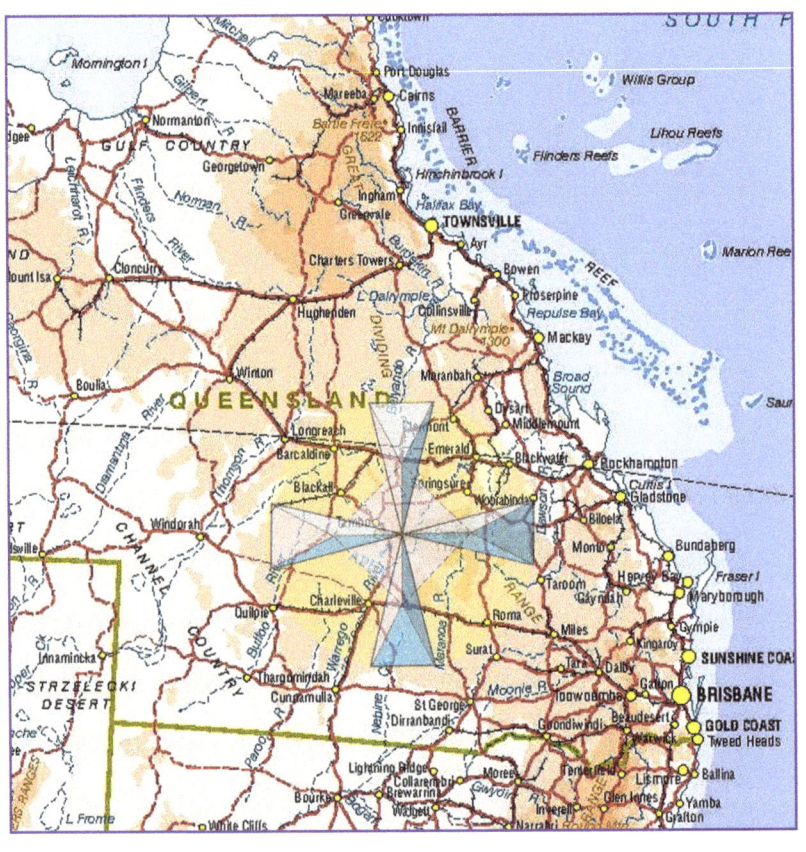

The Greening Map of Ecological Alchemy

Australia and Tasmania

Golden City of SHEAHAH — *Purity, Transmutation*

Golden City of ANGELICA — *City of Divine Love, Twin City to Clayje*

Golden City of FRON — *Focus, Aligns to Gobean*

Golden City of CLAYJE — *City of Many Planets, Universal Oneness*

Golden Cities of Australia and New Zealand

ANGELICA: The Golden City of Angelica is guided by the Elohim Angelica and is affiliated with the Pink Ray. Its eastern adjutant point is Consuelo Peak, and the apex is located in Carnarvon National Park, Queensland. Angelica activates in 2086, and the Star establishes its energies in 2103. Angelica is a sister city to Clayje, the Golden City of Tasmania. (*Pictured above, the Elohim Angelica and Orion.*)

[Above: *The four Golden Cities of Australia.* Right: *The Golden City of Angelica, located in Queensland, Australia.*]

[Left: *The Island of Tasmania.* Below: *The Golden City of Clayje covers the entire Island of Tasmania, Australia.*]

CLAYJE: This Golden City covers the entire island of Tasmania, and like its sister city Angelica, is affiliated with the Pink Ray. Clayje's steward is the Elohim Orion, the divine complement of Angelica. Mount Ossa is the apex and is located near the Franklin-Gordon Wild River National Park on the west side of the island. Forty-two percent of Tasmania's lands are protected with national parks and World Heritage sites. The "City of Many Planets" activates in 2084, and the Star energies are fully developed in 2101.

[Right: *The Golden City of Sheahah is primarily located in the Northern Territory, Australia.*]

SHEAHAH: Australia's Golden City of the White Ray is overseen by the Elohim Astrea. (*Pictured left*.) The Tropic of Capricorn traverses Sheahah's apex, and the center of this Golden City is located south of Haasts Bluff – an indigenous Australian community. Mount Zeil, the highest peak in Australia's Northern Territory, is located on a vital Golden City lei-line. Sheahah activates in 2088, and its Star energies fully establish in 2105. Uluru, known as "Ayers Rock," is located in its Southern Door. Sheahah is metaphysically connected to the United States Golden City of Shalahah, as both Golden Cities promote the development of the Christ Consciousness, Unity, and Oneship.

FRON: Lady Ascended Master Desiree, who

[Right: *Uluru/Ayers Rock is considered a sacred location to the local aboriginal people and is located in the Southern Door of the Sheahah Golden City Vortex.*]

92 I AM AMERICA ATLAS

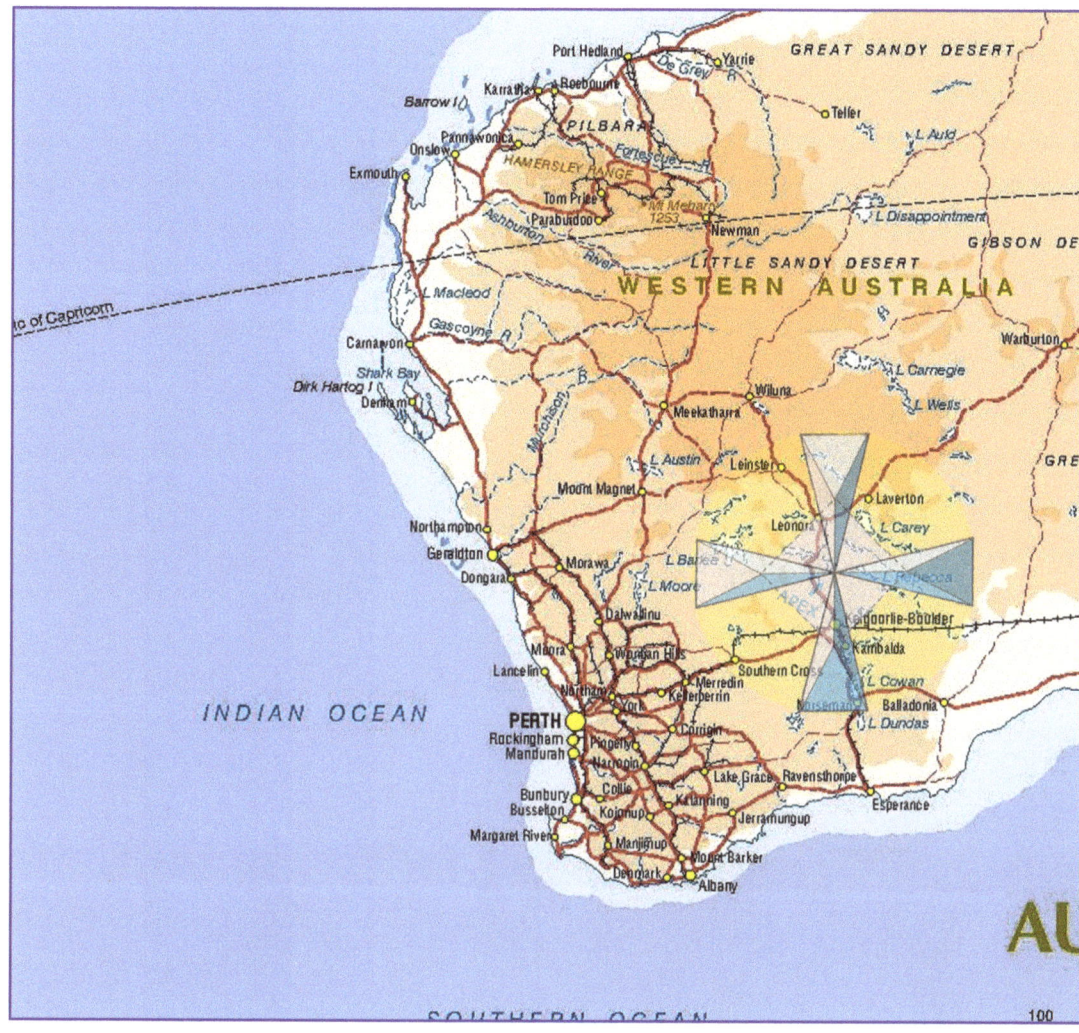

[Left: *The Golden City of Fron, located in Western Australia.*]

works closely with El Morya, is the steward of the Golden City of Fron, located in the Western Australia state, Australia. (*Lady

Desiree pictured above.*) Fron is affiliated with the Blue Ray, and its northern adjutant point is Mount Redcliffe. Its apex is located over Lake Marmion, a salt lake located in the Goongarrie National Park. This Golden City activates in 2090, and the Star matures in 2107.

[Left: *Aoraki/Mount Cook, South Island, New Zealand. Mount Cook is the apex of the Golden City of Grein.*]

I AM AMERICA ATLAS 93

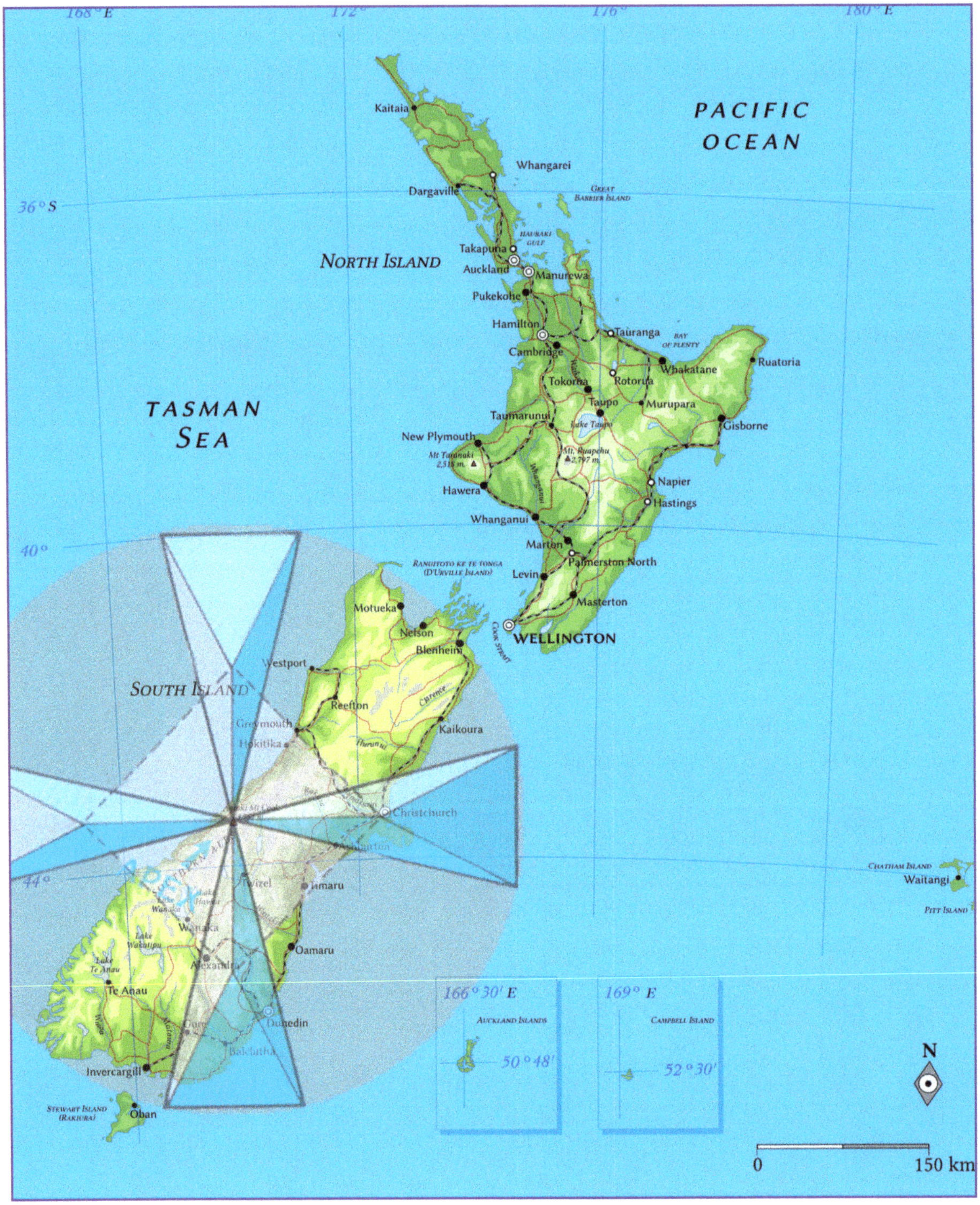

[*Above: The Golden City of Grein, located on South Island, New Zealand.*]

GREIN: Viseria, the Goddess of the Stars and the Divine Complement to Soltec, is the steward of the Golden City of New Zealand. Grein's apex is located at Aoraki/Mount Cook, at 12,218 feet high. A large portion of this Vortex lies over the Tasman Sea where new lands are prophesied to appear. The Golden City is located at the South Island of New Zealand. Grein activates in 2082, and the energies of its Star complete in 2099. It is affiliated with the Green Ray. The city of Churchward, New Zealand is positioned on a vital adjutant point of the Eastern Door. Grein is aligned to the Golden City of Pashacino in Canada. (*Goddess of the Stars pictured to the right.*)

MAP OF EXCHANGES
Golden Cities of Europe

[Above: *The seven Golden Cities of Europe, also known as the Map of Exchanges, are pictured above. Not to scale.*]

Golden Cities of Europe

STIENTA: This Blue Ray Golden City is located on the Island of Iceland and is served by Archangel Michael. Its apex is located at Hofsjokull. The "City of Inner Vision" was activated in 2012, and its star energies complete in 2027. (*Archangel Michael pictured left.*)

GRUECHA: Located in Norway and Sweden, the Golden City of Gruecha focuses upon the truth and strength of the Blue Ray. The Elohim Hercules is its divine steward, and its apex is located at Glittertind, the second highest mountain in Norway. Gruecha activates in 2018, and its Star energies follow in activation seventeen years later in 2035. (*Elohim Hercules pictured above right.*)

I AM AMERICA ATLAS 95

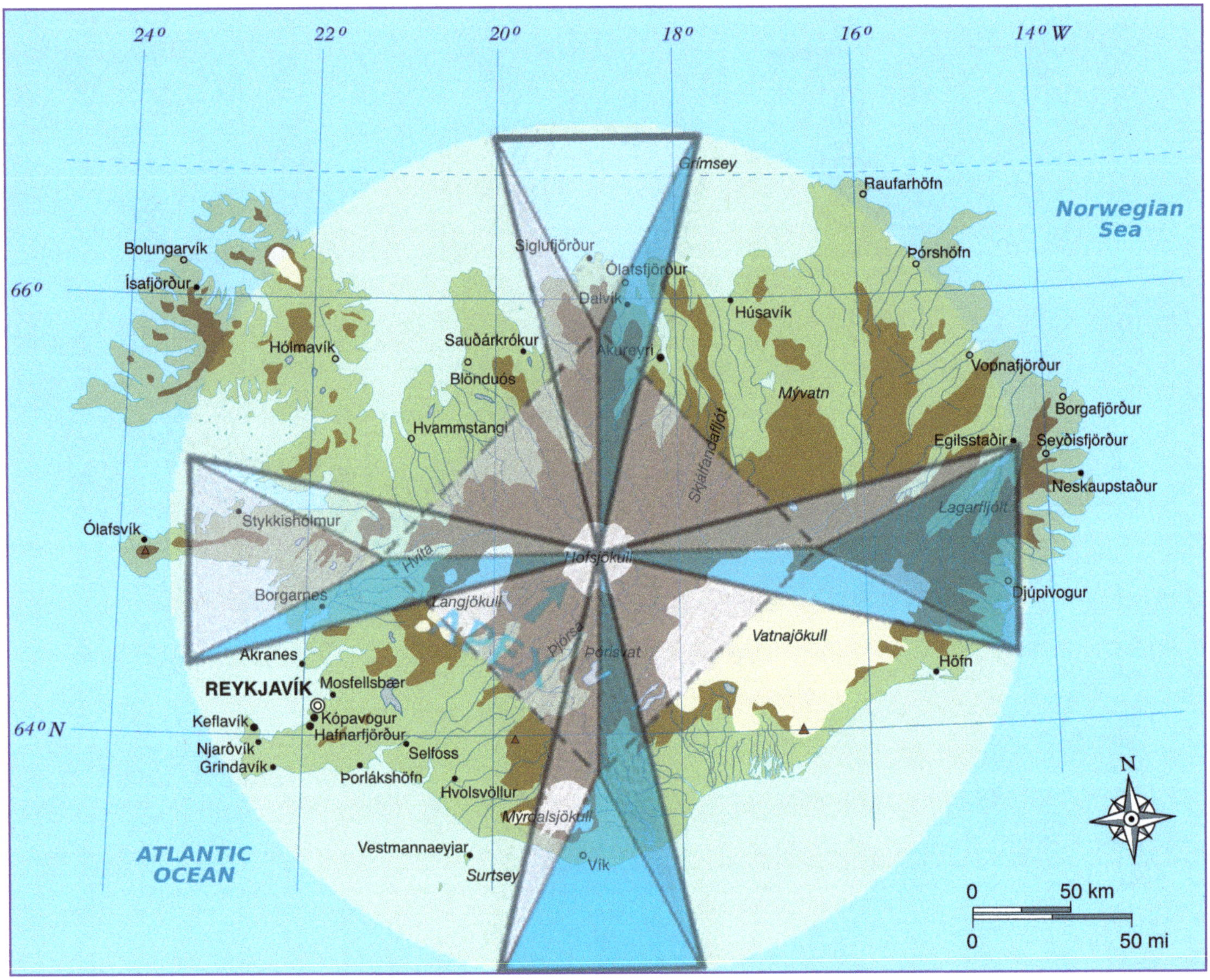

[Above: *The Golden City of Stienta, located in Iceland.*]

DENASHA: The Scotland Golden City of the Yellow Ray is overseen by Ascended Lady Master Nada. Ben Navis, the highest mountain lying at the western end of the Grampian Mountains, is the center of the Vortex. The energies of Denasha activated in 2014, and complete with the further activation of its Star in 2031. (*Lady Nada pictured above.*)

AMERIGO: The Golden City of Spain, Amerigo, is held in the watchful embrace of the Ascended Master Godfre and the unifying Gold Ray. Amerigo's apex is Penalara at 7,996 feet in elevation, the highest mountain peak of the Guadarrama Mountain Range. The Golden City's energies activated in the year 2016, and the Star reaches complete maturity in 2033. (*Godfre and Saint Germain pictured above.*)

[Above: *The Golden City of Gruecha, located in Norway and Sweden.*]

I AM AMERICA ATLAS

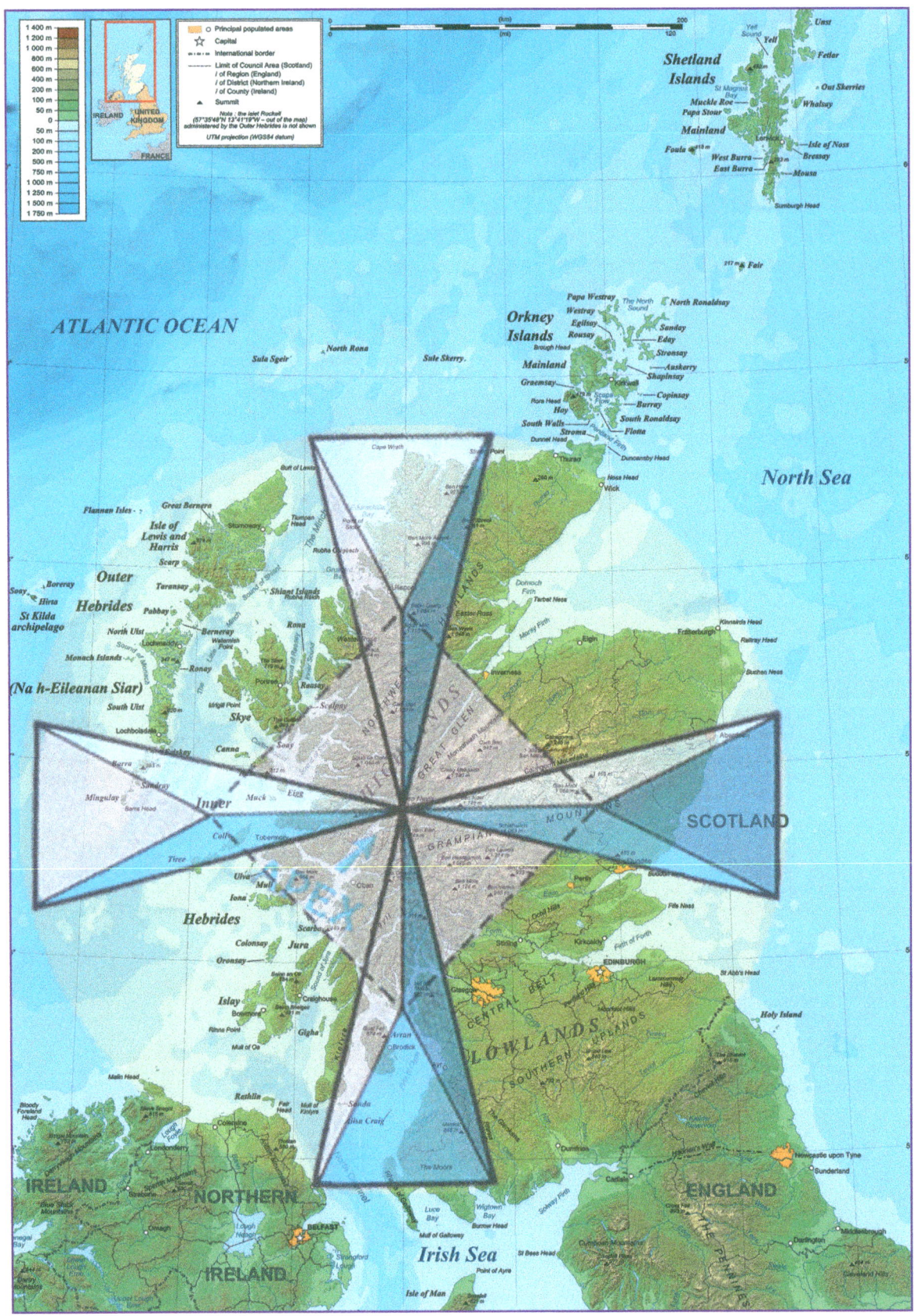

[Above: *The Golden City of Denasha, located in Scotland.*]

[Above: *The Golden City of Amerigo, located in Spain.*]

BRAUN: Mighty Victory of the Yellow Ray is the steward of this European Golden City, primarily located in Germany. Braun's apex is located near Weiden in der Oberpfalz, a city in Bavaria, and just west of the Bohemian Forest. The Golden City of glory and achievement activates in 2020 and its Star reaches maturation in 2037. (*Mighty Victory pictured above.*)

AFROM: The European Golden City of the White Ray of Ascension is located in Hungary and Romania. Its stewards are Claire, the Elohim of Purity, along with the Goddess SeRaya the White Buddha. Afrom's apex is located near Santana, Romania in the Aradului Plateau. This Golden City activates in 2022, and the energies of its Star complete in 2039. (*Claire, the Elohim of Purity pictured above right.*)

I AM AMERICA ATLAS 99

[Above: *The Golden City of Braun, located in Germany, Czech Republic, and Austria.*]

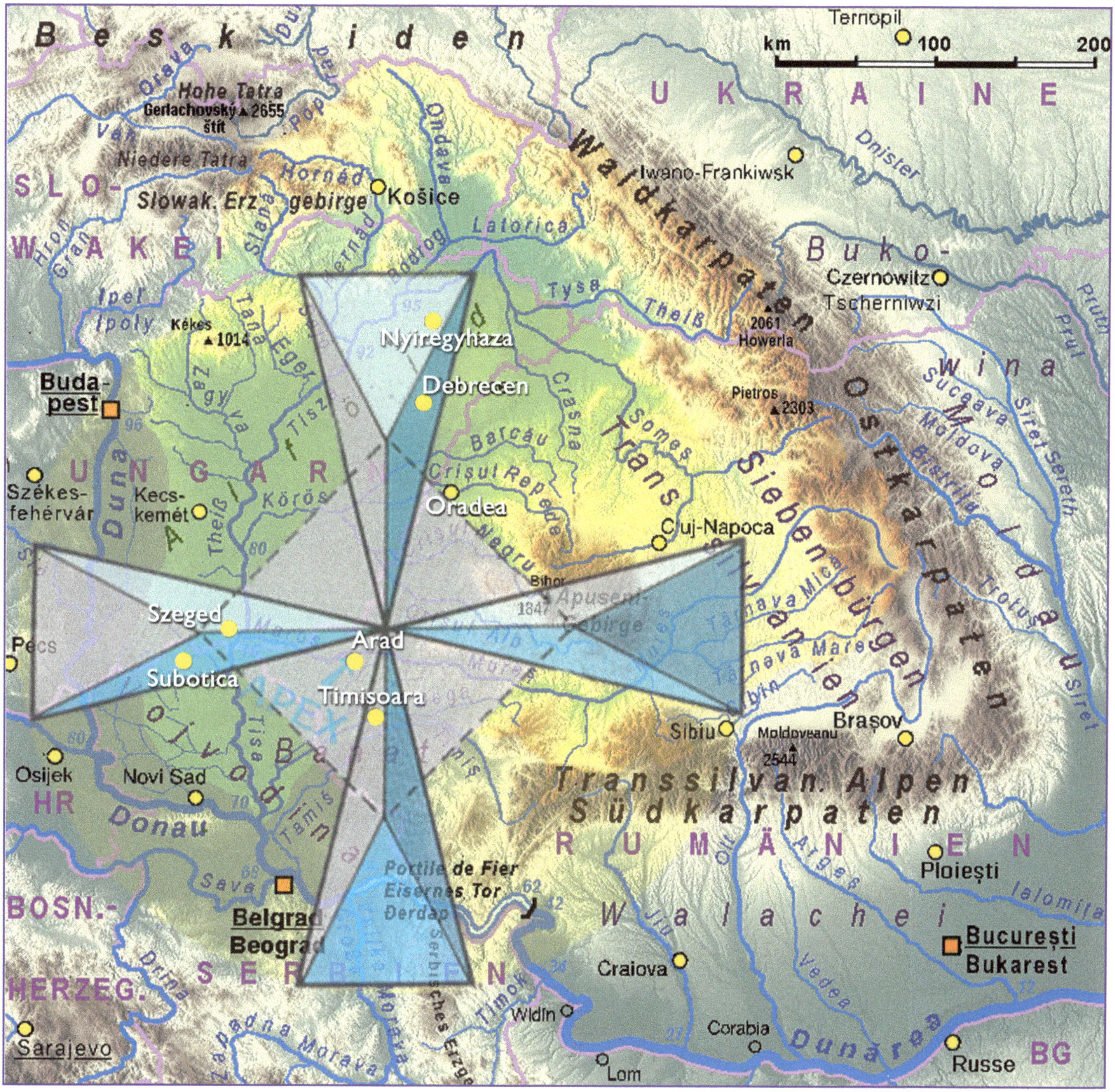

[Above: *The Golden City of Afrom, located in Hungary, Slovakia, Ukraine, Romania, Serbia, and Croatia. Left: SeRaya, the White Buddha.*]

I AM AMERICA ATLAS *101*

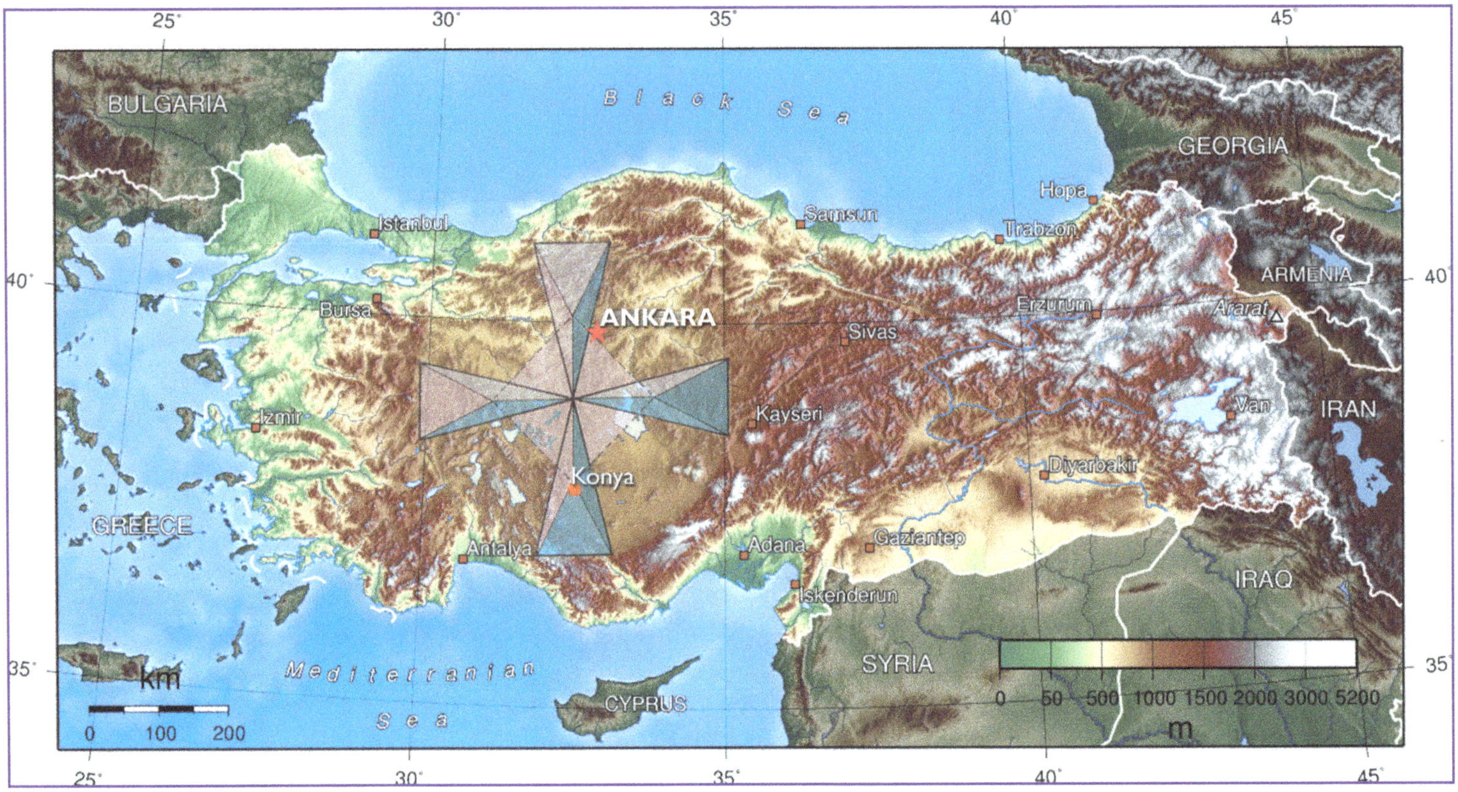

[Above: *The Golden City of Ganakra, located in Turkey.*]

GANAKRA: The Elohim of the Green Ray, Vista, serves this Golden City known as the "All Seeing City," located in Turkey. Its apex is just west of Kulu, in the Konya Province, the central Anatolia region of Turkey. The town of Haymana is also located in the Star of Ganakra, and is famous for its healing waters used in Turkish baths. Ganakra activates in 2024, the Star matures in 2041. (*Vista, pictured left.*)

[Below: *Cappadocia Chimneys, Central Turkey, Eastern Door of Ganakra.*]

SECTION TEN

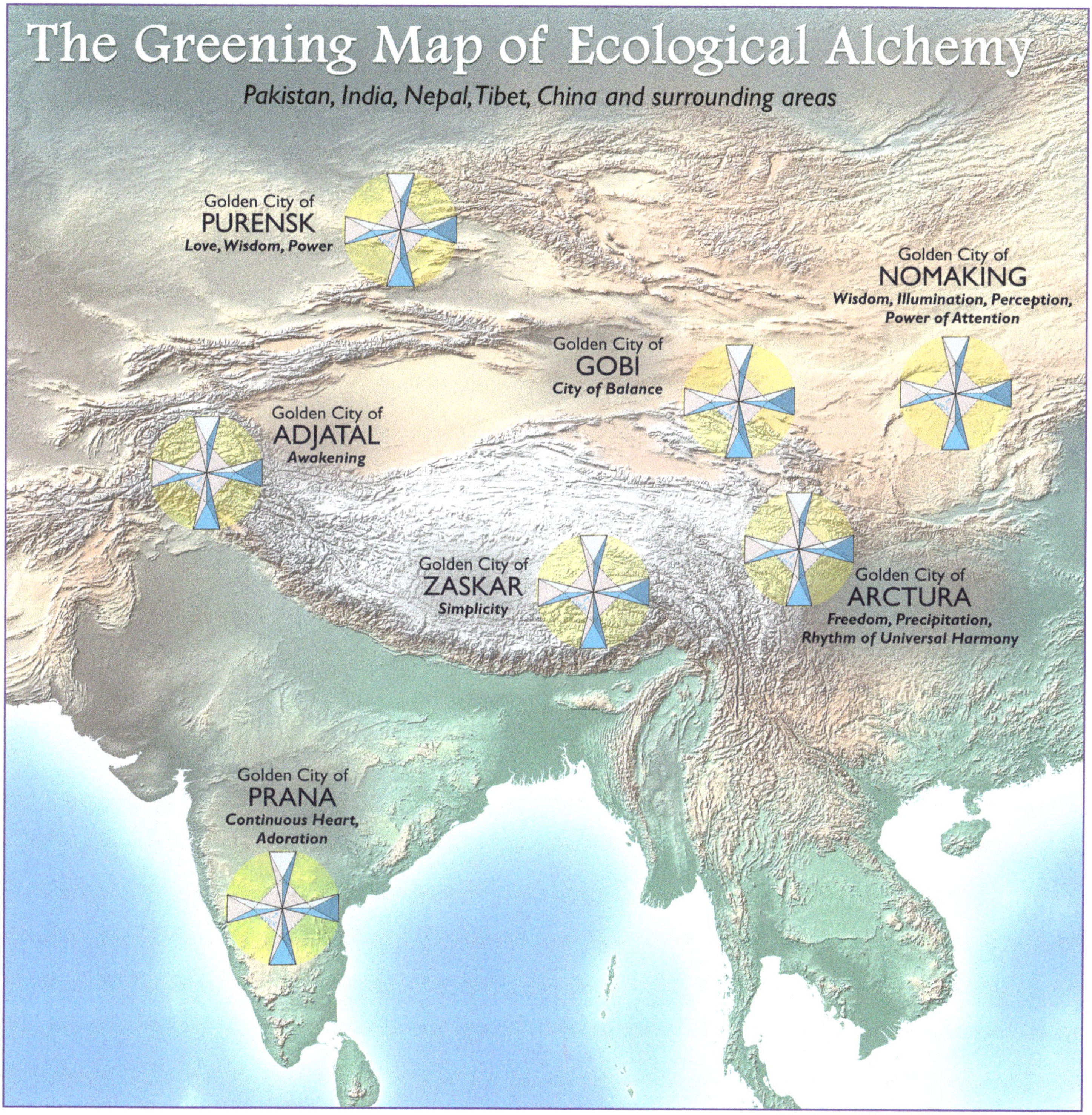

The Greening Map of Ecological Alchemy
Pakistan, India, Nepal, Tibet, China and surrounding areas

Golden City of **PURENSK** — *Love, Wisdom, Power*

Golden City of **NOMAKING** — *Wisdom, Illumination, Perception, Power of Attention*

Golden City of **GOBI** — *City of Balance*

Golden City of **ADJATAL** — *Awakening*

Golden City of **ZASKAR** — *Simplicity*

Golden City of **ARCTURA** — *Freedom, Precipitation, Rhythm of Universal Harmony*

Golden City of **PRANA** — *Continuous Heart, Adoration*

[Above: *The Golden Cities of India, Tibet, and surrounding areas.*]

I AM AMERICA ATLAS 103

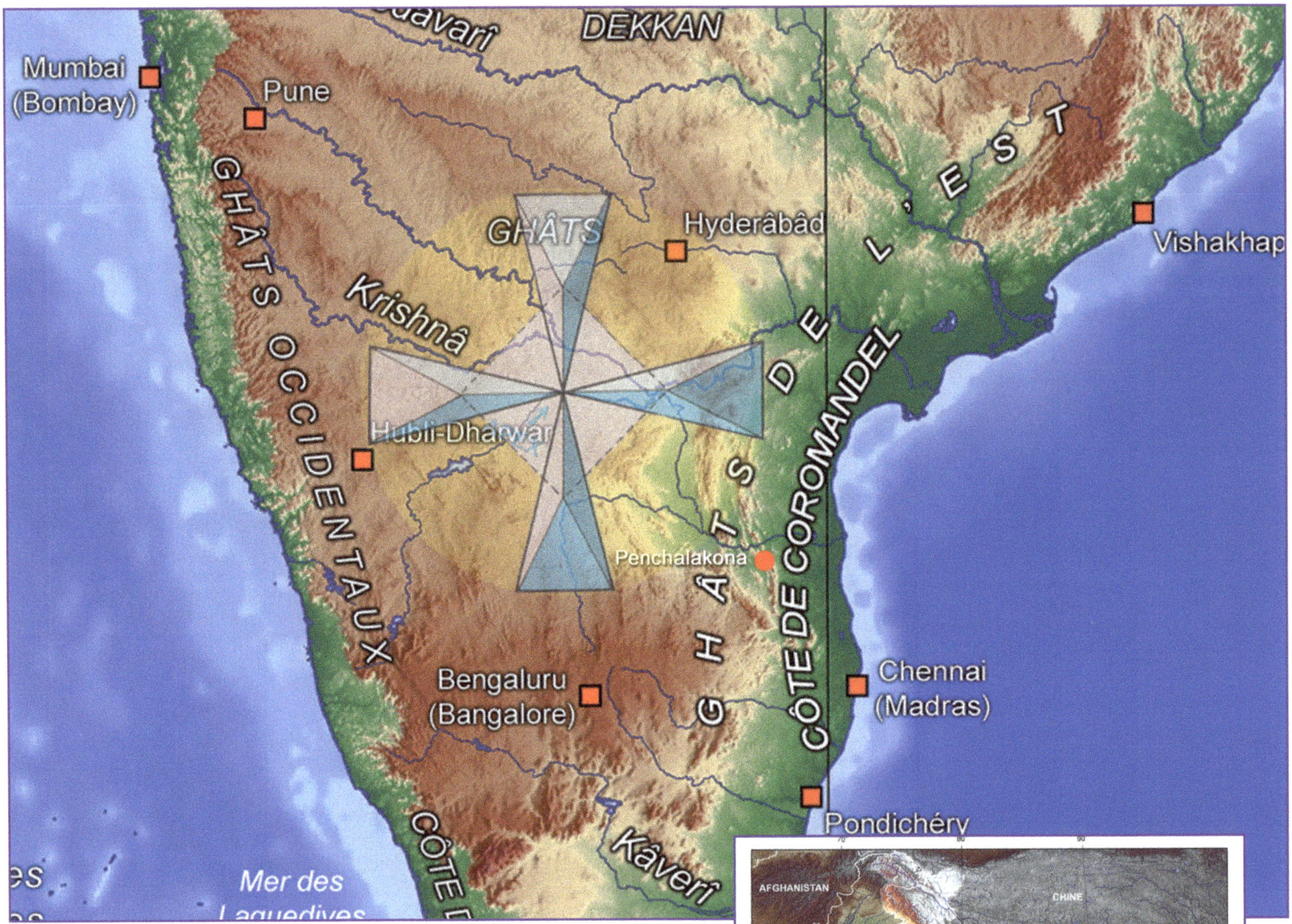

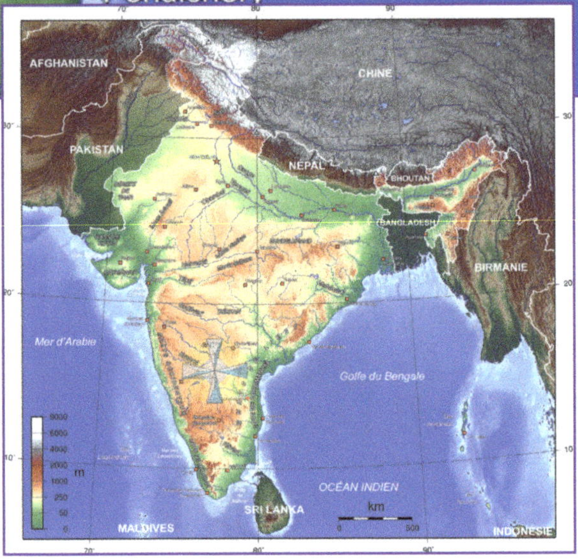

Golden Cities of India, Tibet, and Asia

PRANA: Southern Indian's Golden City is dedicated to the Pink Ray and overseen by the Archangel Chamuel. The apex of this sacred city of the "Continuous Heart" is located in Karnataka. The city of Hubli-Dharwad is in the Eastern Door and Hyderabad is located in the northwest sector of the Golden City. The Krishna River flows throughout the entire Vortex. Mother Karunamayi's spiritual ashram is located near the village of Penchalakona and in the energetic radiance of this sacred city of light. Prana activates in 2034, and the energies of its Star establish in 2051.

[Above: *The Golden City of Prana, located in southern India.* Left: *Archangel Chamuel.*]

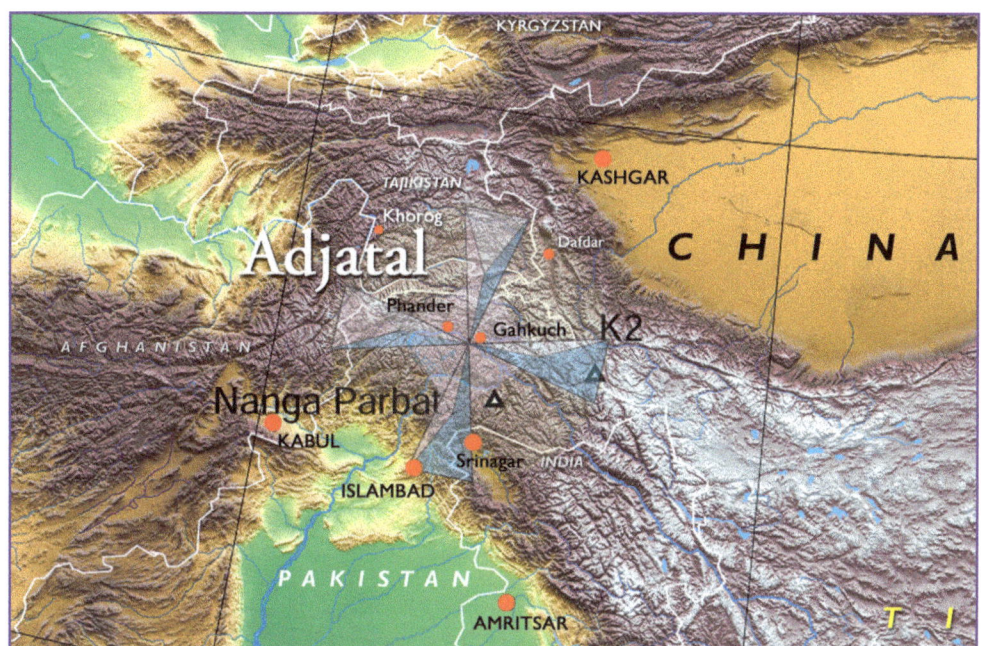

ADJATAL: The mountain peaks of the Himalayan Mountains define this Golden City with K2's presence in the Eastern Door, and Nanga Parbat defining the Southeast Door of the "City of Awakening." Nanga Parbat is the ninth highest mountain in the world at 26,660 feet, and K2 is the world's second highest at 28,251 feet in elevation. Gahkuch, Pakistan, a mountain community of ten thousand, is near the Star of this Golden City of both the Blue and Gold Rays. This Golden City is stewarded by Lord Himalaya, (*pictured above*). Adjatal covers the entire Wakhan Corridor that separates the nations of Pakistan and Tajikistan. The Southern Door is host to the northern Kashmir Valley and is surrounded by the Himalayans on all sides. Srinager is known for its Mughal Gardens, symbolically designed to emphasize the Quarnic concept of paradise. The apex is located near the village of Phander, considered one of the most beautiful sites in Pakistan. Adjatal's uplifting energies activate in 2030, and the Star completes this energetic movement in 2047.

[Upper Right: *Lord Himalaya*. Above: *The Golden City of Adjatal, located in Pakiston, Afghanistan, Tajikistan, China, and India.* Below: *The Golden City of Zaskar, located in Tibet (China), India, and Bhutan.*]

ZASKAR: This Golden City is likely named for the Zanskar Range of Mountains, located in the Golden City of Adjatal. These two Golden Cities are linked as Twin Cities, and Beloved Reya of the White Ray works alongside Lord Himalaya for humanity's spiritual awakening through the ideal of simplicity. The sacred lake of Namtso is located in the Vortex's Western Door, and the apex is near the Tibetan village of Kunggar. The Drigung Monastery is located in the Star of Zaskar. This Golden City activates in 2060, and the energies of the Star follow in activation seventeen years later in 2077. (*Lady Master Reya is also known as Parvati, pictured right.*)

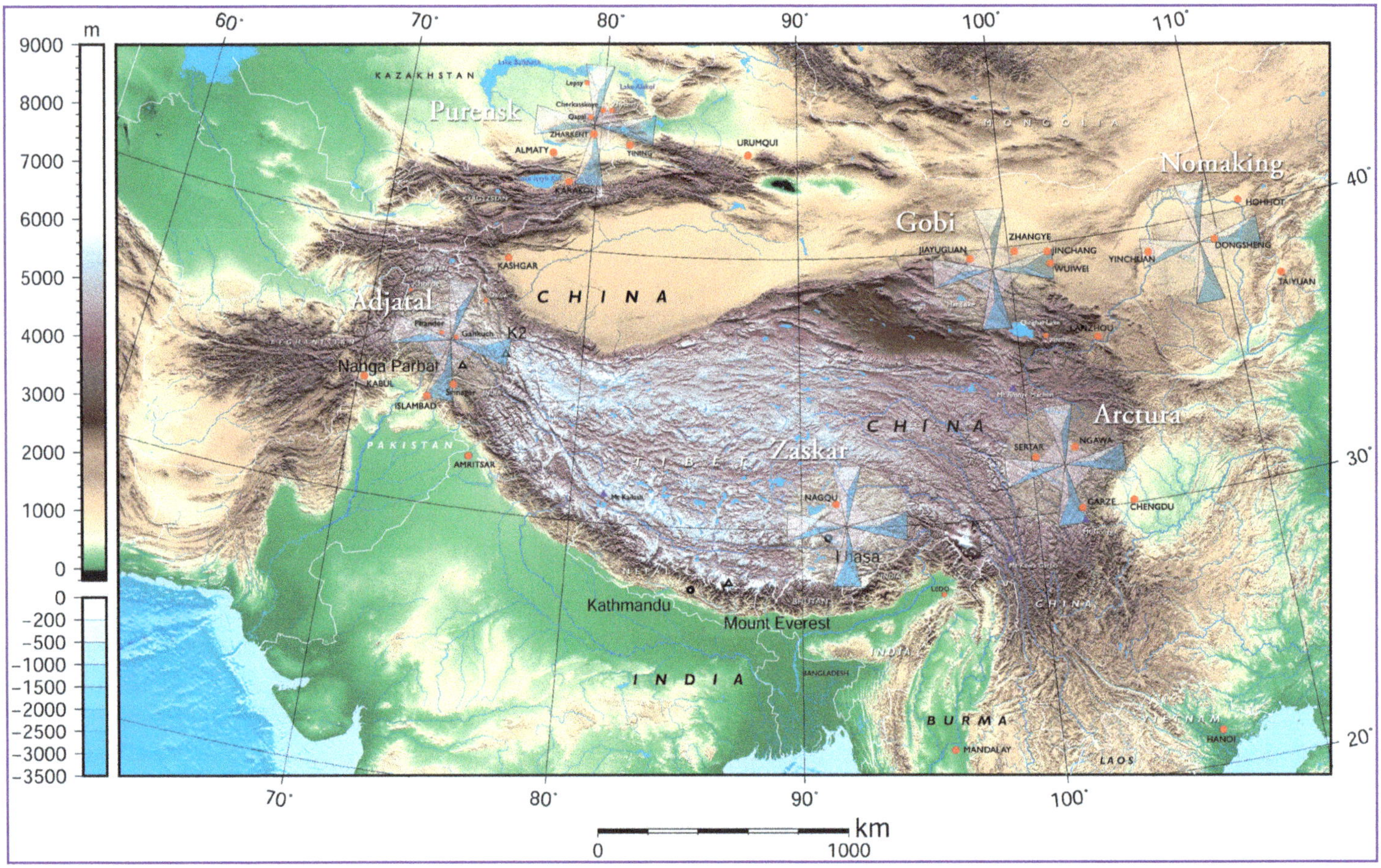

[Above: *Topography Map of Tibet and surrounding areas with Golden Cities.*]

PURENSK: Three Ray Forces of Blue, Yellow, and Pink express their divine qualities through the Divine Beings of Faith, Hope, and Charity in the Golden City of Purensk. (*Threefold Flame pictured left.*) This is a Golden City of many lakes with Lake Balkhash, Lake Alakol, and Lake Issyk-Kul located within the Vortex. The Lepsi River flows through the Southern Door of the "City of Love, Wisdom, and Power." The village of Cherkasskoye is north of the apex and the community of Qpal, Kazakhstan is northeast. Yining, China is located in Purensk's Southeast Door. This Golden City activates in 2032, and its Star reaches maturation in 2049.

GOBI: Lord Meru of the Ruby-Gold Ray oversees the majestic Golden City of Gobi. The apex of the "City of Balance" is located at Quilian Shan Peak at nearly 19,000 feet in elevation. The community of Jiayuguan (near the Jiayu Pass) is

[Left: *Golden City of Purensk, located in Kyrgyzstan, Kazakhstan, and China.*]

located close to a vital adjutant point of Gobi, and marks the end of the Great Wall of China and is the site of thousands of ancient tombs from the Jin Dynasty. The Eastern Door city of Wuiwei in the Gansu province was once a pivotal point along the Silk Road where Buddhism was brought from India to China. Quinghai Lake, located in the Southern Door, is the site of Tibetan Buddhist spiritual pilgrimages. The Golden City of Gobi is seminal to all of the Golden Cities and overshadows all fifty cities with historical provenance, spiritual lineage, and energetic conception. Gobi is especially aligned with its namesake, Gobean, the Golden City of the United States southwest. The magnificent physical Golden City of the Shamballa tradition receives its vital energies directly from the now ethereal, Fifth Dimensional Shamballa, and it will increase in vital energy with further activation in 2062, and in 2079 when the Star of Gobi moves into completion.

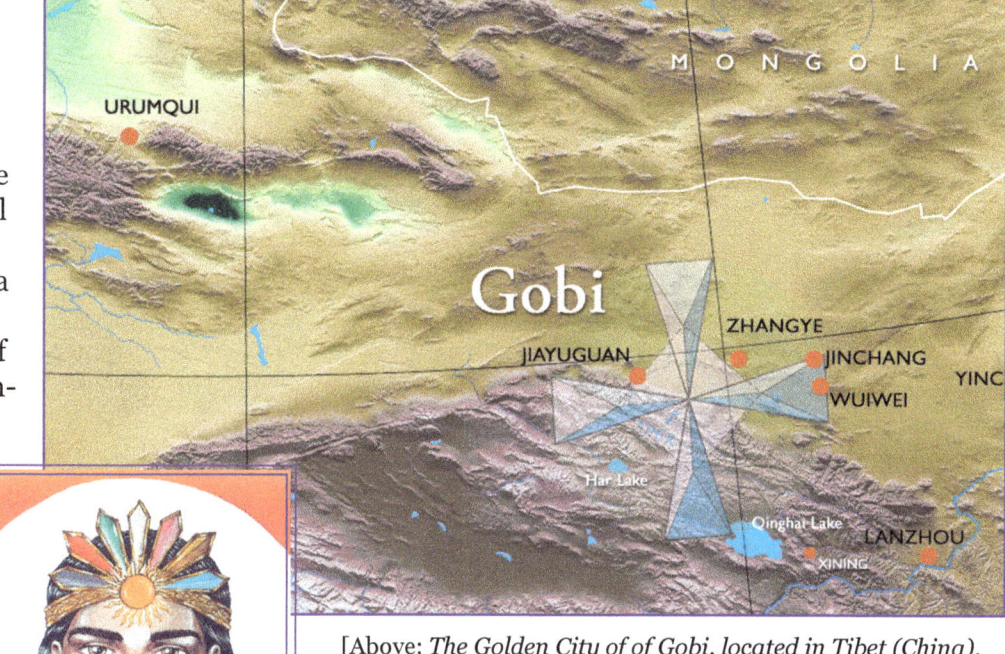

[Above: *The Golden City of of Gobi, located in Tibet (China).* Left: *Lord Meru, steward of the Golden City of Gobi.*]

ARCTURA: The freedom and harmony of the Violet Ray through the Elohim Arcturus and Diana is refined and focused throughout the Golden City of Arctura. Its southerly adjutant point is defined by Mount Gongga – the King of the Sichuan Mountains, a sacred mountain in Tibetan Buddhism. Arctura's apex is located in Zamtag County, China. Ngawa Town and surrounding area includes thirty-seven monasteries with 8,000 Tibetan monks. The Eastern Door of the "City of Freedom" is the location of the Woolong Nature Reserve, home for China's largest pandas. This Golden City activates in 2064, and the Star completes its development in 2081.

[Left: *The Golden City of Arctura, located in China.* Above: *The Elohim Arcturus and Diana.*]

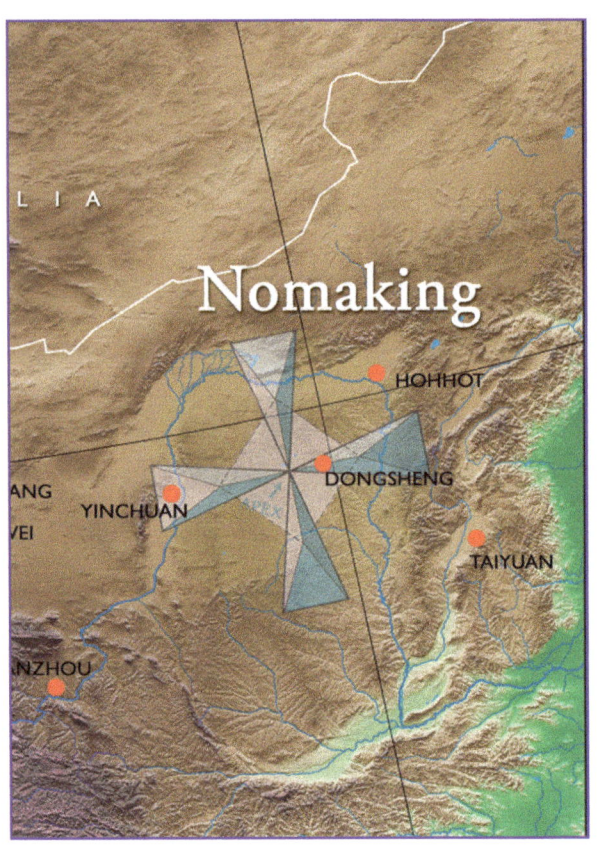

[*Far Left:* Golden City of Nomaking, located in Inner Mongolia, China. *Left:* Yum Chenmo, Asian Wisdom Goddess (a form of Minerva). *Below:* The Elohim Cassiopea.]

NOMAKING: The Beloved Elohim of the Yellow Ray, Cassiopea and Minerva, oversee the Golden City of Nomaking. (*Left*) This Golden City is located east of Bejing in Inner Mongolia, China. Nomaking's apex is east of Dongsheng, that is located in the sublime energies of the Star. The Yellow River flows thoughout all four Golden City Doorways, moving from the West Door to the North Door, then to the East Door and onward through the South Door. The "City of Wisdom and Illumination" activates in 2066; its Star energies reach their full maturity in 2083.

[*Below: Five Pagoda Temple,* Hohhot, Inner Mongolia, China, located in the Golden City of Nomaking.]

[Above: *Sonoran Desert, Golden City of Gobean.*]

SECTION ELEVEN

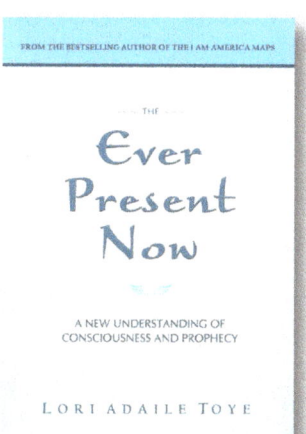

Ever Present Now:
Golden City Names
The names of the Golden Cities are unusual, and each city's meaning is secret knowledge closely held by the Master Teachers. Through the years of our work with the Ascended Masters, several definitions of the names of Golden Cities have emerged, but never in great detail. Yet, each curious name is important and reveals hidden qualities and spiritual characteristics of each Golden City. Some occultists refer to the veiled language of the mystics as Owaspee—the native tongue of Angels. The Divine Language, or the language of the Gods, is referred to in religious traditions including the Adamic language—the language spoken by Adam and Eve; Hebrew—the Jewish language of God; Greek, the mathematical language of harmony; and Sanskrit, the Divine Language of the Gods through Vedic spiritual traditions.

Divine Languages are often known as form languages. My Vedic teacher once explained the etymology of Sanskrit as "a Mother tongue," similar to the syntax and semantics of computer languages. According to Vedic legend, our entire Earth was programmed, or created, through the spoken words of Sanskrit. Speaking a form language is powerful and commanding, and each spoken syllable has the ability to exactly create in form and substance its subject. Perhaps the creation story of Genesis says it best: "Then God said, 'Let there be light,' and there was light." (Genesis 1:3 New American Standard Bible)

The names and meanings of the Golden Cities, which originate in the Causal Plane of the Fifth Dimension, carry their emotive light and sound through the feeling worlds of the Fourth Dimension and integrate their activity to evolve the HU-man—the spiritually enlightened, realized God-man—of Earth's Third Dimension. Golden City names are founded in the multiple languages of Earth. Their individual syllables are based on archetypal words from many cultures of the world, including ancient Sanskrit, Greek, Persian, Phoenician, and the lost tongue of Moriori. Their sounds also include Native American languages: Al-

[Above: *Qilin Mountains, Golden City of Gobi*.]

gonquian, Navajo, Shoshoni, and Cahto. Surprisingly, modern languages appear in the syllables of the names of Golden Cities: the universal language of peace, Esperanto; J. R. R. Tolkein's fictional language of Middle Earth, Elfish; and the contemporary, linguistic Minimalist Language.

The sounds and meanings of the Golden Cities' names are both the evocations and myths for the New Times. Their resonance is the hope and the aspiration for progressive, positive change on behalf of humanity and Earth. The theosophist George William Russell wrote, "The mind of man is made in the image of Deity, and the elements of speech are related to the powers in his mind and through it to the being of the Oversoul. These true roots of language are few, alphabet and roots being identical."

Meanings of the Fifty-One Golden City Vortices

ADJATAL: *The Big Rainbow* derives its meaning from the Suabo-Indonesian word *adja* ("big") and the Pashto-Pakistanian word *tal* ("rainbow"). The Golden City of Adjatal is located in Pakistan, Afghanistan, and India; the historical Khyber Pass (the ancient Silk Road) is located on the western side of this Vortex city.

AFROM: This Golden City name means, "A Devotion." This meaning originates with the word *from*, which in German, Norwegian, and Swedish means "pious" or "devoted." The Ascended Masters claim this Golden City also means "to affirm."

AMERIGO: This European Golden City is Spanish for "I AM Race."

ANDEO: The Golden City of the South American Andes is likely named for this mountain range; however, the source of this Golden City of the Feminine is rooted in the Albanian word *anda*, which means "strong desire," and the Huli (New Guinea) word *andia*, which means "mother." Andeo's meaning translates into this phrase: "the Mother of Desire."

ANGELICA: The Native American Algonquian word *ca* means "at present" or "present"; therefore, Angelica's full meaning is "Angel Present," or "Angels at Present."

ARKANA: The nineteenth-century language of peace—Esperanto, and the Polish language both state that the word *arkana* means "Mystery."

ASONEA: The Golden City of Cuba and ancient Atlantis derives its meaning from the pristine Ason River of the Cantabria province in Spain and its mythological race of supernatural undines—the *Xanas*.

BRAHAM: *Braham* is also known as the Second of Three Sisters who preserves a maternal radiance over South America. Braham is the feminine version of *Brahma*, and this Golden City meaning is the "Mother of the New Manu."

BRAUN: The Golden City of Germany, Poland, Austria, and Czechoslovakia means "the Shining Strong One."

CLAYJE: Dialects from the Netherlands create this Golden City's name through the word *kla*—"clear." The word *je* in Bosnian, Croatian, Serbian, and Slovak languages means "is." The combination of these words constructs this Australian Golden City's meaning: "Is Clear."

CRESTA: In Spanish, Italian, and Brazilian Portuguese the word *cresta* means "the ridge or peak."

CROTESE: Located in the Cradleland of Central America, this Golden City means "the Attentive Cradle." Its meaning is derived from the French *cro*—"cradle," and the Etruscan *tes*—"to care for or pay attention."

[Above: *Petroglyphs along the Snake River, Golden City of Shalahah.*]

DENASHA: This Golden City derives its meaning from the modern English name Denesa, which means the "Mountain of Zeus." This mythological Greek father of both Gods and men is also known in Roman myths as Jupiter, an ideal symbol for this European Golden City of the Yellow Ray.

DONJAKEY: Located on new lands prophesied to rise from the Pacific Ocean in the New Times, this Golden City's name comes from the Italian word *don*—"gift," and the Indonesian word *key*—"tree." Donjakey means "Gift of Trees," and is associated with new species of flora prophesied to appear on Earth.

EABRA: "The Feminine in Eternal Balance." This name is a derivative of several words, namely *bra* or *bodice*, which means "the pair" or the "wearing of pairs." *Ea* has several meanings: in Frisian (German) *ea* means "ever," in Romanian *ea* means "she." The word *pair* numerically indicates two, a number associated with femininity and balance.

FRON: The meaning of this Australian Golden City is "throne" in Albanian. In the Creole language, *fron* means "pious" and "devoted." The combination of these definitions creates Fron's meaning: "the Devoted Throne."

GANAKRA: The ancient Turkish City of Ankara means "anchor" in Greek; in Portuguese *gana* means "desire"; and *kra* is a Creole word for "mind." Ganakra's combined meaning is "Desires Anchored by the Mind," or "Desires of the Mind."

GANDAWAN: From the Sanskrit word *Gondwanaland* means "Forest of the Gonds." Located over the Sahara Desert, this Golden City represents this ancient culture that claimed to survive in present-day India.

[Above: *Ben Navis, Golden City of Denasha*.]

Contemporary Gond legends mirror the emergence stories of Southwest Native American tribes, and the Gond Gods surfaced from a cave and were adopted by the Hindu Goddess Parvati (Divine Mother) and were assisted by their tribal Goddess Jangu Bai. According to myth, the Gonds emerged from their cave in four distinct groups.

GOBEAN: The Ascended Masters claim Earth's first Golden City for the New Times means to "go beyond." However, Gobean's etymology suggests the meaning: "Go Pray." This phrase is derived from the word *bea* or *be*, which in Frisian (German) and Norwegian means "prayer."

GOBI: Named for the Great Desert of China, Gobi in Mongolian means "the waterless place." Ascended Masters claim the Golden City of Gobi is a step-down transformer for the energies of Earth's first Golden City—Shamballa. Gobi's esoteric definition comes from the Chinese translation of "go—across," and *bi* in Indonesian (Abun, A Nden, and Yimbun dialects) means "star." The Golden City of Gobi means "Across the Star," or "Across the Freedom Star." "Freedom Star" is a reference to Earth in her enlightened state.) Gobi aligns energies to the first Golden City of the New Times: Gobean.

GREIN: *Grein* is an Icelandic, Norwegian, and Swedish word which means "branch." The Ascended Masters maintain that the New Zealand Golden City of Grein means "the Green Branch"—a symbol of the peaceful olive branch.

GRUECHA: The Golden City name of Norway and Sweden is a Norwegian word and means "Hearth."

HUE: According to the Ascended Masters, the word *hue* invokes the Sacred Fire, the Violet Flame. In Tibetan dialects, however, the word *hue* or *hu* means "breath."

JEAFRAY: The Golden City of the Ever Present Violet Flame meaning translates to "Yesterday's Brother." This is based on the Gaelic word *jea*, which means "yesterday"; the word *fra* is English for "Brother" (friar). Since Archangel Zadkiel and the Archeia Amethyst serve in this Vortex retreat, "Yesterday's Brother" is a reference to the work of Saint Germain—as Sanctus Germanus (the Holy Brother)—and the many other archetypes of consciousness who tirelessly work

[Above: *Moraine Lake, Golden City of Pashacino.*]

for humanity's freedom and Ascension through the use of the transmuting fire.

JEHOA: It may be that this Golden City's name is based upon the Tetragrammaton YHWH; however, the etymology of this sacred haven of the Caribbean is based on the Russian word *YA*—meaning "I AM"—and *hoa*, which means "friend," from the Tahitian, Hawaiian, Maori, and Rapa Nui (Easter Island) languages. This translation elevates the various interpretations of Jehovah, the jealous God, into the uplifting phrase, "I AM Friend."

KANTAN: This Golden City of China and Russia derives its name from the English (Cornish) word *kan*—which means "song," and the Korean word *tan*, meaning "sweet." The full meaning of this spiritual Vortex is the "Sweet Song."

KLEHMA: The meaning of the fifth Golden City of the United States is based on several Native American words. The first syllable *kle* (pronounced clay) comes from the Navajo word *klê-kai*—which means "white." The second syllable *ma*, is a derivative of the Shoshoni word *mahoi*—around, or encircling. Klehma's esoteric definition is the "Circle of White."

KRESHE: This African Golden City is known to the Ascended Masters as the "Silent Star," an esoteric reference to Venus. *Kres* is also a Celtic word for "peace."

LARAITO: This Ethiopian Golden City's meaning is "Our Home." Laraito's definition comes from the Brazilian, Portuguese, and Spanish word for home—*lar*. *Ito* is a Tanzanian word for "ours."

MALTON: The Ascended Master Kuthumi's Golden City meaning is derived from the Phoenician word *maleth*—which means "a haven."

MARNERO: Mexico's Golden City's steward is Mother Mary and the first syllable of Marnero—*mar*—is a Spanish, Italian, and Portuguese word which means "sea" or "ocean." The remainder of the name—*nero* translates into *ner*, a Hebrew word for "candle." The Golden City of Marnero's meaning is the "Ocean of Candles."

MESOTAMP: The Golden City of Turkey, Iran, and Iraq is likely linked to the ancient word *Mesopotamia*, which means the "land between rivers." The higher

[Above: *Neuschwanstein Castle, Golden City of Braun.*]

meaning of *Mesotamp*, however, is linked to the New Guinea word *meso*—"moon," and the Turkmen word, *tam*—"house." Mesotamp's meaning translates into the "House of the Moon."

Mousee: This Golden City for the New Times means the "Ocean of Fish." This spiritual haven, prophesied to appear near Hawaii, combines the New Guinea word *mou*—"fish," and the Afrikaan word *see*—"sea" or "ocean." New flora and fauna is prophesied to appear as Earth enters the New Times.

Nomaking: This Chinese Golden City means "Name of the King." Its meaning is based on the word *noma* (or *nama*) and in many languages ranging from Italian to Sanskrit simply means "name."

Pashacino: "The Passionate Spirit." This Canadian Golden City's meaning is derived from the English word for "passion"—*pash*, and the Kurdish and Turkish word for "spirit"—*cin*.

Pearlanu: Madagascar's Golden City's meaning is based on the Malagasy (the national language of Madagascar) word *lanosina*, which means "to be swum in." Pearlanu's meaning translates to "Swimming in Pearls."

Prana: Located in the heart of India, this Golden City of the Pink Ray meaning is "Life-giving Energy."

Presching: This Chinese Golden City's meaning is linked to its topography. *Pres* is an English word which means "meadow," and *ching* is a Native American (Cahto) word for "timber and forest." Presching means the "City of Meadows, Grasslands, and Forests."

Purensk: This Golden City means "Pure Intelligence" or the "Pure Message." This Russian and Chinese Golden City derives its esoteric meaning from the Danish, English, German, and French name *pur*—"pure," and the Turkish word, *esk*, for "intelligence" or "message."

Shalahah: Sananda is the steward of this United States Golden City which in Sanskrit means a "Sacred Place Indeed!" The syllables break down with these meanings: *shala*—"sacred place", "sanctuary"; *hah*—"indeed."

Sheahah: The Ascended Masters claim that the meaning of this Australian Golden City is, "I AM as ONE." The etymology of this Vortex meaning is undoubtedly related to the Feminine Energies prophesied to dominate and direct the New Times. The syllable *aha* in Tanzanian and Uganda means "here"; in Czechoslovakian *aha* stands for "I see." Therefore Sheahah's hidden meaning is actually prophetic: "She is here," or "She, I see."

Shehez: This Golden City located in Iran and Afghanistan is a Persian word that means "large," or "grand."

Sircalwe: The Russian Golden City of the White Ray derives its sacred name from the Turkish and Chinese languages—*sir*, which means "secret"; and the Elfish language of Middle Earth—*cal*, meaning "light." The word *we* in the English, Korean, and Italian language is defined as "ours." These languages combine to give this Golden City Vortex name its meaning: "Our Secret Light."

[Above: *The protective magic of Puff the Magic Dragon, the sleeping dragon of Hanalei Bay, is located on the island of Kauai, Hawaii. The Golden City of Mousee, a Golden City Vortex for the aquatic beings is prophesied to manifest in the Pacific Ocean, just northwest of Kauai. Mousee anchors both the Gold and Aquamarine Rays for the New Times.*]

STIENTA: This Golden City's name means "the path" in Norwegian.

TEHEKOA: Since this Golden City represents one of the Three Sister Golden Cities of South America, its meaning springs from the lost Moriori language and the Hebrew word *Teku'a*: "the City of Tents," "secures the tents." These meanings merge and Tehekoa means the "Wise Woman who Secures the City."

UNTE: This Golden City—located in Tanzania and Kenya—means in Brazilian, Spanish, and Portuguese "to anoint."

UVERNO: The Canadian Golden City of the Pink Ray translates in Slovak to "trust well."

WAHANEE: The third Golden City of the United States derives its name from *Wahabu*, the Nigerian name for the "God of Love." The etymological meaning of the final syllable *nee* in English, Italian, and French is "born." Wahanee's esoteric meaning is the "God of Love is born."

YUTHOR: In minimalist language, *Yu* means "union." *Thor* is the Scandinavian God of Thunder—"Power." The Golden City of Greenland's hidden meaning is the "Power of Union."

ZASKAR: This Golden City of the White Ray derives its meaning from the Czech and Slovak word *zas*—"again," "over again"; and the Basque word *kar*, which means "flame." This Chinese Golden City means the "Repeating Flame." ⚜

[Editor's Note: The *Webster's Online Dictionary with Multilingual Thesaurus Translation* was used extensively in creating this translation. For the exact locations of the Golden Cities see also *Freedom Star Map* and *Freedom Star Booklet*.]

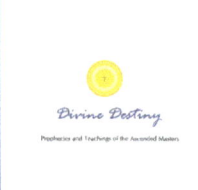

[Above: **Map of the Ancients:** *The Seven Rays and the Nine Civilizations they have formed.*]

Map of the Ancients

SECTION TWELVE

From Divine Destiny

In the I AM America Teachings, Lord Meru, or Lord Macaw, as he prefers to be called at this time, shares one of the eternal records he rescued ages ago from the Lands of Lemuria: the Map of the Ancients. This map of the world simultaneously portrays the lands of Rama, Mu, and Atlantis. No date or timeframe is given for this ancient map; however, its landforms insinuate an epoch before our current geologic period and postdate the theorized existence of the dual continents of Laurasia and Gondwana. These massive continents allegedly broke apart the super-continent of Pangaea and are scientifically estimated to have existed 200 to 180 million years ago. Perhaps Lord Meru purposely left the date off of the ancient map. According to many esoteric teachings, galactic light calibrates scientific development and understanding, and contemporary science may not yet be able to properly interpret this map's geologic and evolutionary implications. However, Lord Meru states that the purpose of the Map of the Ancients is to illustrate the migration and evolution of human consciousness as shaped through the Seven Rays, and

116 I AM AMERICA ATLAS

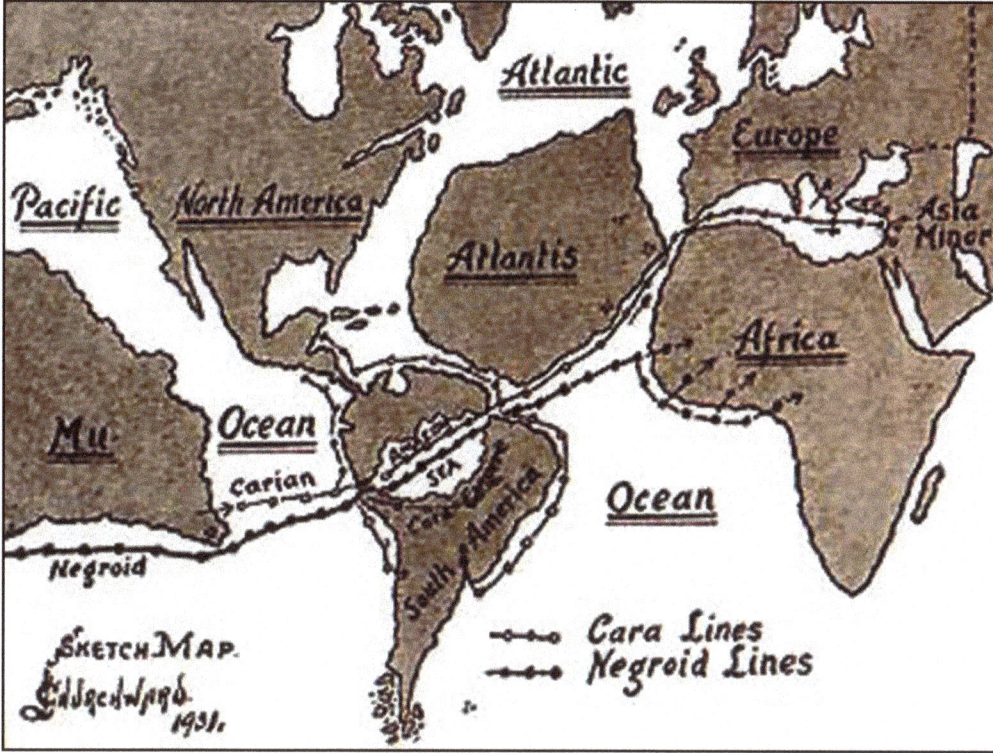

[Right: *The Churchward Map* James Churchward]

Churchward's map showing how he thought Mu refugees spread out after the cataclysm through South America, along the shores of Atlantis and into Africa.

it identifies nine civilizations the Rays have influenced and formed. Geologists who ascribe to the theory of Plate Tectonics and the hypothesis of Continental Drift believe that approximately 135 Mya (million years ago) the South American Plate and the African Plate separated and began to form the familiar map of the Earth we recognize today.

Ameru

Some esoteric historians refer to Ameru as Ameru—the Incan Christ, Quetzalcoatl. From Ameru comes the word America, and, according to Manly P. Hall, "Ameruca is literally translated 'Land of the Plumed Serpent.'" The ancient peoples of America were known as the Red Children of the Sun and worshipped Quetzalcoatl, a prophet of the Christ Consciousness, a messenger from our solar sun.[14]

Ameru and the Right-Hand Path

The provenance of Ameruca—the Land of the Plumed Serpent—is the lost history of Mu, Lemuria, and Atlantis. The Plumed Serpent metaphorically represents the developed Chakra System of the Divine God-man, the Ascended Masters' HU-man. The plume of light atop the head is the developed crown chakra, and the serpent's coils represent the mature Kundalini system, or human energy system comprised of seven chakras. It is claimed that many Lemurians and Atlanteans had the advanced capacity to function in both the Fourth and Fifth Dimension as Spiritual Masters and Shamans where an Alchemical and spiritual battle ensued: the Left-Hand Path versus the Right-Hand Path. Spiritual development at this level of consciousness endows power over the Elemental Kingdom, and the unascended Spiritual Master is often pitted between both malevolent Black Magic and constructive White Magic.

According to Theosophical history, the Lemurian and Atlantean epochs overlap and it is alleged that the lands of Lemuria, also known as Shalmali, existed in the Indian and Southern Pacific Oceans and included the continent of Australia. Lemuria is the remaining culture and civilization of Mu—an expansive continent that once spanned the entire present-day Pacific Ocean.[15] Some esoteric writers place the destruction of Mu around the year 30,000 BC; others place its demise millions of years ago. The apparent discrepancy of these timelines is likely due to two different interpretations of the Cycle of the Yugas—large recurring periods of time employed in the Hindu timekeeping system. The older classical method of calculation literally applies time spans of millions of years; the contemporary method, revealed in 1894, applies cycles that are much shorter.

Lemuria

Short or long, the cycles of the world's ages contain similar archetypes of consciousness and the ever-important ebb and tide of cosmic lessons humanity is destined to learn. The traditional Lemurian was said to live "close to nature" yet was culturally and technologically sophisticated, placing a high value on

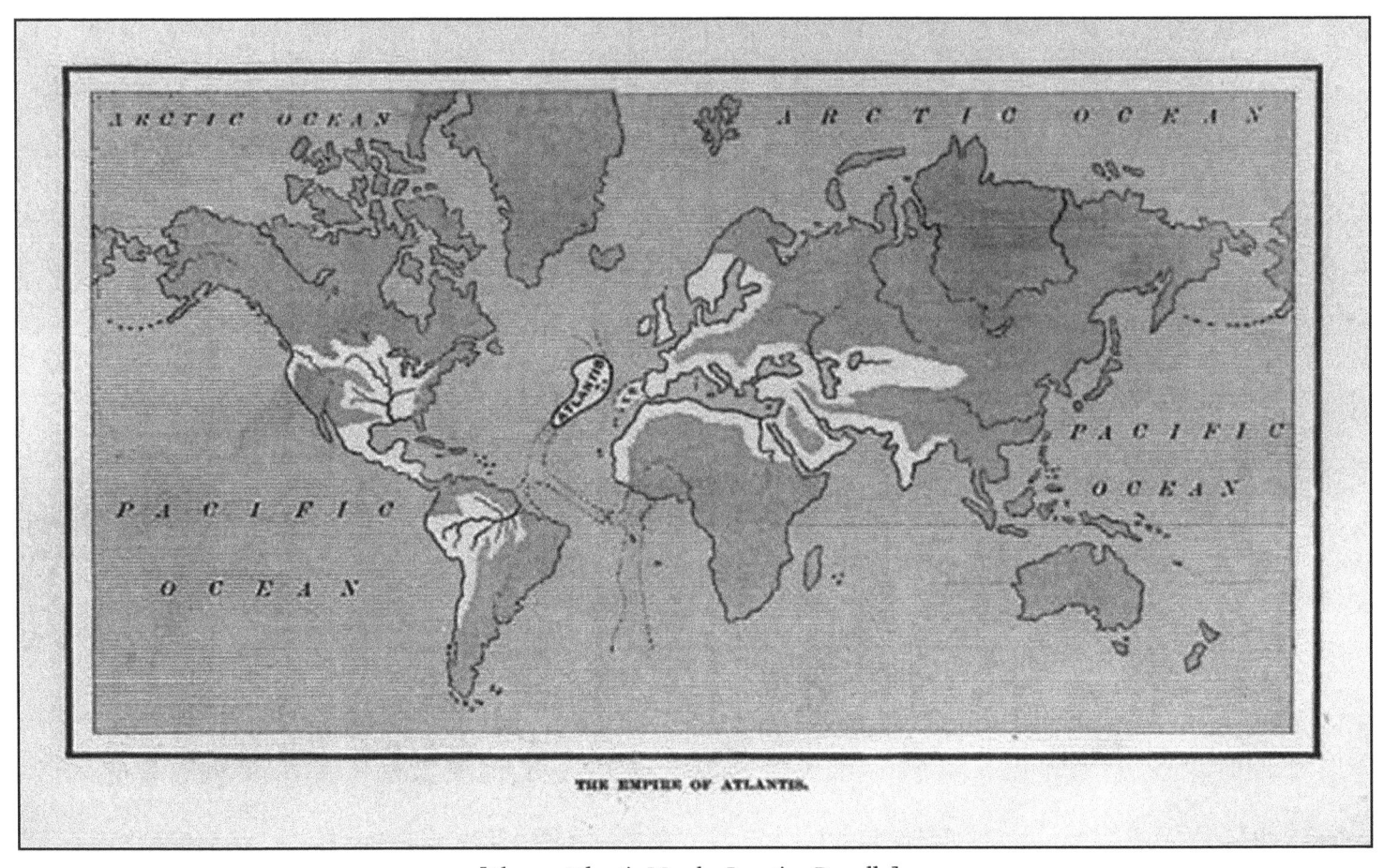

[Above: *Atlantis Map* by Ignatius Donelly]
From Ignatius Donelly's Atlantis: the Antediluvian World, 1882. Image from the Library of Congress.

spiritual and personal growth. Lemurian citizens lived in an esteemed agrarian utopia which attracted migrants from other countries in the ancient pre-Atlantis world. Prior to a polar shift, it is claimed Lemuria suffered civil strife and economic breakdown through illegal immigration. Spiritually and morally unable to expel the foreigners, Lemurians clung to their spiritual aspirations that someday the non-citizens, "who had all the advantages of citizens and cared little about personal growth or taking citizenship training," would later join fellow Lemurians in their spiritual quest.[16] Apparently there was little that could be done. The Lemurian economy could not sustain its empirical growth and needed the immigrant workforce; to further complicate matters, the discontented non-citizenry broke into two conflicting groups: the Pfrees and the Katholis. Inevitably open combat erupted between the two cultures.[17] "The non-citizens eventually divided into two opposing groups: those who prized practicality and those who prized spirituality. The citizenry were more balanced, and valued each equally. The Lemurian Fellowship calls the practical minded non-citizens Pfrees and the spiritually minded non-citizens Katholis," writes David Hatcher Childress in the book Lost Cities of Ancient Lemuria and the Pacific. Hatcher describes the Lemurian cataclysm:

> "The continent had been subsiding for hundreds of years, when a pole shift caused the Pacific continent plate to sink amid much juggling of the tectonic plates. The once great cities were suddenly a thousand feet underwater. The Pfrees had already established their main colony on another continent (actually an island group at that time), Atlantis, while the Katholis established a colony of their own, later to be known as the Rama Empire, in India."[18]

Hatcher claims the venerated Elders of Lemuria also escaped the global tragedy by moving to an uninhabited plateau in central Asia. This similar account mirrors Ascended Master teachings and Lord Himalaya's founding of the Retreat of the Blue Lotus. By Hatcher's explanation, the Lemurian elders re-established their spiritual teachings and massive library as the Thirteenth School. It is claimed these teachings and spiritual records became foundational teachings in the Great White Brotherhood of the mystical lands of Hsi

Wang Mu (the Abode of the Immortals), and the Kuan Yin Lineage of Gurus.[19]

Ameru and the Rise and Fall of Atlantis

During the spiritually enlightened phase of the civilization of Atlantis, the rule of the Toltec Sub-race—the reputed ancestors of today's Native American—created a world society of architectural beauty, unrivaled Earth-friendly technology, with organized armies, governments, and elegant social amenities. The lands of Mu, Ameru, and Atlantis formed the vast empire of the spiritually evolved Atlantean. Spiritual teachings, grand ceremonies, spiritual meditation, and the magnificent Atlantean temples were all dedicated to the worship of the sun.[20] Some esoteric texts allege that the Lands of Mu and the Lands of Rama were home to the spiritual elite—the ancient priesthood of Lemuria; the homeland of Atlantis housed the central government and its wondrous buildings and temples; and the Lands of Ameru remained mostly uninhabited, with a few small cities colonized by Atlanteans. At the height of Atlantean culture, the lands of Ameru were intentionally held in environmental stewardship primarily for agricultural use; fruit and grain crops grew bountifully alongside roaming herds of genetically bred wild game—elk and deer. Frederick Oliver writes about the abundant lands of Ameru colonized by Atlanteans in the esoteric classic A Dweller on Two Planets:

> "Successively we came to the Isthmus of Panama, then over four hundred miles in breadth; to Mexico (South Incalia) and to the immense plains of the Mississippi. These latter formed the great cattle-lands where Poseid drew most of its supplies of flesh-foods, and where, when the modern world discovered it, enormous herds of wild progeny of ancient stock roamed at will. Buffalo, elk, bear, deer and mountain sheep—all off-spring of the remotest ages— to the west lay in what early American days were called the 'great plains.' But in the days of Poseid they had a far different appearance from that which they bear today. Not then arid or very sparsely inhabited, though vastly colder in winter, owing to the nearness of the vast glaciers of the north. The Nevada lakes were not then mere dried up beds of borax and soda, nor the 'Great Salt Lake' of Utah a bitter, brackish body of water of its present comparatively small size. All lakes were large bodies of fresh water and the Great Salt Lake was an inland sea of fresh floods, bearing icebergs from

[Above: *Temple Ruins at Chichen Itza*, 1918 (approx.)]
Author Edward Thompson theorizes that the Temple of the Tables, "takes its name from a table-like altar supported on the uplifted arms of small Atlantean figures." [40]

the glaciers on its northern shores. Arizona, that treasure-house of the geologist, had its now marvelous desert covered with the waters of Miti, as we called the great inland sea of that region . . . On the shores of Miti was a considerable population, and one city of no small size—colonists all, from Atl."[21]

It is claimed that secluded Atlantean Temples were established in the lands of Ameru. Oliver describes an Atlantean Temple in the Teton Mountains of Idaho discovered in an 1870s expedition of the Yellowstone region led by the U.S. geologist Ferdinand V. Hayden:

> "On its top he found a roofless structure of granite slaps, within which, he said, that 'granite detritus was a depth indicating that for eleven thousand years it had been undisturbed' . . . He was examining a structure made by Poseid hands one hundred and twenty-seven and a half centuries ago . . ."[22]

Religious teachings and colorful motifs of the Children of the Sun allegedly migrated into the preceding cultures of ancient Egypt, the Mayan, and are said to have influenced both the Aztec of Mexico and the Native American tribes of North America. Occultists link Atlantean culture to North Africa and the surrounding areas of the Mediterranean: Greece, Italy, Portugal, and Spain. Perhaps one of the best known accounts of ancient Atlantis was written by Ignatius Donnelly in 1882. His book Atlantis, the Antediluvian World was revised in 1949 by mythologist Egerton Sykes (1894–1983). Hugh Cayce, son of the renowned psychic Edgar Cayce writes:

> "Donnelly's arguments are based largely on evidence of similarities between the culture of Egypt and the Indian cultures of Central and South America. On both sides of the Atlantic one finds the use of a 365-day calendar, the practice of embalming, the building of pyramids, legends of a flood, etc. Donnelly argues that both the ancient Egyptian and American Indian cultures originated in Atlantis, and spread east and west when Atlantis was destroyed. An Atlantean heritage, Donnelly suggests, would explain the fact that the Basques of the Spanish Pyrenees differ from all their neighbors in appearance and language . . . Donnelly says Spain, Portugal, and the Canary Islands would be likely landing spots for refugees from sinking Atlantis."[23]

Land of Rama

The Land of Rama grew and developed alongside the great Atlantean civilization, and was ruled by magnificent kings—spiritual priests, adepts, and Master Teachers known in Sanskrit as Rishis. It is claimed that seven great cities emerged in the Rama Empire, known as the Seven Rishi Cities. David Childress writes, "The Rama Empire spread out to include most of the Indian sub-continent. It probably extended as far west as Iran or so, and as far east as Burma."[24] The Rama Empire rivaled Atlantean culture with its technology and it is claimed both countries developed sophisticated air-flight; however the Rama Empire was known for its creation of the Vimana, a double-decked aircraft that flew "with the speed of the wind," and "weapons such as fireballs that could destroy a whole city."[25] Many ancient Indian texts including the Ramayana and the Mahabharata describe Rama's splendor and beauty alongside its endurance of horrific wars and battles. Perhaps one of the most eclectic accounts of this prehistoric civilization, from the Lemurian Fellowship, uniquely describes the clash between Lemurian rivals, now world-powers, the once practical Pfrees—Atlanteans; and the Katholis—the spiritually adept Rama Empire.[26]

> "The Atlanteans (sent) a well-equipped army to India in order to subjugate the Rama Empire and bring it under the sovereignty of Atlantis. Equipped with a formidable array of weapons the Atlanteans landed their valixi (aircraft) outside one of the Rishi Cities . . . sent a message to the ruling Priest-King of the city that they should surrender. The Priest-King sent word back to the Atlantean general, 'We of India have no quarrel with you of Atlantis. We ask that we be permitted to follow our own way of life.'"[27]

The Atlanteans, equipped with advanced weaponry and technology, perceived their enemy weak, sensed an easy victory, and replied, "We shall not destroy your land with the mighty weapons at our command provided you pay sufficient tribute and accept the rulership of Atlantis."[28] The Priest-King responded, "We of India do not believe in war and strife, peace being our ideal. Neither would we destroy you or your soldiers who but follow orders. However, if you persist in your determination to attack us without cause and merely for the purpose of conquest, you will leave us no recourse but to destroy you and all of your leaders. Depart, and leave us in peace."[29]

The Atlantean army began their invasion, while the great Rishi watched from his hilltop palace. The Priest-King of Rama raised his arms upwards and spiritually evoked the power of heaven through yogic technique. The Atlantean General and each of his descending officers dropped dead to the ground—their hearts burst. The Atlantean force, without leadership and organization, panicked and retreated.[30]

Inevitably after the humiliating defeat, the government of Atlantis, instead of subjugating the ancient Indians, decided to destroy the major cities of the Rama Empire with nuclear attacks. Hatcher claims the Mahabharata is a historical account of the use of nuclear weaponry, and the Atlantean destruction of the magnificent Rishi Cities.[31]

> "Gurkha, flying a swift and powerful Vimana,
> Hurled a single projectile
> Charged with all the power of the Universe.
> An incandescent column of smoke and flame,
> As bright as ten thousands suns,
> Rose with all its splendor."
> –the Mahabharata

H. P. Blavatsky claims that prior to the invasion of the Rama Empire, a new sub-race of Atlanteans incarnated on Earth: the Turanians. According to Theosophical history, the Turanian sub-race was a young group of souls: selfish, materialistic, and inevitably they overcame the wise stewardship of the Atlantean Toltecs.[32] The advanced science and technology of Atlantis sadly morphed into egotistical self-indulgence with continued violence and cruelty against other

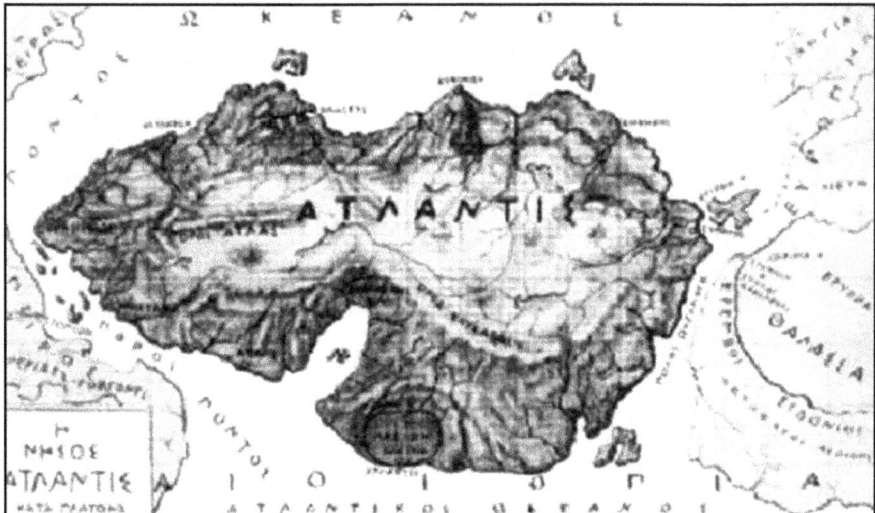

[Right: *Atlantis* by Patroclus Kampankis]

Fictional map of Atlantis by Patroclus Kampanakis. Originally drawn in 1891, first published in his book "The pro-cataclysm *Communication of the Two Worlds via Atlantis*," Constantinople 1893.

nations. Extreme supernatural experience prevailed during the Atlantean cultural downturn and led Atlantean geneticists to create a bizarre sub-race of Animal-Humans—chimeras. The chimeras were abused as sex slaves and later bred into vicious armies of cruel, blood-thirsty warriors.[33] The psychic readings of Edgar Cayce reiterate the myths of the chimeras, and the moral conflict their presence created in Atlantis between the Sons of the Law of One and the Sons of Belial.

> "In Atlantis when there (was turmoil) between children of the Law of One and Sons of Belial, found Sons of Belial desirable for gratification of material emotions and desires."[34]

The account of this conflict describes the Sons of the Law of One seeking higher consciousness to spiritually affect the Group Mind of Atlantis and lift the spiritual consciousness of the nation to overcome the conflict,

> ". . . through the concentration of the Group Mind of the children of the Law of One, they entered into a fourth-dimensional consciousness—or were absent from the body."[35]

Clearly, the Sons of the Law of One saw the chimeras as developing souls; the Sons of Belial saw these creations merely as property—common chattel. The Cayce readings further explain:

> "This is not intended to indicate that there is transmigration or transmutation of the soul from animal to human; but the comparison is made as to trait, as to mind, as to how those so domesticated in the present are dependant upon their masters for that consideration of their material as well as mental welfare—yet in each there is still the instinct, the predominant nature of that class or group-soul impregnation into which it has pushed itself for self-expression."[36]

Atlantean spiritual life spiraled downward into the polarized misuse of occult energy and black wizardry, and sorcery denigrated the great Mystery Schools; in the later Atlantean period human sacrifice and gross idolatry disabled the once mighty civilization, facilitating its inevitable destruction through massive Earth Changes.

The demise of Atlantis was unavoidable; however modern-day geologists, archaeologists, and occultists disagree about its timing. Ascended Master teachings affirm that Atlantis—a continent whose geo-physical and political existence probably spanned well over 100,000 years—experienced several phases of traumatic Earth Change. This same belief is held by occult historians who claim that the Earth repeatedly cycles through periods of massive Earth Change and cataclysmic pole shifts that activate tectonic plates and subsequently submerge whole continents and create vital new lands for Earth's successors. Theosophists and the psychic readings of Edgar Cayce agree that a massive deluge occurred in Atlantean times somewhere between 75,000 and 50,000 BC; this was followed by another period of Earth's instability around 28,000 BC.[37, 38] However, both groups conclude that the Atlantis finale took place around 10,000 BC, and it was described by the Greek philosopher Plato in the historic dialogues Timaeus and Critias.

Prior to the Atlantean epoch, Mu and Lemuria had suffered a similar fate; yet the sinking of Atlantis remains to this day etched in humanity's archetypal consciousness. The Edgar Cayce readings claim that many of the souls who once walked, lived, and loved the lands and the mystical times of Atlantis are today reincarnated in America—Ameru, the beloved land of the Toltecs. Hugh Cayce writes, "Along with technological abilities, they bring tendencies for being extremists. Often they exhibit individual and group karma associated with selfishness and exploitation where others are concerned. Many of them lived during one of the periods of destruction, or geological change in Atlantean history. If Edgar Cayce's prophecies are correct, a similar period of Earth Changes is imminent."[39]

[Above: **Map of the Ancients:** *The influence of the Seven Rays on nations.*]

The Colonization of the Earth as Taught by Lord Meru

The first souls to inhabit schoolhouse Earth originally came from other planets. This colonization process was energetically orchestrated by the Great Central Sun in a threefold process. First, the energies established themselves upon the Earth through the Emanation-Radiation Process of the Rays. Once a single Ray Force established a stronghold in the collective planetary consciousness, the attraction of various lifestreams from other planets toward Earth ensued, and various Ray(ces) populated on Earth through the incarnation process—sometimes esoterically referred to as the Transmigration of Souls. Others arrived physically as space-travelers from our Solar System. Altogether, Meru claims souls and life forms from eight planets originally colonized Earth. While other Master Teachers have mentioned the presence of souls and lifestreams from other solar systems and galaxies, Lord Meru focuses on the esoteric history of the extraterrestrial immigration from these planets: Saturn, Jupiter, our Sun, the Earth's Moon, Mercury, Venus, Uranus, and Mars.

The spiritual and physical leaders of each immigrant group of Ray(ce) Souls in Ascended Master teachings is referred to as a Lord. Meru claims Lord Rama led the first wave of immigrants from the planet Saturn to Earth. Today portions of the geological area where the Saturnians (also known as the Blue Ray) once colonized are present-day India. In the Lineage of Manus, Lord Rama is known as the Manu of the Aryan Race.

Ray Forces from Saturn, the Sun, and the Great Central Sun assisted the rise of this great civilization.

According to Lord Meru, the second Ray(ce) to populate Earth originated from Jupiter—the Yellow Ray. Meru refers to this civilization as the Land of Brihaspati—Brihaspati is a Sanskrit term and astronomically refers to Jupiter—a term likely coined by the colonial Ramans. This group of souls is alleged to have originally settled on lands which today geologically comprise the Japanese Archipelago. It is claimed that the mountain range of the Lands of Brihaspati eventually morphed into the Himalayas, and the genetic seed of this Ray(ce) are the ancient Kirata and Tibetan cultures. The Mahabharata recounts this mythological race of people as "gold-like . . . unlike the Dasas (Ramans) who were dark (dark blue)."[41] It is claimed that the I-Ching (the sixty-four hexagrams) is the foundation of the lost language of Mu, which likely originated with the Brihaspatites.[42] The Raman and Brihaspati cultures produced the post-diluviun Elders of Lemuria who later migrated to the Himalayans during cyclic Earth Changes. [Editor's Note: See Lord Meru.] Hsi Wang Mu—a name assigned to the mystical lands West of the Lands of ancient Brihaspati—became synonymous for the goddess Kuan Yin as the Goddess Hsi Wang Mu: the Merciful Guardian, Queen Mother of the West. Lao Tzu was said to travel to Hsi Wang Mu (the Thirteenth School), and before he embarked on the spiritual journey from which he would never return, he wrote in the famous book Tao Te Ching, "The Ancient Masters were subtle, mysterious, profound, responsive. The depth of their knowledge is unfathomable. All we can do is describe their appearance; watchful, like men crossing a winter stream. Alert, like men aware of danger; courteous, like visiting guests; yielding, like ice about to melt; simple, like uncarved blocks of wood."[43]

Lord Meru claims that the lands of Earth were once one large super-continent, similar to the scientific theories of Pangaea. Geologists estimate Pangaea to exist about 250 million years ago. During this time of greater spiritual light on Earth, esoteric myths maintain the continent floated over one continuous ocean. The land drifted on a blissful, calm sea and followed the ever-present light of the sun. The land, its nature kingdoms, and its peoples never experienced the duality of day and night until the super-continent broke apart and permanently affixed to the Earth. [Editor's Note: Lord Meru does not place a date on the Map of the Ancients, yet it is possible that this map depicts the Earth after the birth or destruction of continental land masses known as Mu. Also, lands located Southwest of Atlantis are described by Meru to have once been above the ocean. It is wrong to presume Lord Meru's representation of the world would remain unchanged. It is likely new lands emerged in short periods of time as this geologic epoch developed and ended; whole continents changed or disappeared as yet another geological epoch ensued. The idea of Earth Change embraces the concept that Earth experiences and is susceptible to constant cycles of descending and ascending galactic light through the Cycle of the Yugas; therefore, humanity is simultaneously changing and adapting to these phases.]

Ancient Timeline

The following timeline may help us understand potential timeframes and geographical possibilities:

4.6 Billion Years BC: This is the estimated time of creation of the Earth theorized by geologists and scientists.[44]

250 MYA (Million Years Ago): Pangaea exists.

200–180 MYA: Earth experiences the breakup of Pangaea and two super-continents emerge: Laurasia and Gondwana.

145–65 MYA: Laurentia exists as an independent continent which is known today as North America.[45]

135 MYA: South America and Africa split. [Editor's Note: Ancient Earth entered Dvapara Yuga at approximately 135.5 MYA—the estimated date of Lord Meru's Map of the Ancients. Kali Yuga follows Dvapara Yuga around 136.3 MYA and this event likely marked Kali's entrance with global Earth Change.]

65.95 MYA: A mass extinction occurs on Earth of all life; scientists refer to this as the Cretaceous-Tertiary Extinction. Eighty-five per cent of all species on Earth died including the dinosaurs; and scientists believe this catastrophe was likely caused by asteroid impacts alongside massive volcanic activity.[46] [Editor's Note: Scientists have recently improved their process for dating rocks and fossils, and according to Paul Renne, director of the UC Berkeley Geochronology Center, the "best date for the Cretaceous-Tertiary boundary is now 65.95 million years ago, give or take 40,000 years."[47] This gives plausible evidence as to the accuracy of the Cycle of the Yugas, which places the beginning of a Kali Yuga at 66.2 MYA. According to the Vedic succession of the Classical Yugas, Kali Yuga is identified as a period of Earthly decline and strife, which is immediately overcome once the Kreta

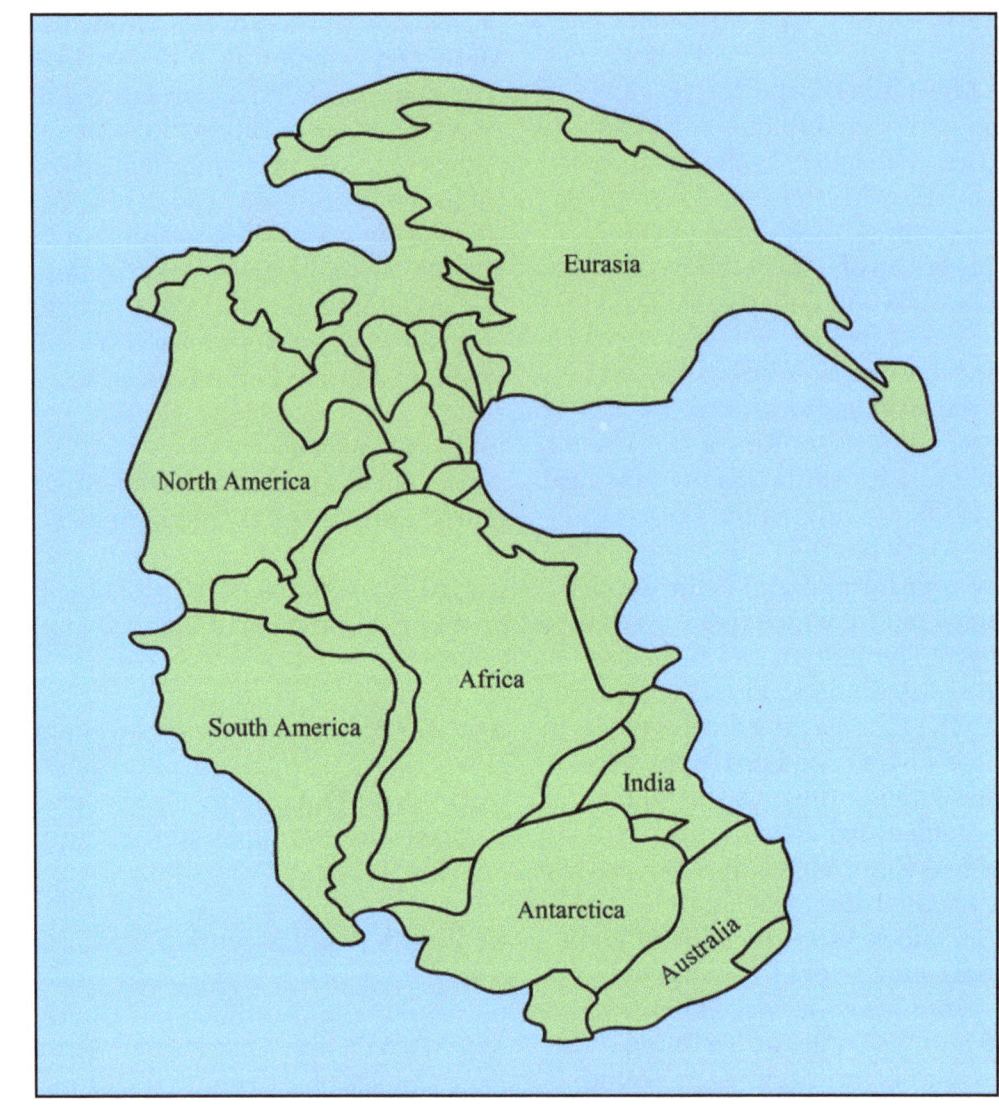

[*Pangaea:* A depiction of Pangaea.]

Yuga (Golden Age) begins. According to the Puranic method of Yuga calculation, Earth entered this vulnerable period at approximately 66.2 MYA. Since a Kali Yuga lasts for a period of 432,000 years, the episode of destruction was likely endured until 67.6 MYA. Applying the slop-factor of 40,000 years, the Cretaceous-Tertiary Extinction could be placed as early as 66.35 MYA, during a Kali Yuga period on Earth.]

55–39 MYA: Europe, Greenland, and North America drift apart.

34–23 MYA: The continents continue to drift to their present locations.

23–.5 MYA: The land-bridge between South America and North America disappears and reappears. North America (Laurentia) crashes into South America and forms the super-continent America.[48]

3,891,102 BC: The last Kreta Yuga (full-force Golden Age) on Earth ensues, using the Puranic, or classical timing of Yugas.

2.58 MYA to Present: The Earth enters its fourth Ice Age: the Quaternary Ice Age. Scientists believe Earth entered its worst Ice Age from 850 to 635 MYA, when ice covered the entire globe. The Ascended Masters prophesy that as we enter the New Times, Earth will enter a phase of Global Warming and the polar ice-caps may melt.[49]

2,163,102 BC: Treta Yuga begins. According to the revered Sanskrit poet Valmiki, Ramayana (the Lands of Rama) flourish in this time period.

2 to 1.5 Million Years BC: The civilization of Mu develops at the end of Treta Yuga (a Silver Age on Earth).

1.8 MYA: The Pleistocene Ice Age—a subdivision of the Quaternary Ice Age—begins and glaciers form on all continents of Earth. This glacial period ends almost 12,500 years ago as ice sheets and continental glaciers retreat.[50]

867,102 BC: Dvapara Yuga begins and the races of men that will eventually civilize the societies of Lemuria and Atlantis are born.

780,000 BC: Earth's magnetic field reverses.

778,000 to 400,000 BC: Ancestral human remains exist. Present-day archaeologists have found and dated them within this time span; locations of remains include: Ancient Israel, Ancient Britain, Northern Europe, Ethiopia, Indonesia, and Germany.[51]

638,000 BC: The massive Yellowstone Caldera erupts in North America. Scientists believe the Supervolcano also erupted in 2.1 MYA and 1.3 MYA.[52]

300,000 BC: According to author and researcher Zecharia Sitchen, the Annunaki—a race of extraterrestrials on Earth—genetically engineer through in-vitro fertilization a race of genetic workers to labor in their gold mines.[53]

[*North American Craton* by the United States Geological Survey Geology of Ameru, also known by geologists as Laurentia.]

(North American craton. The brown area shows the part of the North American continent that has been stable for over 600 million years. This region is made up of a basement older Precambrian metamorphic and igneous rock.)
United States Geological Survey.

278,000 to 250,000 BC: Ancestral human remains exist. Present-day archaeologists have found and dated them within this time span; locations include: China, Northern Siberia, Central Mexico.

200,000 BC: According to James Churchward, Lemuria is inhabited by over sixty million people, consisting of ten diverse tribes, united by one government.[54]

128,000 BC: Humans are voyaging across the Ancient Mediterranean Sea, according to evidence discovered by present-day archaeologists.[55]

100,000 BC to 50,000 BC: Lord Meru claims that by 100,000 BC civilizations of Atlantis co-exist with the civilizations of Lemuria.

73,000 BC: The super volcano Toba erupts in Indonesia. Scientists theorize that the global temperature drops five degrees for many years on Earth, substantially reducing its population.[56]

70,000 BC: According to James Churchward, the Uighur Empire of Lemuria flourishes as a world power, just north of present-day Burma.[57]

40,000 to 24,000 BC: The Great Barrier Reef is above water—according to Aboriginal myths.[58]

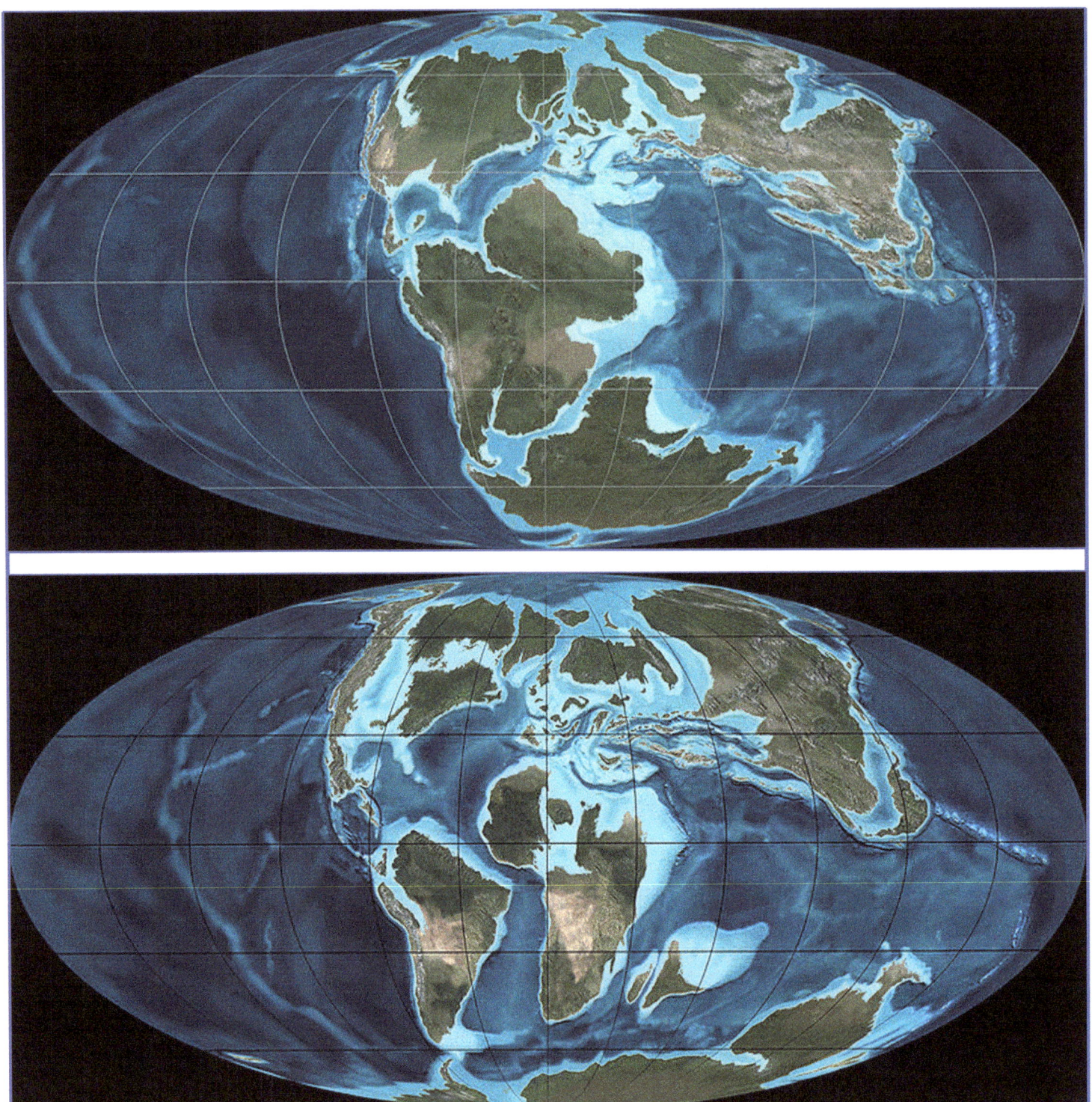

[*Prehistoric Earth:* A geologist's depiction of prehistoric Earth, before and after South America and Africa split.]

24,000 BC: Lemuria, also known as Mukulia, Rutas, Hiva (Polynesian), and Pacifica, undergoes massive Earth Changes.[59]

20,000 BC: Geologists estimate sea levels begin to rise on the Great Barrier Reef and coral skeletons initiate the construction of the present-day natural wonder on an older platform estimated to be over 600,000 years old.[60]

10,000 to 15,000 BC: An Ice Age ensues, and remaining coastlines of Lemuria disappear under the ocean waters. Today, present-day Australia also known by ancient Egyptian gold-miners as the ancient Land of Punt, is the remainder of the once great continent of Mu and Lemuria.[61]

10,000 BC: Earth enters the Holocene geological epoch regarded as a warmer period, also known as an interglacial period, within the Quaternary Ice Age.

Scientists credit the stable climate of the Holocene period to the development of humanity and its current urbanization. Many believe this era marks a permanent end to the current Ice Age.[62]

9,628 BC: Atlantis sinks; although many esoteric texts claim Atlantis' geologic Earth Changes occurred in three partial cataclysms. 9,628 BC is the estimated year of Atlantis' final demise.

3,102 BC: Kali Yuga begins.

360 BC: Plato writes about the lost continent of Atlantis.[63]

Lord Meru claims the teachings of the Map of the Ancients is for esoteric students to grasp the interaction of Ray Forces, and how their natural power and energy sculpts societies, cultures, and the civilizations of Earth. Ray Forces work together in a harmonic, instead of a defined, focus. For example, Lord Meru teaches that civilizations from the Moon, Venus, and Mercury appeared simultaneously. The civilizations from these Ray Forces developed in ancient America, Atlantis, and the prehistoric lands of South America and Africa.

Venus is perhaps one of the most unique planets in our Solar System. Meru claims Venus is not originally from our solar scheme, and initially functioned like a large, planetary satellite that was intentionally placed in our Solar System by members of the Galactic Brotherhood to resurrect and restore impoverished Ray Forces throughout our Solar System. No date is given for this event; however, Meru claims this action alone saved the Earth from imminent annihilation through spiritual depravity. Lord Meru states a similar spiritual intervention by Venus; in the twentieth century, it gave humanity yet another reprieve from obliteration; and the construction of the spiritual infrastructure of the Golden City Vortices by the Spiritual Hierarchy ensued.

The Ray Forces of the Moon and Mercury aided the birth and growth of an ancient civilization claimed to once exist in the present-day Sahara Desert of Africa. Meru states this empire was intellectually adept and communication was primarily telepathic; although an alphabet and written language were also developed. The same energies and their influence gave rise to the Osirian Culture of Egypt and initiated ancient settlements of present-day Central and South America. The pre-American civilizations were conceived millions of years ago on the super-continent of conjoined South America and Africa. [Editor's Note: These Native American cultures likely flourished in the early centuries of Dvapara Yuga.]

The Greater and Lesser Antilles chain of islands, along with the island of Cuba was once a land mass where Lord Meru claims the pre-American civilizations of Quetzalcoatl developed. This society was sponsored by the Ray Force of the Moon and the White Ray; its culture was inordinately feminine.

The esoteric Christian tradition finds its roots under the sway of the Ruby-Gold Ray and to this day many Christians are deeply impacted by the healing benevolence of this religious faith. However, the esoteric, historical influence of this Ray split its effect over two continents: the Lands of Mu, which later evolved into Lemuria and present-day Australia; and lands located near the North Pole—present day Russia. Meru claims this Ray developed the healing arts which profoundly influenced the spiritual cultures of Mu and Lemuria. The Ray Force draws its energy from Mars and our Sun, with overtones from the White and Green Rays—the planets Venus and Mercury. Altogether the Rays formed an aggregate energy which became the nexus for two new Ray(ces)—the Lemurian and Atlantean—both birthed on the Motherland of Mu.

Prehistoric Tectonic Plate

Lord Meru refers to this geological plate, which is in reference to the Pacific Plate, as an oceanic tectonic plate beneath the Pacific Ocean. Esoteric historians theorize that the Pacific Plate, through periodic geologic upheaval and Earth Changes formed the submerged lost continent of Lemuria. Some Earth Changes theories claim pole shifts caused entire continents to rise or fall due to Tectonic Plate Theory.[64]

Flora and Fauna of the Ancient Lands of the Plumed Serpent

Plants: According to Lord Meru, plants grow in harmony and cooperation with the Mineral Kingdom. Since humanity subsists primarily on a vegetarian diet at this time—likely due to the increased light and the spirituality of Dvapara Yuga—ancient species of nuts, grains, and fruits are harvested after their maturation process. According to scientific theory, this time frame marks the evolution of flowering plants—angiosperms. Honey is collected through domestic beekeeping, and many occult teachings claim bees were brought to Earth from their homeland planet of Venus. The evolved cultures of Earth ate certain foods to enhance or strengthen specific Ray Forces, according to health needs.

Animals: Meru claims few wild animals (mammals) existed in the ancient land of Earth during the Dvapara Yuga millions of years ago, however certain animal species were cultivated domestically as pets and were likely wiped out in the Cretaceous-Tertiary Extinction. The group-souls of these animal companions still exist today as the domesticated horse, dog, and cat. Meru describes a domestic ox that once existed millions of years ago on Earth. It is claimed that colonies of ancient dolphins and whales habituated the ancient oceans, and their presence increased the spiritual vibration of the Earth.

Diet: A vegetarian diet prevailed throughout the ancient Dvapara Yuga, due to the highly sensitized human Kundalini system which could not bear the vibration of flesh-eating. Since foods were chosen to compliment specific Ray Forces, this resulted in the deepening of spiritual knowledge and development alongside the "demonstration of the physical laws of cooperation." Lord Meru states that the land resonated with Beauty and Harmony.

Insects: It is claimed the Lords of Venus introduced butterflies and bees to our Earth. The golden nectar of honey is claimed to support the human intellect in obtaining enlightenment and spiritual illumination. ✣

RAY SYSTEMS

From Light of Awakening:
Some Ray Systems include up to forty singular Rays, it is best to stick with and memorize the basic seven Rays. Also, discard confusing numbering systems. Instead, focus on the color of the Ray to grasp its core meaning.

Below is a Ray System based on Ascended Master teachings and Vedic or Hindu astrology—Jyotish. In Sanskrit, Jyotish coincidentally means science of light. I have incorporated the Vedic system with the Ascended Master teachings for several reasons. First, it is perhaps the oldest astrology system on Earth (Jyotish traces back to 4,000 BC), and it articulates information on the Rays. Second, Jyotish and the Seven Ray System are uniquely compatible. It is likely the Vedic system is the same arrangement once studied by many of our contemporary Master Teachers.

Please note, the following two levels of attributes are given for each Ray: common qualities and cosmic qualities. The understanding of astrological planets is vital to grasping how Ray forces work in our solar system.

• **Blue Ray**
Common Attributes: steady, calm, persevering, transforming, harmonizing, diligent, determined, austere, protective, humble, truthful, self-negating, stern
Cosmic Attribute: Divine Will or Choice
Planet: Saturn

• **Yellow Ray**
Common Attributes: studious, learned, expansive, optimistic, joyful, fun-loving, generous, proper, formal
Cosmic Attribute: Spiritual Enlightenment
Planet: Jupiter

• **Pink Ray**
Common Attributes: loving, nurturing, hopeful, heartfelt, compassionate, considerate, communicative, intuitive, friendly, humane, tolerant, adoring
Cosmic Attribute: Divine Mother
Planet: Moon

• **White Ray**
Common Attributes: beautiful, pure, elegant, refined, sensitive, charming, graceful, creative, artistic, cooperative, uplifting, strong, piercing, blissful
Cosmic Attribute: Divine Feminine
Planet: Venus

• **Green Ray**
Common Attributes: educated, thoughtful, communicative, organized, intellectual, objective, scientific, discriminating, practical, discerning, adaptable, rational, healing, awakened
Cosmic Attribute: Active Intelligence
Planet: Mercury

• **Ruby (Red) and Gold Ray**
Common Attributes (Ruby): energetic, passionate, devoted, determination, dutiful, dependable, direct, insightful, inventive, technical, skilled, forceful
Cosmic Attribute (Ruby): Divine Masculine
Planet (Ruby): Mars
Common Attributes (Gold): warm, perceptive, honest, confident, positive, independent, courageous, enduring, vital, leadership, responsible, ministration, authority, justice
Cosmic Attribute (Gold): Divine Father
Planet (Gold): Sun

• **Violet Ray**
Common Attributes: forgiving, transmuting, alchemizing, electric, intervening, diplomatic, magical, merciful, graceful, freedom, ordered service
Cosmic Attribute: Divine Grace
Planet: Currently undetermined, but some systems place Uranus, the higher vibration of Saturn, or both under this Ray force.

Invocation of the Violet Flame for Sunrise and Sunset

I invoke the Violet Flame to come forth in the name of I AM that I AM,
To the Creative Force of all the realms of all the Universes, the Alpha, the Omega, the Beginning, and the End,

To the Great Cosmic Beings and Torch Bearers of all the realms of all the Universes,
And the Brotherhoods and Sisterhoods of Breath, Sound, and Light, who honor this Violet Flame that comes forth from the Ray of Divine Love—the Pink Ray, and the Ray of Divine Will—the Blue Ray of all Eternal Truths.

I invoke the Violet Flame to come forth in the name of I AM that I AM! Mighty Violet Flame, stream forth from the Heart of the Central Logos, the Mighty Great Central Sun! Stream in, through, and around me.

Awakening Prayer

Great Light of Divine Wisdom,
Stream forth to my being,
And through your right use
Let me serve mankind and the planet.
Love, from the Heart of God.
Radiate my being with the presence of the
Christ
That I walk the path of truth.
Great Source of Creation.
Empower my being,
My Brother,
My Sister,
And my planet with perfection
As we collectively awaken as one cell.
I call forth the Cellular Awakening.
Let wisdom, love, and power stream forth to this
cell,
This cell that we all share.
Great Spark of Creation awaken the Divine Plan
of Perfection.
So we may share the ONE perfected cell,
I AM.

Glossary

Adjatal: This Golden City of the Blue and Gold Rays is overseen by Lord Himalaya and promotes Spiritual Awakening. It is located primarily in Pakistan and Tajikistan, and is a twin to the Golden City of Zaskar.

Afrom: A Golden City of the White Ray that is located mainly in Hungary and Romania. Its stewards are Claire, the Elohim of Purity, along with the Goddess SeRaya, also known as the White Buddha. Afrom assists Earth's Ascension through the spiritual attribute of purity.

Amerigo: Ascended Master Godfre serves in this Golden City, located in Spain. Amerigo facilitates the spiritual ideal of, "God in All," through its alignment to the Gold Ray.

Ameru: The ancient lands of America from which the word Ameruca is derived, and means, "Land of the Plumed Serpent." Esoteric historians allege Ameru is the beloved land of the Toltecs, the ancestral forefathers of today's Native American; geologists suppose the lands of Ameru are the North America Craton, the ancient continent of Laurentia.

Andeo: The thirtieth Golden City located in Peru, Columbia, and Brazil, South America. Its qualities are consistency; its Ray Force is Pink and Gold; and its Master Teachers are the Goddesses Meru and Constance. The Golden City of Andeo is also known as the City of the Feminine.

Angelica: The Golden City of Angelica is guided by the Elohim Angelica and is affiliated with the Pink Ray. It is located in Queensland, Australia, and is paired to the Golden City of Clayje.

Archangel Chamuel: The Archangel of the Pink Ray is associated with all aspects of Divine Love.

Archangel Crystiel: The Archangel who protects the ongoing spiritual evolution and enlightment of humanity. Crystiel's angelic complement is the Archeia Clarity who works with the principles of precision and transparency. Crystiel's color ray is aquamarine and gold. His weapon is a heavenly laser. He serves in the Golden City of Cresta, located in Antarctica.

Archangel Michael: Masculine leader of the angels of the Blue Ray, Archangel Michael is the steward of the Golden City of Stienta, located in Iceland. A primary protector of aspiring HU-mans through the Blue White Flame, Archangel Michael is known for binding demons and foreign entities from the Earth Plane and Planet. As an agent of God Protection, he attentively guards the two poles of our Earth.

Archangel Zadkiel: Masculine leader of the angels of the Violet Ray, Archangel Zadkiel is the steward of the Golden City of Jeafray, located in Canada. Archangel Zadkiel is associated with the spiritual attributes of transmutation, alchemy, freedom, and mercy.

Archeia Constance: Feminine leader of the angels of the Yellow Ray, Archeia Constance is also affiliated with the Gold Ray. She is a steward of the Golden City of Andeo, and a protector and defender of the conception and birth of the New Children, prophesied to incarnate in the New Times. She is associated with wisdom, understanding, expansion, courage, and leadership.

Arctura: The thirty-seventh Golden City is located in China. Arctura's stewards are the twin Elohim Arcturus and Diana of the Violet Ray. This Golden City is associated with freedom, precipitation, and the rhythm of universal harmony.

Arkana: This Golden City is overseen by Archangel Gabriel of the White Ray. Located in East Siberia, Russia, this sacred Vortex radiates and transfigures the HU-man for Ascension.

Aryan: The fifth Root Race of humanity is identified primarily with Active Intelligence, and the development of the prefrontal lobes of the brain (prefrontal cortex). This is the dominant Root Race currently incarnated on Earth.

Ascended Masters: Once an ordinary human, an Ascended Master has undergone a spiritual transformation over many lifetimes. He or she has Mastered the lower planes—mental, emotional, and physical—to unite with his or her God-Self or I AM Presence. An Ascended Master is freed from the Wheel of Karma. He or she moves forward in spiritual evolution beyond this planet; however, an Ascended Master remains attentive to the spiritual well-being of humanity, inspiring and serving the Earth's spiritual growth and evolution.

Ascension: A process of Mastering thoughts, feelings, and actions that balance positive and negative karmas. It allows entry to a higher state of consciousness and frees a person from the need to reincarnate on the lower Earthly planes or lokas of experience. Ascension is the process of spiritual liberation, also known as moksha.

Ascension Valley: According to the I AM America Prophecies, Ascended Masters appear in physical form in the Golden City Vortices during and after a prophesied twenty-year period. At that time, Mass Ascensions occur in the Golden Cities, at the Golden City Star locations, and in select geophysical locations around the world, which are hosted by the complimentary energies of Mother Earth. A model of this geophysical location is Ascension Valley, located in the Shalahah Vortex. The energy of Ascension Valley prepares students to integrate their light bodies and spiritual consciousness into the Oneship, the divinity within, and further prepares the body, mind, and spirit to experience and travel into the New Dimensions.

Asonea: The Twelfth Golden City of the Americas is located in Cuba. Its qualities are alignment and regeneration; its Ray Force is Yellow; and its Master Teacher is Peter the Everlasting.

Atlantis: An ancient civilization of Earth, whose mythological genesis was the last Puranic Dvapara Yuga—the Bronze Age of the Yugas. Its demise occurred around the year 9628 BCE. Esoteric historians suggest three phases of political and geophysical boundaries: the Toltec Nation of Atlantis (Ameru); the Turian Nation of Atlantis (the invaders of the Land of Rama); and Poseid, the Island Nation of the present-day Atlantic Ocean.

The early civilizations of Atlantis were ruled by the spiritually evolved Toltec. Their spiritual teachings, ceremonies, and temples were dedicated to the worship of the Sun. According to Theosophical thought, Atlantis' evolving humanity brought about an evolutionary epoch of the Pink Ray on the Earth, and the development of the Astral-Emotional bodies and Heart Chakra. Ascended Master provenance claims that the Els—now the Mighty Elohim of the Seven Rays—were the original Master Teachers to the spiritual seekers of Atlantis. Atlantean culture later deteriorated through the use of nuclear weapons and cruelty toward other nations, including the use of genetic engineering. The demise of Atlantis was inevitable; however, modern-day geologists, archaeologists, and occultists all disagree to its factual timing.

Ascended Master teachings affirm that Atlantis—a continent whose geophysical and political existence probably spanned well over 100,000 years—experienced several phases of traumatic Earth Change. This same belief is held by occult historians who allege that Earth repeatedly cycles through periods of massive Earth Change and cataclysmic pole shifts, which activate tectonic plates and subsequently submerge whole continents, creating vital New Lands for Earth's successors.

Awakening Mountains: The name ascribed by the Spiritual Teachers to the Himalayan Mountains. This mountain range is prophesied to rise in greater elevation during the "Time of Change." These mountains separate the lands of the Indian subcontinent from the Tibetan Plateau. They are located primarily throughout Pakistan, India, Nepal, Bhutan and Tibet (China).

Babajeran: A name for the Earth Mother that means, "Grandmother rejoicing."

Blissful Sea: During the "Time of Change," the continent of Australia is prophesied to split in half and form a new sea in its interior lands named the Blissful Sea.

Blue Ray: A perceptible light and sound frequency. The Blue Ray not only resonates with the color blue, but is identified with the qualities of steadiness, calm, perseverance, transformation, harmony, diligence, determination, austerity, protection, humility, truthfulness, and self-negation. It forms one-third of the Unfed Flame within the heart—the Blue Ray of God Power—which nourishes the spiritual unfoldment of the human into the HU-man. Use of the Violet Flame evokes the Blue Ray into action throughout the light bodies, where the Blue Ray clarifies intentions and assists the alignment of the Will. In Ascended Master teachings, the Blue Ray is alleged to have played a major role in the physical manifestation of the Earth's first Golden City, Shamballa. Six of fifty-one Golden Cities emanate the Blue Ray's peaceful, yet piercing frequencies. The Blue Ray is esoterically linked to the planet Saturn, the development of the Will, the ancient Lemurian Civilization, the Archangel Michael, the Elohim Hercules, the Master Teacher El Morya, and the Eastern Doors of all Golden Cities.

Braham: The fourteenth Golden City of the Americas is located in Brazil, South America. Its quality is nurturing; its Ray Force is Pink; and its Master Teacher is the Goddess Braham or Yemanya, progenitor of the New Manu. Braham literally means *the nurturer* and this Golden City is the second of the Three Sisters in South America.

Braun: Mighty Victory overshadows and radiates the Yellow Ray of glory and achievement in this Vortex. The fifteenth Golden City is located in Germany, Austria, and the Czech republic.

Christ, or Christ Consciousness: The highest energy or frequency attainable on Earth. The Christ, or Christ Consciousness, is a step-down Transformer of the I AM energies, which enlightens, heals, and transforms all human conditions of degradation and death.

Clayje: This is known as the *Golden City of Many Planets* through its divine quality of Universal Oneness. Clayje is the forty-seventh Vortex and is associated with the Elohim of Divine Love – Orion, and the Pink Ray. Clayje covers the entire island of Tasmania in Australia, and is a Twin Golden City to Angelica.

Co-creation: Creating with the God-Source.

Collective Consciousness: The higher interactive structure of consciousness as two or more.

Cooperation Mountains: A new chain of mountains, prophesied to appear during and after the "Time of Change." This future mountain range is expected to rise in the following North American States: Colorado, Kansas, and Texas. This chain of mountains is also prophesied to rise south into Mexico, and onward into Central America.

Cosmic Wave Motion: Belts of energy that weave a pattern throughout the universe and originate from the sun.

Cradleland Map: Central America, and especially its Golden Cities that help to gestate the consciousness of Earth to receive new energies. It is also alleged that these new frequencies help many new, higher evolved beings to incarnate on Earth – the New Children.

Creation Grid: A grid of receptive and susceptible universal energies comprising many different types of Earth's lei-lines. It is alleged that at certain intersections of Earth's Creation Grid, energy is uniquely sensitive and different forms and patterns of DNA are able to collect ethereal energies that can physically manifest. Since new DNA can enter through this unique grid of energy, established forms of DNA can become responsive to mutation and change through Earth's Creation Grid. The Golden City Grid is but one aspect of Earth's Creation Grid.

Cresta: The fifty-first and final Golden City to be activated serves the uplifting and evolutionary Gold and Aquamarine Rays. Beloved Archangel Crystiel is the hierarch of this sublime Vortex of eternal protection, healing, and clarity for humanity, located in Antarctica on Eternity Range.

Crotese: The sixteenth Golden City of the Americas is located in the Heartland countries of Costa Rica and Panama, Central America. This Golden City's qualities are divinity and the Heart of Love; its Ray Force is Pink; and the resident Master Teacher is Paul.

Crystone: The prophesied new capitol city of the United States, located in the mountains of Colorado.

Denasha: The Golden City of Denasha is primarily located over Scotland, and the Ascended Masters assert this Vortex holds the energies of Divine Justice for all of humanity. Denasha is also the Sister Golden City to Malton (Illinois and Indiana, USA) and both Vortices mutually distribute energies to the Nature and Elemental Kingdoms during the New Times. The Master Teacher is Lady Nada; the Ray Force is Yellow; and Denasha's translation means, "Mountain of Zeus."

Donjakey: This Golden City currently presides over the Pacific Ocean and prophesied new land that rise in the New Times – New Lemuria. The Elohim Pacifica guards and protects this Golden City of both the Gold and Aquamarine Rays.

Eabra: The seventh Golden City located in Canada in the Yukon and Northwest Territories. Its qualities are joy, balance, and equality; its Ray Force is Violet; and its Master Teacher is Portia.

Earth Changes: A prophesied Time of Change on the Earth, including geophysical, political, and social changes, alongside the opportunity for spiritual and personal transformation.

Earth's Grid: Geometrical patterns that cover the Earth and follow symmetrical links to sacred geometry and crystalline shapes.

El Morya: Ascended Master of the Blue Ray, associated with the development of the will.

Elohim: Creative beings of love and light that helped manifest the Divine idea of our solar system. Seven Elohim (the Seven Rays) exist on Earth. They organize and draw forward Archangels, the Four Elements, Devas, Seraphim, Cherubim, Angels, Nature Guardians, and the Elementals. In Ascended Master teaching, the Silent Watcher—the Great Mystery—gives them direction. It is also claimed the Elohim magnetize the Unfed Flame at the center of the Earth. Some esoteric historians perceive the Elohim—also referred to as the Els—as the Ancient Gods, or the Master Teachers of Lemuria and Atlantis.

Ecological Alchemy: A process of Earth transmutation and transformation. The innate power of Mother Earth restores and heals her own sensitive environments and internal systems. These are currently compromised by global warming and climate change, anthropogenic climate change, and various forms of pollution. This natural, restorative process reinstates the natural cycles and rhythms of Mother Earth and nature, in conjunction with the worldwide appearance of new flora and fauna.

Fertile Plain: An enormous agricultural area prophesied to rise in central China and Mongolia. It is claimed that this area will produce abundant and rich crops that feed millions of people. But the Fertile Plain's existence is not wholly physical. The Fertile Plain is the result of a shift of humanity's consciousness into the ideals of harmony, cooperation, and subsequent abundance. This new consciousness enjoins new political, ecological, economical, and social systems.

Fire Triplicity: Energies from the Great Central Sun, or Galactic Center triangulate to our Solar System through these three planets: the Sun, Mars, and Jupiter. These three planets are known as the Fire Triplicity and represent three forms of spiritual fire: the Sun is the spiritual leader; Mars is the spiritual pioneer; and Jupiter is the spiritual teacher.

Fourth Dimension: A dimension of vibration associated with telepathy, psychic ability, and the dream world. This is the dimension of the Elemental Kingdom and the development of the super senses.

Freedom Star World Map: The Ascended Masters' map depicts prophesied global Earth Changes and the locations of worldwide Golden City Vortices. This map's spiritual teachings are divided into three unique maps of prophesied social, cultural, and geophysical changes. The Americas Map is composed of Greenland, Canada, the United States, Mexico, Central and South America, and New Atlantis. The Greening Map is composed of India, Pakistan, Afghanistan, Russia, China, Japan, Malaysia, Australia, and New Zealand. The Map of Exchanges is composed of Iceland, Europe, the Middle East, Africa, Antarctica, and New Lemuria. The Map of the Americas, including the I AM America Map, is sponsored by Saint Germain. The Greening Map is sponsored by Kuan Yin, and the Map of Exchanges is sponsored by Lady Nada, Kuthumi, and El Morya.

Each distinctive map depicts the location of seventeen Golden Cities. Three sets of seventeen Golden Cities comprise a total of fifty-one Golden City Vortices. Fifty-one is a pentagonal number and is esoterically connected to Divine Man, Divine Intervention, perfect harmony, and the planet Venus. Gobean, the first Golden City Vortex, was activated in 1981. Cresta, the fifty-first Golden City Vortex, activates in the year 2092 AD.

Fron: Beloved Desiree of the Blue Ray guides and overshadows this Golden City located in Western Australia. This Vortex is fiftieth in the activation pattern, and assists aspirants, chelas, and developing HUman's to spiritually focus upon their inner balance.

Galactic Light: Energy streams from the Great Central Sun, or Galactic Center, as the Seven Rays of Light and Sound to Earth. Galactic Light calibrates the level of intelligence on Earth through memory function; the ability to absorb, recognize, and respect spiritual knowledge; the length of lifespans; and our ability to access the Akashic Records. The amount of Galactic Light streaming to Earth at any given time is classically measured through the Hindu Puranic timing of the Yugas, and through a contemporary method—the Electric Cycle—advocated by the Eastern Indian guru Sri Yuteswar.

Galactic Sun: *See Great Central Sun*

Galactic Web: A large, encircling galactic grid, created by the consciousness of all things in the galaxy–human, animal, plant, and mineral. Magnetic Vortices, namely the Golden Cities, appear at certain intersections of the Galactic Web.

Ganakra: The seventeenth Golden City is located in Turkey and is overseen by the Elohim Vista of the Green Ray. Ganakra is known as the "All Seeing City," and is affiliated with the qualities of Divine Focus and concentration.

Gandawan: The Master Kuthumi oversees the Golden City of Gandawan, also identified as the *Infinite Garden*. This Golden City of the Ruby and Gold Rays is located in Africa.

Glory Ocean: A large ocean, prophesied to exist in the New Times, which covers the present-day Arabian Ocean (northern Indian Ocean). This new coastline includes the African countries of Somalia, Kenya, and Ethiopia; the Middle-East countries of Yemen, Oman, Saudi Arabia, Iraq, and Iran; and the south Asian countries of Pakistan and India. It is prophesied that the submarine Mid-Indian Ridge and the Carlsberg Ridge erupts and forms a large group of small islands in the Glory Ocean called the "Shimmering Islands."

Gobean: The first United States Golden City located in the states of Arizona and New Mexico. Its qualities are cooperation, harmony, and peace; its Ray Force is Blue; and its Master Teacher is El Morya.

Gobi: Steps-down the energies of Shamballa into the entire Golden City Network. This Golden City is located in the Gobi Desert. It is known as the City of Balance, and means *Across the Star*; its Master Teachers are Lord Meru and Archangel Uriel.

Golden Age: A peaceful time on Earth that is prophesied to occur after the Time of Change. It is also prophesied that, during this age, human life spans will increase and sacred knowledge will be revered. During this time, the societies, cultures, and the governments of Earth will reflect spiritual enlightenment through worldwide cooperation, compassion, charity, and love. Ascended Master teachings often refer to the Golden Age as the Golden-Crystal Age and the Age of Grace.

Golden Age of Kali Yuga: According to the classic Puranic timing of the Yugas, Earth is in a Kali-Yuga period that started around the year 3102 BCE the year that Krishna allegedly left the Earth. During this time period, which according to this Puranic timing lasts a total of 432,000 years—the ten-thousand year Golden Age period, also known as the Golden Age of Kali Yuga, is not in full force. Instead, it is a sub-cycle of higher light frequencies within an overall larger phase of less light energy.

This Golden Age is prophesied to raise the energy of Earth as additional light from the Galactic Center streams to our planet. This type of light is a non-visible, quasar-type light that is said to expand life spans and memory function, and nourish human consciousness, especially spiritual development. There are many theories as to when this prescient light energy began to flow to our planet. Some say it started about a thousand years ago, and others claim it began at the end of the nineteenth century. No doubt its influence has changed life on Earth for the better, and according to the I AM America Teachings, its effect began to encourage and guide human spiritual evolution around the year 2000 CE.

The Spiritual Teachers say that living in Golden Cities can magnify Galactic Energies and at their height, the energies will light the Earth between 45 to 48 percent—nearly reaching the light energies of a full-spectrum Treta Yuga or Silver Age on Earth. The Spiritual Teachers state, "The Golden Age is the period of time where harmony and peace shall be sustained."

Golden City Doorway: The four doorways of a Golden City. They comprise the North Door (or the Black Door); the East Door (or the Blue Door); the South Door (or the Red Door); the West Door (or the Yellow Door). The center of a Golden City is known as the "Star" and is affiliated with the color white.

Golden City Vortex: According to the prophecies, these large Vortex areas are havens of safety and spiritual growth during the Time of Change.

Gold Ray: The Ray of Brotherhood, Cooperation, and Peace. The Gold Ray produces the qualities of perception, honesty, confidence, courage, and responsibility. It is also associated with leadership, independence, authority, ministration, and justice. The Gold Ray vibrates the energies of Divine Father on Earth. Its attributes are: warm; perceptive; honest; confident; positive; independent; courageous; enduring; vital; leadership; responsible; ministration; authority; justice. The Gold Ray is also associated with the Great Central Sun, the Solar Logos, of which our Solar Sun is a Step-down Transformer of its energies. According to the Master Teachers, the Gold Ray is the epitome of change for the New Times. The Gold Ray is the ultimate authority of Cosmic Law, and carries both our personal and worldwide Karma and Dharma (purpose). Its presence is designed to instigate responsible spiritual growth and planetary evolution as a shimmering light for humanity's aspirations and the development of the HU-man. The Gold Ray, however, is also associated with Karmic justice, and will instigate change: constructive and destructive. The extent of catastrophe or transformation is contingent on humanity's personal and collective spiritual growth and evolutionary process as we progress into the New Times.

Great Central Sun: The great sun of our galaxy, around which all of the galaxy's solar systems rotate. The Great Central Sun is also known as the Galactic Center, which is the origin of the Seven Rays of Light and Sound on Earth.

Great White Brotherhood and Sisterhood: A fraternity of ascended and unascended men and women who are dedicated to the universal uplifting of humanity. Its main objective includes the preservation of the lost spirit, and the teachings of the ancient religions and philosophies of the world. Its mission is to reawaken the dormant ethical and spiritual sparks among the masses. In addition to fulfilling spiritual aims, the Great White Lodge pledges to protect mankind against the systematic assaults – which inhibit self-knowledge and personal growth – on individual and group freedoms.

Greening Map: The second Map of Earth Changes Prophecies. It contains a total of seventeen Golden City Vortices and is sponsored by Ascended Master Kuan Yin. It entails all of Asia, Japan, and Australia. New land is prophesied to appear near New Zealand, New Guinea, Hawaii, and the Easter Islands, and is referred to as "New Lemuria" by the Spiritual Teachers. The Greening Map signifies personal and transpersonal healing of the feminine. It balances Mother Earth through the awakening of Ecological Alchemy. During the Greening Map's Time of Change, Earth is healed and rejuvenated with new flora and fauna appearing throughout the planet.

Green Ray: The Ray of Active Intelligence is associated with education, thoughtfulness, communication, organization, the intellect, science, objectivity, and discrimination. It is also adaptable, rational, healing, and awakened. The Green Ray is affiliated with the planet Mercury. In the I AM America teachings the Green Ray is served by the Archangel Raphael and Archeia Mother Mary; the Elohim of Truth, Vista—also known as Cyclopea, and Virginia; the Ascended Masters Hilarion, Lord Sananda, Lady Viseria, Soltec, and Lady Master Meta.

Grein: Viseria, the Goddess of the Stars and Divine Compliment to Soltec serves in Grein, the Golden City of New Zealand's South Island. The Vortex radiates the energies of the Green Ray and is associated with Divine Consecration, and service to humanity's upliftment through scientific development.

Group Mind: A conscious intelligent force formed by members of distinguished cultures, societal organizations, and more prominently, by religious church members. The Group Mind is held together by rituals and customs that are typically peculiar to its members; newcomers instantly sense the energies of the atmosphere, and will either accept or reject their influence. The physics of the Group Mind are important to comprehend, as this collective intelligence is purposely formed to aid the Aspirant to raise human consciousness beyond present limitations.

Gruecha: Gruecha is Norway and Sweden's Golden City of the Blue Ray. The Elohim Hercules serves in this sacred refuge, and its qualities produce spiritual strength through the principle of truth.

Heart of the Dove: Also known as the Center of Fire, this energy anomaly is prophesied to exist Northwest of Kansas City, Missouri. It is here that Master Teachings claim an umbilicus connection between Earth and the Galactic Center exists, creating time anomalies and the potential for time travel in the New Times. The Heart of the Dove is also prophesied to become a spiritual center for learning and self-actualizing the consciousness of Quetzalcoatl—the Christ.

Hilarion: Ascended Master of the Green Ray and associated with the attainment of personal truth and the development of faith.

Hue (Golden City): This Golden City is also known as the *City of Many Spiritual Paths*, and is aligned with the Violet Ray. This Vortex's steward is Lord Gautama and its sacred quality is earnestness. It is located in Siberia, Russia.

HU-man: The God-Man.

I AM America Map: The Ascended Masters' Map of prophesied Earth Changes for the United States, Canada, Mexico, Central and South America.

Jeafray: The eighth Golden City located in Quebec, Labrador, and Newfoundland, Canada. Its qualities are stillness and the celebration of the Violet Flame;

its Ray Force is Violet; and its Master Teachers are Archangel Zadkiel and Amethyst.

Jehoa: The seventeenth Golden City of the Americas is prophesied to exist over new lands that rise in the Time of Change. The Golden City of Jehoa is located over the Lesser Antilles Islands of: Guadeloupe, Dominica, Martinique, Saint Lucia, Barbados, and Grenada. Its qualities are compassion, acts of love, and gratitude; its Ray Force is Violet; and its Master Teacher is Kuan Yin.

Kali Yuga: The Age of Iron, or Age of Quarrel, when Earth receives twenty-five percent or less galactic light from the Great Central Sun.

Kantan: The city of regeneration, assimilation, and dedication is located in Russia and China. This Golden City Vortex is overseen by Great Divine Mother and the Archangel Raphael. Kantan is affiliated with the Green Ray.

Klehma: The fifth United States Golden City located primarily in the states of Colorado and Kansas. Its qualities are continuity, balance, and harmony; its Ray Force is White; and its Master Teacher is Serapis Bey.

Kreshe: Overseen by the Lord of Nature and Lady Amaryllis – the Goddess of Spring. It is associated with the Ruby and Gold Rays and is located Botswana, Namibia, Angola, and Zambia. Kreshe aligns its energies to the silent star and is in perpetual service to elemental life.

Kuan Yin: The Bodhisattva of Compassion and teacher of Saint Germain. She is associated with all the Rays and the principle of femininity.

Kuthumi: An Ascended Master of the Pink, Ruby, and Gold Rays. He is a gentle and patient teacher who works closely with the Nature Kingdoms.

Lady Master Nada: The Ascended Goddess of Justice and Peace is associated with Mastery of speech (vibration), communication, interpretation, and the sacred Word. Nada is also known as a divine advocate of Universal Law and she is often symbolized by the scales of blind justice. She is associated with the Yellow Ray of Wisdom and the Ruby and Gold Rays of Ministration, Brotherhood, and Service. Lady Nada is the hierarch of Denasha, a Golden City located in Scotland.

Lake of Deep Truth: This Russian Lake is prophesied to develop in several stages of Earth Changes. The lake's size and volume will increase due to melting glaciers and climate change. Eventually, the northern shores will erode, and salt waters will enter the lake, creating a bay of the northern Ocean of Balance. The lake's waters are prophesied to have unique properties, and will be used for irrigating new varieties and species of fruit and nut trees. This lake is located near present-day Lake Baikal.

Land of Brihaspati: A mythical land and civilization that according to Lord Meru originated and thrived on the ancient Japanese Archipelago whose civilizations later migrated to the present-day Himalayans. It is claimed the ancient Kirata and Tibetan cultures came from the Land of Brihaspati, and the Mahabharata recounts the ancient people as, "Gold-like."

Land of the Plumed Serpent: The ancient lands of Ameru, from which the word America is derived. The ancient peoples of America were known as the Red Children of the Sun and worshipped Quetzalcoatl, a Prophet of the Christ Consciousness, a messenger from our solar Sun. The Plumed Serpent metaphorically represents the developed Chakra System of the Divine God-man, the Ascended Masters' HU-man. The plume of light atop the head is the developed crown chakra, and the serpent's coils represent the mature Kundalini system, or human energy system comprised of seven chakras.

Land of Rama: The ancient civilization of India once co-existed with Ancient Atlantis and is claimed to have extended as far West as present-day Iran, and as far East as present-day Burma. The Land of Rama is claimed to have been a nation of spiritual adepts, priests, and Masters—Rishis.

Larito: Beloved Lanto and Laura share their Divine Service in this Golden City of the Yellow Ray. This sacred Vortex is located in Ethiopia and is affiliated with spiritual understanding and illumination.

Lei-line: Lines of energy that exist among geographical places, ancient monuments, megaliths, and strategic points. These energy lines contain electrical or magnetic points.

Law of Love: Per the Ascended Master tradition, to consciously living without fear, without inflicting fear on others. Perhaps every religion on Earth is founded on the Law of Love, per the notion of "treating others as you would like to be treated." The Fourth of the Twelve Jurisdictions instructs us that Love is the "Law of Allowing, Maintaining, and Sustainability." All of these precepts distinguish love from an emotion or feeling, and observe Love as action, will, or choice. The Ascended Masters affirm, "If you live love, you will create love." This premise is fundamental to understanding the esoteric underpinnings of the Law of Love. The Master Teachers declare that through practicing the Law of Love, one experiences acceptance, understanding, and tolerance, alongside detachment. Metaphysically, the Law of Love allows different and varied perceptions of ONE experience, situation, or circumstance to exist simultaneously. From this viewpoint, the Law of Love is the practice of tolerance.

Lemuria: A continent that primarily existed in the Pacific Ocean before it was submerged by Earth Changes. It is deemed to have been the remaining culture and civilization of Mu – an expansive continent that once spanned the entire present-day Pacific Ocean. It is alleged that the lands of Lemuria, also known as Shalmali, existed in the Indian and Southern Pacific Oceans, and included the continent of Australia.

Thus, it is believed to have integrated with the Lands of Rama, and is to be considered one the earliest cultures of humanity. Sri Lanka is alleged to have been one of the empire's capital cities. Esoteric historians theorize that the tectonic Pacific Plate formed this lost continent. Asuramaya is one of the great Manus of Lemuria's Root Race.

Some esoteric writers place the destruction of Mu around the year 30,000 BCE; others place its demise millions of years ago. According to Theosophical history, the Lemurian and Atlantean epochs overlapped. The apparent discrepancy of these timelines is likely due to two different interpretations of the Cycle of the Yugas. It is claimed that the venerated Elders of Lemuria escaped the global tragedy by moving to an uninhabited plateau in central Asia. This account mirrors Ascended Master teachings and Lord Himalaya's founding of the Retreat of the Blue Lotus.

The Lemurian elders re-established their spiritual teachings and massive library as the Thirteenth School. Spiritual teachers claim that the evolutionary purpose of this ancient civilization was to develop humanity's Will (the Blue Ray of Power). Lemurian culture also venerated the Golden Disk of the Sun and practiced the Right-hand Path. It is claimed that these teachings and spiritual records became foundational teachings for the Great White Brotherhood of the mystical lands of His Wang Mu (the Abode of the Immortals) and the Kuan Yin Lineage of Gurus. Present-day Australia – once known by Egyptian gold-miners as the ancient Land of Punt – is considered the remainder of the once great continent of Mu and Lemuria, which likely existed in the time period of Dvapara-Yuga, over 800,000 years ago.

Lord Meru or Lord Macaw/Machah: An Ascended Master of the Ruby and Gold Ray is also known as the great Sage of Ancient Mu. Lord Meru is a teacher of the ancient civilizations of the Earth and considered a spiritual historian of their mythological records. Lord Meru is also known as Lord Machah—the parrot—a symbol of beauty, wisdom, and spiritual knowledge. Lord Machah's dark skin is contrasted by a colorful headdress filled with parrot, trogon, and quetzal bird feathers, a symbol of Quetzalcoatl—the Christ Consciousness. In the New Times, Lord Meru is prophesied to steward the Golden City of Gobi.

Love: "Light in action." The fourth of the Twelve Jurisdictions evolves our understanding of love as the Law of Allowing, Maintaining, and Sustainability.

Malton: The second United States Golden City located in the states of Illinois and Indiana. Its qualities are fruition and attainment; its Ray Force is Gold and Ruby; and its Master Teacher is Kuthumi.

Map of Exchanges: The Ascended Masters' Map of prophesied Earth Changes for Europe and Africa. Its seventeen Golden City Vortices focus on the self-realization of the HU-man through the exchange of heavenly energies on Earth, which usher in the Golden Age.

Map of the Ancients: Lord Meru rescued this ancient map ages ago from the Lands of Lemuria: the Map of the Ancients. This map of the world simultaneously portrays the lands of Rama, Mu, and Atlantis. According to Lord Meru the Map of the Ancients illustrates the migration and evolution of human consciousness as shaped through the Seven Rays, and identifies the nine civilizations the Rays have influenced and formed.

Marnero: The eleventh Golden City of the Americas is located in Mexico. Marnero means Virtue; its Ray Force is Green; and its Master Teacher is Mother Mary.

Mesotamp: The eighteenth Golden City is overseen by Mohammed and the Yellow Ray. This sacred site radiates spiritual happiness for humanity.

Motherland Map: South America and prophesied Earth Changes including its three vital, feminine Golden Cities, and Mother Mary's Swaddling Cloth of protected lands. The Motherland in Ascended Master teaching considers it a land of origin. The Ascended Masters refer to South America as the Motherland.

Mother Mary: Ascended Goddess of the Feminine who was originally of the angelic evolution. She is associated with the Green Ray of Healing, Truth, and Science, and the Pink Ray of Love.

Mousee: Located in the Pacific Ocean, northwest of the Hawaiian Island of Kauai. It is served by the Ascended Master Kona and the Gold and Aquamarine Rays. Mousee's attribute is "the eye of spiritual fire," and assists Earth's aquatic beings to instigate or achieve Ascension.

New Age: Prophesied by Utopian Francis Bacon, the New Age would herald a United Brotherhood of the Earth. This Brotherhood/Sisterhood would be built as Solomon's Temple, and supported by the four pillars of history, science, philosophy, and religion. These four teachings would synergize the consciousness of humanity to Universal Fellowship and Peace.

New Children: *see Seventh Manu*

New Lemuria: Ancient Lands of Lemuria, and entirely new lands, which will rise in the Pacific Ocean during the Time of Change. These new lands and continents are prophesied to appear near New Zealand, New Guinea, Hawaii, and the Easter Islands.

New Dimensions: As humanity enters the New Times, subtle elements and aspects physically appear and spiritually and simultaneously enable HU-man consciousness to embrace allowing, alignment, transformation, and self-knowledge. The Ascended Masters claim this spiritual growth is the result of New Dimensions.

Nomaking: Located in China, this Golden City of the Yellow Ray is overseen by Cassiopeia, the Elohim of Wisdom, and Minerva, the Goddess of Wisdom. This is the thirty-eighth Golden City in activation and is affiliated with the spiritual qualities of wisdom, illumination, the power of attention, and perception.

Ocean of Balance: A large ocean prophesied to be formed throughout Northern Russia, the Barents Sea, the Norwegian Sea, and large sections of Eastern Europe. Its waters are prophesied to flood France, the Netherlands, Poland, Ukraine, Denmark, Sweden, and Finland. The metaphysical and spiritual meaning of this massive ocean is that "balance begets life."

Pashacino: The sixth Golden City is located in Alberta and British Columbia, Canada. Its quality serves as a Bridge of Brotherhood for all people; its Ray Force is Green; and its Master Teacher is Soltec.

Paul the Devoted: A spiritual son of the three divine Suns: Krishna, Buddha, and Christ; this Ascended Master Paul represents the Eternal Heart of Love. He is associated with the White Flame of the Sun through the principles of purity, order, clarity, and mirroring the true nature of the soul. Paul is affiliated with the Pink and White Rays, and is the hierarch of the Golden City of Crotese, the Golden City of Costa Rica.

Paul the Venetian: An Ascended Master of the Pink, White, and Green Rays. Paul the Venetian identifies with the qualities of cooperation and beauty through art, architecture, music, and literature.

Pearlanu: Lady Master Lotus serves in the Golden City of Pearlanu, located on Madagascar. This is the twenty-fifth Golden City, is affiliated with the Violet Ray, and the transmuting quality of forgiveness.

Peter the Everlasting: This Ascended Master lived several controversial lifetimes on Earth; however, he found liberation through these everlasting spiritual precepts: balance, simplicity, and stability. He is also known as the consummate Master of Change and manages insecurity and unpredictability with the ever present wisdom of love and friendship. Master Peter is affiliated with the Yellow Ray.

Pink Ray: The Pink Ray is the energy of the Divine Mother and associated with the Moon. It is affiliated with these qualities: loving; nurturing; hopeful; heartfelt; compassionate; considerate; communicative; intuitive; friendly; humane; tolerant; adoring. In the I AM America teachings the Pink Ray is served by the Archangel Chamuel and Archeia Charity; the Elohim of Divine Love Orion and Angelica; and the Ascended Masters Kuan Yin, Mother Mary, Goddess Meru, and Paul the Venetian.

Portia: The Goddess of Justice and Opportunity. She represents Divine Justice on Earth. Her action is balance, expressed as the scales. Harmony holds balance. Some say her electronic pattern, a mandala, is the Maltese Cross. Portia serves as hierarch of Eabra, a

Golden City for feminine balance of the Earth, located in the Yukon and a part of the Land of Co-creation.

Prana: The Golden City of India is overseen by its hierarch, Archangel Chamuel. It is affiliated with the Pink Ray and serves through adoration and the continuous heart.

Presching: Archangel Jophiel of the Yellow Ray serves in this Golden City located in North Korea. It is the thirty-eighth sacred Vortex and is known as, "The City for the Angels." It is also associated with the enduring love of ordered service.

Prophecy: A spiritual teaching given simultaneously with a warning. It's designed to change, alter, lessen, or mitigate the prophesied warning. This caveat may be literal or metaphoric; the outcome of these events are contingent on the choices and the consciousness of those willing to apply the teachings.

Protective Field: An ethereal aura or energy field that shields and defends, especially noted within the Stars of the Golden Cities.

Purensk: The Divine Beings of Faith, Hope, and Charity serve the Blue, Yellow, and Pink Rays of the Unfed Flame in this twenty-first Golden City. Purensk radiates the spiritual gifts of love, wisdom, and power. It is located in Russia and China.

Quetzalcoatl: The Quetzalcoatl Energies, as explained and taught by Lord Meru, are akin to the Christ energies when applied in the esoteric Western Christian tradition. This ancient spiritual teacher, however, predates Christianity and likely has its roots in alchemic Atlantean (Toltec) teaching. Quetzalcoatl, in contemporary terms, is the Incan Christ.

Ray: A force containing a purpose, which divides its efforts into two measurable and perceptible powers, light and sound.

Ring of Fire: A geographical area, which encircles the basin of the Pacific Ocean, prone to volcanic eruptions and earthquakes.

Ruby Ray: The Ruby Ray is the energy of the Divine Masculine and Spiritual Warrior. It is associated with these qualities: energetic; passionate; devoted; determination; dutiful; dependable; direct; insightful; inventive; technical; skilled; forceful. This Ray Force is astrologically affiliated with the planet Mars and the Archangel Uriel, Lord Sananda, and Master Kuthumi. The Ruby Ray is often paired with the Gold Ray, which symbolizes Divine Father. The Ruby Ray is the evolutionary Ray Force of both the base and solar chakras of the HU-man; and the Gold and Ruby Rays step-down and radiate sublime energies into six Golden Cities.

Saint Germain: Ascended Master of the Seventh Ray, Saint Germain is known for his work with the Violet Flame of Mercy, Transmutation, Alchemy, and Forgiveness. He is the sponsor of the Americas and the I AM America material. Many other teachers and Masters affiliated with the Great White Brotherhood help his endeavors. Saint Germain serves in the Golden City of Wahanee, a Vortex that helps humanity to spiritual apply justice, liberty, and forgiveness.

Sananda: The name used by Master Jesus in his ascended state of consciousness. Sananda means joy and bliss, and his teachings focus on revealing the savior and heavenly kingdom within. Sananda is associated with Christ Consciousness and the Golden City of Shalahah.

Sanat Kumara: Sanat Kumara is a Venusian Ascended Master and the venerated leader of the Ascended Masters, best known as the founder of Shamballa, the first Golden City on Earth. He is also known in the teachings of the Great White Brotherhood as the Lord of the World, and is regarded as a savior and eminent spiritual teacher. Sanat Kumara is the guru of four of the Twelve Jurisdictions: Cooperation, Charity, Desire, and Stillness. These spiritual precepts are based on the principles of Co-creation, and are prophesied to guide human consciousness into the New Times. These four Jurisdictions reiterate the symbolic revelation of Sanat Kumara's four-fold identity as the Cosmic Christ, which assist humanity's evolutionary process into the New Times. As Kartikkeya, the commander of God's Army, Sanat Kumara teaches Cooperation to overcome the lower mind; as Kumar the holy youth, Sanat Kumara imparts Charity to conquer the darkness of disease and poverty; as Skanda, the son of Shiva and the spiritual warrior, Sanat Kumara offers Desire as the hopeful seed of God's transformation; and as Guha, the Jurisdiction Stillness restores the cave of all hearts.

Sea of Grace: A large European and Russian Sea, that is prophesied to exist within the Sea of Balance. It is allegedly formed when the Himalayan Mountains rise and the Black Sea, Azov, Sea, the Caspian Sea, and Aral Sea combine into the Sea of Grace. It is metaphysically and spiritually linked to humanity's spiritual transformation of greed into non-judgment, political freedom, and spiritual human rights.

Serapis Bey: An Ascended Master from Venus who works on the White Ray. He is the great disciplinarian—essential for Ascension; and works closely with all unascended humanity who remain focused for its attainment. He oversees and serves in the Golden City of Klehma, to promote cooperation and the attainment of Ascension.

Seven Rays of Light and Sound: The traditional Seven Rays of Light and Sound are: the Blue Ray of Truth; the Yellow Ray of Wisdom; the Pink Ray of Love; the White Ray of Purity; the Green Ray of Healing; the Gold and Ruby Ray of Ministration; and the Violet Ray of Transmutation.

Seventh Manu: Highly evolved lifestreams that embody on Earth between 1981 to 3650. Their goal is to anchor freedom and the qualities of the Seventh Ray to the conscious activity on this planet. They are prophesied as the generation of peace and grace for the Golden Age. South America is their forecasted home, though small groups will incarnate in other areas of the globe.

Shalahah: The fourth United States Golden City located primarily in the states of Montana and Idaho. Its qualities are abundance, prosperity, and healing; its Ray Force is Green; and its Master Teacher is Sananda.

Shaman: A shaman has developed the ability to leave their body to work for spiritual transformation at many levels. An intermediary between the natural world and the spirit world. Indigenous Shaman place a strong emphasis on their environments; nature spirits and animals play important roles and act as omens, messengers, and spirit guides.

Shamballa: Venusian volunteers, who arrived 900 years before their leader Sanat Kumara, and built the Earth's first Golden City. Known as the City of White, located in the present-day Gobi Desert, its purpose was to hold conscious light for the Earth and to sustain her evolutionary place in the solar system.

Sheahah: Located in Australia, this Golden City is the forty-ninth in activation. Its steward is the Elohim Astrea, the twin force to the Elohim of Purity – Claire. Sheahah is associated with the White Ray and its spiritual qualities are transmutation and purity. This Vortex is affiliated with the Golden City of Shalahah, located in Idaho and Montana, United States.

Shehez: The steward is Tranquility, the Elohim of Peace, and is the nineteenth Golden City. Located primarily in Iran and Afghanistan, this sacred site radiates the Ruby and Gold Ray. Its spiritual qualities are peace, serenity, and calm.

Shimmering Islands: *see Glory Ocean*

Shiny Pearl: The present-day Ural Mountains form this prophesied islands, surrounded by the Ocean of Balance, with the Sea of Grace to the southwest. Its metaphysical properties help to hold the spiritual principle of balance for Russia, during the Time of Change and onward into the New Times.

Sircalwe: The Group of Twelve, also known as an ever-changing and anonymous group of Ascended Masters of Light, serve this Golden City of the White Ray. Located in East Siberia Russia, Sircalwe is known as the *Circle of Life*.

Six Map Scenario: A series of six maps of the United States. The Ascended Masters prophesied this schematic to illustrate choice, consciousness, and their relationship to Earth Changes.

Soltec: An Ascended Master of science and technology who is affiliated with the Green Ray. Soltec is the hierarch of Pasahcino, located primarily in Alberta, Canada.

Spiritual Awakening: Conscious awareness of personal experiences and existence beyond the physical, material world. Consequently, an internalization of one's true nature and relationship to life is revealed, freeing one of the lesser self (ego) and engendering contact with the higher (Christ) self and the I AM.

Star (Golden City): The apex, or center of each Golden City.

Stienta: The eleventh Golden City of the Blue Ray is served by Archangel Michael and is located in Iceland. It is known as the *City of Inner Vision*.

Swaddling Cloth: An area of over one million square miles. It is located in Brazil, South America. According to the Ascended Masters, this area is the primary prophesied physical location for the incarnation of the children of the Seventh Manu. The Swaddling Cloth is protected by the Ascended Master Mother Mary.

Tehekoa: The fifteenth Golden City of the Americas is located in Argentina, South America. Its quality is devotion; its Ray Force is Pink and Violet; and its Master Teacher is Panchamama, the Third Sister of South America.

Three Sisters: Three Goddesses assisted by the Archeia Constance. The Three Sisters represent the three feminine aspects of consistency, devotion, and nurturing to oversee and protect South America – the Motherland – during the Time of Change and guide her entry into the New Times.

Time Compaction: An anomaly produced as we enter into the prophesied Time of Change. Our perception of time compresses; time seems to speed by. The unfolding of events accelerates, and situations are jammed into a short period of time. This experience of time will become more prevalent as we get closer to the period of cataclysmic Earth Changes.

Time of Change: The period of time currently underway. Tremendous changes in our society, cultures, and politics in tandem with individual and collective spiritual awakenings and transformations will abound. These events occur simultaneously with the possibilities of massive global warming, climactic changes, and seismic and volcanic activity—Earth Changes. The Time of Change guides the Earth to a New Time, the Golden Age.

Transportation Vortex or Center: Prophesied to develop as we enter the New Times, a model of this energy anomaly will exist in the Golden City of Shalahah hear Coeur d'Alene, Idaho (USA). This interdimensional portal functions through the developed projection of the mind. As our understanding of Ray Forces evolves, our bodies take on a finer quality in light and substance and we are able to bi-locate through these energy Vortices. In the New Times this becomes an accepted form of travel.

Unte: Known as the City of Grace, this Golden City is served by Donna Grace, the Archeia of the Ruby and Gold Rays. It is located Tanzania and Kenya and cultivates the spiritual principle of ministration and service to humanity.

Uverno: The Canadian Golden City of the Pink Ray. Also known as the *Song of God*, the Golden City Vortex is located primarily in Ontario, and Manitoba, Canada. This Golden City is served by Paul the Venetian, an ascended being associated with music, art, and literature.

Violet Flame: The Violet Flame is the practice of balancing karmas of the past through Transmutation, Forgiveness, and Mercy. The result is an opening of the Spiritual Heart and the development of bhakti—unconditional love and compassion. It came into existence when the Lords of Venus first transmitted the Violet Flame, also knows as Violet Fire, at the end of Lemuria to clear the Earth's etheric and psychic realms, and the lower physical atmosphere of negative forces and energies. This paved the way for the Atlanteans, who used it during religious ceremonies and as a visible marker of temples. The Violet Flame also induces Alchemy. Violet light emits the shortest wavelength and the highest frequency in the spectrum, so it induces a point of transition to the next octave of light.

Violet Ray: The Seventh Ray is primarily associated with Freedom and Ordered Service alongside Transmutation, Alchemy, Mercy, Compassion, and Forgiveness. It is served by the Archangel Zadkiel, the Elohim Arcturus, the Ascended Master Saint Germain and Goddess Portia.

Vortex: A Vortex is a polarized motion body that creates its own magnetic field, aligning molecular structures with phenomenal accuracy. Vortices are often formed where lei-lines (energy meridians of the Earth) cross. They are often called power spots as the natural electromagnetic field of the Earth is immensely strong in this type of location.

Wahanee: The third United States Golden City located primarily in the states of South Carolina and Georgia. Its qualities are justice, liberty, and freedom; its Ray Force is Violet; and its Master Teacher is Saint Germain.

White Ray: The Ray of the Divine Feminine is primarily associated with the planet Venus. It is affiliated with beauty, balance, purity, and cooperation. In the I AM America teachings the White Ray is served by the Archangel Gabriel and Archeia Hope; the Elohim Astrea and Claire; and the Ascended Masters Serapis Bey, Paul the Devoted, Reya, the Lady Master Venus, SeRaya the White Buddha, and the Group of Twelve.

Yellow Ray: The Ray of the Divine Wisdom is primarily associated with the planet Jupiter and is also known as the Divine Guru. It is affiliated with expansion, optimism, joy, and spiritual enlightenment. In the I AM America teachings the Yellow Ray is served by the Archangel Jophiel and Archeia Constance, (also known as Christine); the Elohim of Illumination Cassiopeia and Lumina; and the Ascended Masters Lady Nada, Peter the Everlasting, Confucius, Lanto, Laura, Minerva, and Mighty Victory.

Yuthor: The tenth Golden City is located in Greenland. Its quality is abundance of choice; its Ray Force is Green; and its Master Teacher is Hilarion.

Zaskar: Located in Tibet, this Golden City is overseen by Lady Master Reya. Zaskar radiates the energies of the White Ray and is affiliated with the guiding spiritual principle of simplicity.

Endnotes

1. Bosonic. "Canada Political-Geo." Map. Wikimedia.org. November 8, 2008. Accessed April 10, 2016.
2. Balarezo, Manuel. "File:Mexico Map (english).svg." - Wikimedia Commons. January 15, 2016. Accessed April 10, 2016. https://commons.wikimedia.org/wiki/File:Mexico_map_%28english%29.svg.
3. CIA World Factbook. "Political Central America." Map. Wikimedia.org. April 5, 2015. https://commons.wikimedia.org/wiki/File:%22Political_Central_America%22_CIA_World_Factbook.jpg.
4. Ksiom. "East Asia Topographic Map." Wikimedia.org. August 17, 2008. Accessed April 10, 2016.
5. Rkitko. "File:WGSRPD Siberia.svg." - Wikimedia Commons. May 6, 2015. Accessed April 10, 2016. https://commons.wikimedia.org/wiki/File:WGSRPD_Siberia.svg.
6. CIA World Factbook. "Political Southeast Asia." Wikimedia.org. April 5, 2014. Accessed April 10, 2016. https://commons.wikimedia.org/wiki/File:%22Political_Southeast_Asia%22.jpg.
7. Cacahuate. Wikimedia.org. Accessed April 10, 2016. https://commons.wikimedia.org/wiki/File%3AMap_of_Central_Asia.png.
8. Denniss. "Tibet-claims.jpg." Https://commons.wikimedia.org/wiki/File:Tibet-claims.jpg#file. Accessed April 10, 2016. https://commons.wikimedia.org/wiki/File:Tibet-claims.jpg#file.
9. Jose, S. "Europe Topography." Map. Wikimedia.org. July 3, 2010. https://commons.wikimedia.org/wiki/File:Europe_topography_map_en.png.
10. CIA World Factbook. "Middle East." Map. Wikimedia.org. January 9, 2008. https://commons.wikimedia.org/wiki/File:Middle_East.png.
11. Maksim. "Russia Topography." Map. Wikimedia.org. February 3, 2006. https://commons.wikimedia.org/wiki/File:Russland_topo.png.
12. Bamse. "Africa Topography with Borders." Map. Wikimedia.org. February 25, 2008. Accessed April 10, 2016. https://commons.wikimedia.org/wiki/File:Africa_topography_map_with_borders.png.
13. Szczureq. "Deglaciated Antarctic Topography." Map. Wikimedia.org. June 16, 2015. Accessed April 10, 2016. https://commons.wikimedia.org/wiki/File:Antarctica_Without_Ice_Sheet.png. "This is the topographic map of Antarctica after removing the ice sheet and accounting for both isostatic rebound and sea level rise. Hence this map suggests what Antarctica may have looked like 35 million years ago, when the Earth was warm enough to prevent the formation of large-scale ice sheets in Antarctica. Isostatic rebound is the result of the weight of the ice sheet depressing the land under it. After the ice is removed, the land will rise over a period of thousands of years by an amount approximately 1/3 as high as the ice sheet that was removed (because rock is 3 times as dense as ice). Approximately half the uplift occurs during the first two thousand years [1]. If the ice sheet is removed over more than a few thousand years, then it is possible that a majority of the uplift will occur before the ice sheet fully disappears."
14. Manly P. Hall, The Secret Teachings of All Ages: An Encyclopedic Outline of Masonic, Hermetic, Qabbalistic and Rosicrucian Symbolical Philosophy (The Philosophical Research Society, Inc., 1988, Los Angeles, CA), Diamond Jubilee Edition, page 194.
15. Wikipedia, Root Race, http://en.wikipedia.org/wiki/Root_race, (2011).
16. David Hatcher Childress, Lost Cities of Ancient Lemuria and the Pacific (Adventures Unlimited Press, 1988, Stelle, IL), page 47.
17. Ibid.
18. Ibid.
19. Ibid., page 48.
20. Wikipedia, Root Race, http://en.wikipedia.org/wiki/Root_race, (2011).
21. Frederick Spencer Oliver, A Dweller on Two Planets or The Dividing of the Way by Phylos the Thibetan (Harper and Row Publishers, 1974, San Francisco, CA), page 170.
22. Ibid., page 173.
23. Hugh Lynn Cayce, Edgar Cayce on Atlantis (Warner Books, 1968, New York, NY), page 18.
24. David Hatcher Childress, Lost Cities of Ancient Lemuria and the Pacific (Adventures Unlimited Press, 1988, Stelle, IL), page 70.
25. Ibid., page 71.
26. Ibid.
27. Ibid., page 72.
28. Ibid.
29. Ibid.
30. Ibid.
31. Ibid.
32. Wikipedia, Root Race, http://en.wikipedia.org/wiki/Root_race, (2011).
33. Ibid.
34. Hugh Lynn Cayce, Edgar Cayce on Atlantis (Warner Books, 1968, New York, NY), page 102.
35. Ibid., page 103.
36. Ibid.
37. Ibid., page 28.
38. Wikipedia, Root Race, http://en.wikipedia.org/wiki/Root_race, (2011).
39. Hugh Lynn Cayce, Edgar Cayce on Atlantis (Warner Books, 1968, New York, NY), page 27.
40. Temple of the Jaguars. 1918 (approx). American Museum of Natural History. By Edward H. Thompson. Accessed April 14, 2016. https://commons.wikimedia.org. "View of the North Temple of the Ball Court, showing the two cylindrical columns. The figures on the sculpted walls have never been drawn or carefully studied. In general the carvings show processions of warriors and priests similar to those of the lower chamber of the Temple of the Jaguars partly excavated. One of the most interesting is the Temple of the Tables which takes its name from a table-like altar supported on the uplifted arms of small Atlantean figures."
41. Wikipedia, Kirata http://en.wikipedia.org/wiki/Kirata, (2011).

42. David Hatcher Childress, Lost Cities of Ancient Lemuria and the Pacific (Adventures Unlimited Press, 1988, Stelle, IL), page 95.
43. Ibid, page 48.
44. Wikipedia, Geological History of Earth, http://en.wikipedia.org/wiki/Geological_history_of_Earth, (2011).
45. Wikipedia, Laurentia, http://en.wikipedia.org/wiki/Laurentia, (2011).
46. Wikipedia, Cretaceous-Tertiary Extinction Event, http://en.wikipedia.org/wiki/Tertiary_extinction_event, (2011).
47. Science Daily, "When Did Dinosaurs Go Extinct? Cretaceous-Tertiary Boundary Dating Refined," http://en.wikipedia.org/wiki/Kirata, (2011).
48. Wikipedia, Laurentia, http://en.wikipedia.org/wiki/Laurentia, (2011).
49. Wikipedia, Geological History of Earth, http://en.wikipedia.org/wiki/Geological_history_of_Earth, (2011).
50. Wikipedia, Last Glacial Period, http://en.wikipedia.org/wiki/Last_glacial_period, (2011).
51. Etznab Mathers, Historical Timeline 4 Million B.C., http://mirrorh.com/timline4mbc.html, (2011).
52. Wikipedia, Yellowstone Caldera, http://en.wikipedia.org/wiki/Yellowstone_Caldera, (2011).
53. Etznab Mathers, Historical Timeline 4 Million B.C., http://mirrorh.com/timline4mbc.html, (2011).
54. Ibid.
55. Ibid.
56. Ibid.
57. Ibid.
58. David Hatcher Childress, Lost Cities of Ancient Lemuria and the Pacific (Adventures Unlimited Press, 1988, Stelle, IL), page 128.
59. Ibid., page 152.
60. Wikipedia, Great Barrier Reef, http://en.wikipedia.org/wiki/Great_Barrier_Reef, (2011).
61. David Hatcher Childress, Lost Cities of Ancient Lemuria and the Pacific (Adventures Unlimited Press, 1988, Stelle, IL), page 95.
62. Wikipedia, Holcene, http://en.wikipedia.org/wiki/Holcene, (2011).
63. Wikipedia, Atlantis, http://en.wikipedia.org/wiki/Atlantis, (2011).
64. David Hatcher Childress, Lost Cities of Ancient Lemuria and the Pacific (Adventures Unlimited Press, 1988, Stelle, IL), page 36.

Illustrations of Hierarchs

Section Four

"El Morya," Hall, Manly P., *The Phoenix: An Illustrated Overview of Occultism and Philosophy,* Los Angeles, CA: Philosophical Research Society, 1983.

"Kuthumi," Ibid.

Boulet, Susan Seddon. "Saint Germain." Digital image. *Turning Point Gallery.* Accessed July 07, 2018. http://www.turningpointgallery.com/saint_germain.htm.

"Sananda," Toye, Lori. *Freedom Star: Prophecies That Heal Earth.* Payson, AZ: I AM America Publishing, 1995.

Ascension Now. "Serapis Bey." Digital image. Accessed July 07, 2018. https://anow.org/.

Section Five

"The Art of Receiving by Lady Portia." "Archangel Zadkiel." Digital image. Accessed July 07, 2018. http://www.crystalwind.ca/awaken-the-soul/channeled-messages/the-ascended-masters/the-art-of-receiving-by-lady-portia.

Faget, Caroline. "Archangel Zadkiel." Digital image. *Message De L'ange Haziel.* http://www.carolinefaget.fr/message-de-lange-haziel/.

Korsolm, Celeste. "Soltec." Digital image. *Art Gallery Portraits by Celeste.* Accessed July 07, 2018. http://www.artsedona.net/albums/album_image/3958827/7245023.htm.

"Paul the Venetian." Digital image. *Paul the Venetian Prayer.* Accessed July 07, 2018. https://monthly-slov.rf/pavel-venetsianets-molitva/.

Fox, Jon C. "Hilarion." Digital image. *The Hilarion Page.* Accessed July 07, 2018. http://hilarion.com/.

Section Six

"Mother Mary." Digital image. *The Rainbow Scribe.* Accessed July 07, 2018. http://www.therainbowscribe.com/mothermaryjune2017.htm.

"Peter." Digital image. *Peter Fought Against Fear and Doubt.* Accessed July 07, 2018. https://www.jw.org/en/publications/books/true-faith/peter-fought-fear-doubt/.

"Saint Paul the Apostle." Digital image. *The Newman Connection.* Accessed July 07, 2018. http://www.newmanconnection.com/faith/saint/saint-paul-the-apostle.

Halstenberg, Sue. "Kuan Yin." Digital image. *Kuan Yin, the Way of the Bodhisattva.* Accessed July 07, 2018. http://mykuanyin.blogspot.com/p/kuan-yin-quotes.html.

Section Seven

"Lord and Goddess Meru." Digital image. *My Own Universe.* Accessed July 07, 2018. http://noarosauniversoespiritual.blogspot.com/2015/07/conociendo-los-maestros-ascendidos-el.html.

"Archangel Jophiel." Digital image. Accessed July 07, 2018. https://i.pinimg.com/736x/76/7b/f1/767bf147b881e4022e5e69427b5875c3--angels-beauty-heavenly-angels.jpg.

"Yemanya." Digital image. *Flavors of Brazil.* Accessed July 07, 2018. https://flavorsofbrazil.blogspot.com/2012/02/february-second-festival-of-yemanja.html.

"Pachamama." Digital image. *Pachamama, Astral Flowers.* Accessed July 07, 2018. https://chordify.net/chords/pachamama-astral-flowers-dany-matos.

Section Eight

Matthews, Pamela. "Orion and Angelica." Digital image. Accessed July 07, 2018. https://www.grail.co.nz/shop/prints/orion-and-angelica/.

"Astrea, Goddess of Purity." Digital image. *Prayers/Angels of Pure Love.* Accessed July 08, 2018. https://pure-love.org/prayers-and-angels/.

"Star Goddess." Digital image. Accessed July 07, 2018. https://fineartamerica.com/art/goddess.

Section Nine

"Archangel Michael." *Https://Mysticcircle.wordpress.com/Tag/Archangel-Michael/*, 8 July 2018.

"Elohim Hercules." Digital image. Accessed July 08, 2018. https://librosmetafisica.com/elohim-hercules-lamina-imagen/.

"Lady Nada." Digital image. Accessed July 08, 2018. https://padmadiva.wordpress.com/2014/10/17/ascended-heart-by-lady-nada/.

"Godfre and Saint Germain." Digital image. *Saint Germain Foundation.* Accessed July 08, 2018. http://www.saintgermainfoundation.org/SGF_08_TheOrigTeachings.html.

Suvorov, Valdimir. "Mighty Victory." Digital image. Accessed July 08, 2018. https://www.pinterest.com/pin/473440979554315271/.

"Claire, Elohim of Purity." Digital image. *I AM That I AM YouTube Channel.* Accessed January 6, 2018. https://www.youtube.com/watch?v=XqojGswJlnw.

"SeRaya, the White Buddha." Digital image. *Eat Till Tummy Full.* Accessed July 08, 2018. http://tummyfull.blogspot.com/2010/05/temples-visit-in-tumpat-kelantan.html.

"Vista, Elohim of the Green Ray." Digital image. *YouTube Channel, Servers of the New Era: Personal Prayer to the Supreme Creator*, 16 Aug. 2015, www.youtube.com/watch?v=dw1WgR35Gkg.

Der Wolf. "Cappadocia Chimneys." Digital image. Wikimedia Commons. February 2, 2011. https://commons.wikimedia.org/wiki/File:Cappadocia_Chimneys.jpg.

Section Ten

"Archangel Chamuel." Digital image. *YouTube Channel, Bram Ardianto: How to Recognize Archangel Chamuel*, 31 Oct. 2016, www.youtube.com/watch?v=4yvEwWTJHvI.

"Lord Himalya." Digital image. *Land of Lord Shiva*, Accessed 8 July 2018, landoflordshiva.blogspot.com/2011/07/embodiment-of-welfare-0-lord-shiva.html.

"Lady Master Reya, the Goddess Parvati." Digital image. *Ganesha, the Supreme Lord*, Accessed 8 July 2018, thesecretsoflordganersha.wordpress.com/2012/09/10/wallpapers-of-lord-ganesha/goddess-parvati/.

"Threefold Flame." Digital image. *Balancing Your Threefold Flame.* Accessed July 08, 2018. https://www.summitlighthouse.org/balancing-your-threefold-flame/.

"Lord Meru." Digital image. *Metaphysical School of Maitreya.* Accessed July 08, 2018. http://metafisicacdelu.blogspot.com/2012/08/lunes-dia-de-iluminacion-dioses-meru.html.

"Elohim Arcturus and Diana." Digital image. *Metaphysical School of Maitreya.* Accessed July 08, 2018. http://metafisicacdelu.blogspot.com/2012_12_15_archive.html.

"Goddess of Wisdom Yum Chenmo, a Form of Minerva." Digital image. *Okar Research*, balkhandshambhala.blogspot.com/2015/06/yum-chenmo-shenlha-okar.html. Accessed 8 July 2018.

"Cassiopea, Elohim of the Yellow Ray." Digital image. *The Power of Prayer, Appeal to the Elohims.* Accessed July 08, 2018. http://holisticocromocaio.blogspot.com/2013/10/0-poder-da-oracao-apelos-aos-elohins.html.

Golden City Maps

Section Five

Nzeemin. "Relief Map of Canada." Digital image. Wikimedia Commons. September 28, 2012. https://commons.wikimedia.org/wiki/File:Relief_map_of_Canada.png.

Shaund. "Yukon Region Map." Digital image. Wikimedia Commons. November 18, 2012. https://commons.wikimedia.org/wiki/File:Yukon_region_map_(fr).png.

Gaba, Eric. "Quebec Province Topographic Map." Digital image. Wikimedia Commons. March 3, 2009. https://commons.wikimedia.org/wiki/File:Quebec_province_topographic_map-fr.svg.

Natural Resources Canada. "Elevation Map Ontario, Canada." Digital image. EMaps World. June 28, 2018. https://fabulousbydesign.net/elevation-map-ontario-canada/.

Skew. "Topographic_map_of_Greenland_bedrock.jpg." Digital image. Wikimedia Commons. May 25, 2010. https://commons.wikimedia.org/wiki/File:Topographic_map_of_Greenland_bedrock.jpg.

Holl, Kaspar. "Greenland, Danish Commonwealth." Digital image. Wikimedia Commons. March 25, 2006. https://commons.wikimedia.org/wiki/File:The_Danish_Commonwealth.gif.

Section Six

Unpocoloco. "Central America, Mexico, Caribbean." Digital image. Wikimedia Commons. February 26, 2010. https://commons.wikimedia.org/wiki/File:CentralAmerica-Mexico-Caribbean2.png.

Halldin, Mats. "Map of Mexico." Digital image. Wikimedia Commons. December 20, 2006. https://commons.wikimedia.org/wiki/File:Map_of_Mexico_Demis.png.

Eirik. "Map of Cuba." Digital image. Wikimedia Commons. Accessed May 11, 2005. https://commons.wikimedia.org/wiki/File:Cu-map.png.

Electionworld. "Costa Rica Shaded Relief Map." Digital image. Wikimedia Commons. December 7, 2006. https://commons.wikimedia.org/wiki/File:Costa_Rica_map_shaded_relief.png.

Section Seven

Botev. "South America Map." Digital image. Wikimedia Commons. March 27, 2009. https://commons.wikimedia.org/wiki/File:South_America_map.png.

Brian0918. "Peru." Digital image. Wikimedia Commons. October 27, 2005. https://commons.wikimedia.org/wiki/File:Peru_rel1991.gif.

Brian0918. "Map of Brazil." Digital image. Wikimedia Commons. October 27, 2005. https://commons.wikimedia.org/wiki/File:Brazil_rel94.jpg.

Janitoalevic. "Relief Map of Argentina." Digital image. Wikimedia Commons. May 18, 2018. https://sco.m.wikipedia.org/wiki/File:Relief_Map_of_Argentina.jpg.

Celestino, Pablo. "Valle Grande, Argentina." Digital image. Wikimedia Commons. November 26, 2012. https://commons.wikimedia.org/wiki/File:Valle_grande,_San_Rafael_,_Mendoza,_Argentina.jpg.

Section Eight

"World Map." Digital image. Natural Earth. 2012. https://www.naturalearthdata.com/.

Victor V. "Australia Relief Map." Digital image. Wikimedia Commons. November 14, 2010. https://commons.wikimedia.org/wiki/Datei:Australia_relief_map.jpg.

Geoscience Australia, Government of Australia. "Australia General Reference Map." Digital image. Wikimedia Commons. June 20, 2013. https://commons.wikimedia.org/wiki/File:GA20891.pdf.

Kelisi. "Tasmania." Digital image. Wikimedia Commons. February 4, 2006. https://commons.wikimedia.org/wiki/File:Tazziemap.

Weyf. "Ayers Rock." Digital image. Wikimedia Commons. December 20, 2011.

Riden, James. "Mount Cook." Digital image. Wikimedia Commons. January 9, 2006. https://commons.wikimedia.org/wiki/File:Aoraki_-_Mount_Cook_and_Mount_Hicks.jpg.

Bohwaz. "Map of New Zealand." Digital image. Wikimedia Commons. March 31, 2014. https://commons.wikimedia.org/wiki/File:Map_New_Zealand-en.svg.

Section Nine

Alexrk2. "Relief Map of Europe." Digital image. Wikimedia Commons. July 4, 2018. https://commons.wikimedia.org/wiki/File:Europe_relief_laea_location_map.jpg.

Pethrus. "Map of Iceland." Digital image. Wikimedia Commons. March 25, 2010. https://commons.wikimedia.org/wiki/File:Map_of_Iceland_highlands-en.svg.

"Relief Map of Norway." Digital image. Carte-Monde. Accessed July 09, 2018. http://www.carte-monde.org/maps-of-norway/?lang=en.

ManuelGR. "Spain Topography Map." Digital image. Wikimedia Commons. October 13, 2016. https://commons.wikimedia.org/wiki/File:Spain_topo.jpg.

NordNordWest. "Germany General Map." Digital image. Wikimedia Commons. December 29, 2012. https://en.wikipedia.org/wiki/File:Germany_general_map.png.

Ulamm. "Basin of Tisza River." Digital image. Wikimedia Commons. April 21, 2016. https://commons.wikimedia.org/wiki/File:Tisza_Karte.png.

Taragui. "Turkey Topography Map." Digital image. Wikimedia Commons. October 20, 2005. https://commons.wikimedia.org/wiki/File:Turkey_topo.jpg.

Section Ten

"World Map." Digital image. Natural Earth. 2012. https://www.naturalearthdata.com/.

Sting. "India Topography Map." Digital image. Wikimedia Commons. March 7, 2006. https://commons.wikimedia.org/wiki/File:India_topography-fr.jpg.

Darekk2. "Tibet and Surrounding Areas." Digital image. Wikimedia Commons. June 11, 2015. https://commons.wikimedia.org/wiki/File:Tibet_and_surrounding_areas_topographic_map_2.png.

Unatnight. "Temple in Hohhot." Digital image. Wikimedia Commons. September 27, 2012.

Illustrations

Section Twelve

Churchward, James. "File:Lemuria Mumap2.jpg." Wikimedia Commons. 29 July 2009. Web. 21 Mar. 2011. <http://commons.wikimedia.org/wiki/File:Lemuria_mumap2.jpg>. (1851—1936). Book: The Lost Continent of Mu.

Donelly, Ignatius. "File:Atlantis Map 1882.jpg." Wikimedia Commons. 29 Dec. 2005. Web. 21 Mar. 2011. <http://commons.wikimedia.org/wiki/File:Atlantis_map_1882.jpg>.

Kampanakis, Patroclus. "File:Atlantis Map Kampanakis.jpg." Wikimedia Commons. 9 Jan. 2006. Web. 21 Mar. 2011. <http://commons.wikimedia.org/wiki/File:Atlantis_map_Kampanakis.jpg>.

"File:North America Craton Nps.gif." Wikipedia, the Free Encyclopedia. 16 Sept. 2005. Web. 20 Apr. 2011. <http://en.wikipedia.org/wiki/File:North_america_craton_nps.gif>.

Kieff. "File:Pangaea Continents.svg." Wikipedia, the Free Encyclopedia. 21 Oct. 2009. Web. 20 Apr. 2011. <http://en.wikipedia.org/wiki/File:Pangaea_continents.svg>.

Blakey, Ron. *Prehistoric Earth.* "File:TectonicReconstructionGlobal2.gif." Wikipedia, the Free Encyclopedia. 17 Mar. 2010. Web. 20 Apr. 2011. <http://en.wikipedia.org/wiki/File:TectonicReconstructionGlobal2.gif>.

Bibliography

1. Bailey, Alice Anne. *A Treatise on the Seven Rays*. New York: Lucis Publishing, 1971.

2. Blavatsky, H. P. *The Secret Doctrine*. Adyar: Theosophical Publishing House, 1978.

3. Campbell, Joseph, and Bill D. Moyers. *The Power of Myth*. New York: Doubleday, 1988.

4. Cayce, Edgar Evans., and Edgar Cayce. *Edgar Cayce on Atlantis*. New York: Warner Communications, 1968.

5. Childress, David Hatcher. *Lost Cities of Ancient Lemuria & the Pacific*. Stelle, IL: Adventures Unlimited Press, 1988.

6. Frawley, David. *The Astrology of Seers: A Comprehensive Guide to Vedic Astrology*. Salt Lake City, UT: Passage Press, 1990.

7. Hall, Manly P. *The Secret Teachings of All Ages: An Encyclopedic Outline of Masonic, Hermetic, Cabbalistic and Rosicrucian Symbolical Philosophy*. Los Angeles: Philos. Research Soc., 1988.

8. Luk, A. D. K. *Law of Life and Teachings by Divine Beings*. Pueblo, CO: ADK Luk Publications, 1978.

9. Mails, Thomas E. *The Hopi Survival Kit*. New York, NY: Penguin Group, 1997.

10. Phylos, and Frederick Spencer Oliver. *A Dweller on Two Planets: Or the Dividing of the Way*. Alhambra, CA: Borden Pub., 1952.

11. Toye, Lori A. "I AM America 6-Map Scenario." Map. Payson, AZ: I AM America Seventh Ray Publishing, 1996. *United States Earth Changes Progression*

12. Toye, Lori A. *Divine Destiny*. Vol. 3. Golden City Series. Payson, AZ: I AM America Seventh Ray Publishing 2012.

13. Toye, Lori A. *Freedom Star: Prophecies That Heal Earth*. Payson, AZ: I AM America Seventh Ray Pub., 1992.

14. Toye, Lori A. "Freedom Star World Map." Map. Payson, AZ: I AM America Publishing, 1994.

15. Toye, Lori A. "I AM America Map." Map. Payson, AZ: I AM America Seventh Ray Publishing, 1989.

16. Toye, Lori A. "I AM America United States Golden Cities Map." Map. Payson, AZ: I AM America Seventh Ray Publishing, 1998.

17. Toye, Lori A. *Light of Awakening*. Vol. 2. Golden City Series. Payson, AZ: I AM America Seventh Ray Publishing, 2011.

18. Toye, Lori A. *New World Wisdom*. Vol. 1. New World Wisdom Series. Payson, AZ: I AM America Seventh Ray Publishing, 2016. *Formerly New World Atlas, Volume One.*

19. Toye, Lori A. *New World Wisdom*. Vol. 2. New World Wisdom Series. Payson, AZ: I AM America Seventh Ray Publishing, 2016. *Formerly New World Atlas, Volume Two.*

20. Toye, Lori A., and Lenard Toye. *New World Wisdom*. Vol. 3. New World Wisdom Series. Payson, AZ: I AM America Seventh Ray Publishing, 2016. *Formerly New World Atlas, Volume Three.*

21. Toye, Lori A. *Points of Perception*. Vol. 1. Golden City Series. I AM America Seventh Ray Publishing, 2008.

22. Toye, Lori A. *The Ever Present Now*. Payson, AZ: I AM America Seventh Ray Publishing, 2014.

23. Yukteswar. *The Holy Science. Kaivalya Darsanam*. Los Angeles: Self-Realization Fellowship, 1972.

Resources & Reading

Websites:
iamamerica.com
loritoye.com

iamamericaearthchanges.blogspot.com

I AM America Teachings by Lori Toye

Violet Flame I AM

Earth Changes

Stan Deyo: Earth Changes and practical preparedness. standeyo.com

(Left: Hopi Waterline Map by Stan Deyo)

Earthquake: usgs.gov
Climate Change and Global Warming NASA: climate.nasa.gov
Climate Science from climate scientists: realclimate.com

Vedic Prophecies: *A New Look into the Future*
Stephen Knapp: stephen-knapp.com/vedic_prophecies.htm

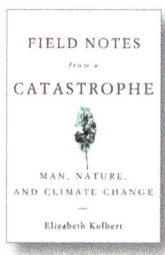

Elizabeth Kolbert: *The Sixth Extinction* and *Field Notes from a Catastrophe*

James Hansen: *Storms of My Grandchildren*

Naomi Klein: *This Changes Everything*
naomiklein.org

I AM AMERICA ATLAS **149**

Anthropogenic Climate Disruption

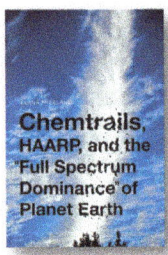

Elana Freeland: *Chemtrails, HAARP, and the Full Spectrum Dominance of Planet Earth*

feralhouse.com/chemtrails
geoengineeringwatch.org

Plant Based Diet

T. Colin Campbell: *The China Study*
nutritionstudies.org

Forks over Knives Movie
forksoverknives.com

Food Storage, Herbs, and Seeds

foodstoragemadeeasy.net
naturalsociety.com/emergency-food-organic/
herbstoponline.com
nativeseeds.org
seedalliance.org
territorialseed.com

Index

A

Abundant Sea 34, 36
Achilles
   Detroit, MI 25
Addis Ababa, ETH 49
Adelaide, AUS 45
Adjatal 105
   and Zaskar 105
"A Dweller on Two Planets" 119
Afghanistan 44
   Map 105
Africa 50, 127
   East Coast 51
   Map 52
     Topography 53
African Plate 117
Afrom 99
agricultural areas 31
   United States 31
Aktobe, KAZ 49
Alabama 30
Alaska
   and the North Slope 35
   Map 31
Albania 49
Alberta, CAN 34, 36
Albuquerque, NM 21
Alchemical Battles of Ancient Shamans and Spiritual Masters 117
Aleppo, SYR 50
Aleutian Islands 36
Alexandria, Egypt 49
Algeria 51, 52
Alice Springs, AUS 41
Amazon River 38
America
   ancient 127
   Red Children of the Sun 117
Amerigo 96
Ameru 119
   Atlantean Temples 119
   definition 131
   geology of
     illustration 125
Amsterdam, NL 47
Anchorage, AK 36
ancient cultures
   Six Map Scenario 59
Ancient Egypt
   and Klehma 76
Andeo 86
Angelica 90
Angola 51, 52
animals
   ancient 127
Annunaki 125
Antarctica 54
   Deglaciated Topography Map 54
Aoraki/Mount Cook, NZL 93
Appalachian Mountains 30
   Six Map Scenario 58

aquatic life
   new species 81, 115
Aradului Plateau, ROU 99
Aral Sea 49
Archangel Chamuel 104
   definition 131
Archangel Crystiel
   definition 131
Archangel Michael 95
   definition 131
Archangel Zadkiel 77
   definition 131
Archeia Constance 86
   definition 131
Arctic temperatures 60
Arctura 107
Argentina 38, 39, 87
Arizona 21, 28
   new Grand Canyon 63
Arkansas 24
Aryan 122
   definition 131
Ascended Masters 24
   definition 131
ascension
   definition 132
   Six Map Scenario 64
Ascension Valley 19, 22
   definition 132
   Map 75
Asia
   Central
     Map 43, 44
   East
     Map 40, 41
   North
     Map 42
   Southeast
     Map 43
Asonea 82
asteroid 27
   a second moon 63
Athens, GRC 49
Atlantean
   invasion of Rama Empire 120
Atlantic Ocean
   thermohaline current 48
Atlantis 116
   advanced culture 117
   Atlantis Map 118, 119
   co-exists with Lemuria 125
   definition 132
   demise 121
   illustration 121
   pre-Atlantean culture 118
   records 30
   sinks 127
   Sons of the Law of One 121
   the rise and fall 119
"Atlantis, the Antediluvian World" 119
Australia 41, 45, 89
   Land of Punt 126
   Map 45
Austral Seamount Chain 53

Austria 46
   Map 100
Awakening Mountains 44, 48
   definition 132
Azov Sea 49

B

Babajeran
   definition 132
   the Earth Mother 69
Baffin Island, CAN 36
Baikonur, Kazakhstan 49
Baja Peninsula 27, 36, 66
Bangalore, IND 41
Bangladesh 40, 45
Baton Rouge, LA 31
Bay of
   Bengal 41
   Deliverence 34
   Golden Sun 37
   Harmony 21, 22
     river passage 31
   Holy Prayer 49
   Many Forms 34
   Mystery 45
   Prosperity 19, 20
   Scented Flowers 40, 45
bees 128
Beirut, LBN 49
Bejing, CHN 40
Belarus 46, 50
Belgium 46
Benghazi, Libya 49
Ben Navis, SCT 96, 112
Berdichev, UA 48
Berlin, DEU 47
Bhutan 40
   Map 105
Bismarck, ND 23
Black Sea 49
Blakey, Ron 126
Blavatsky, H. P.
   and Atlantean History 120
Blazing Bay 41
Blissful Sea 45
   definition 132
Blue Islands 19, 22
Blue Mountains 28
Blue Ray 122, 128
   Adjatal 105
   Archangel Michael 95
   definition 132
   Desiree 93
   Divine Beings of Faith, Hope, and Charity 106
   Fron 92
   Gobean 71
   Gruecha 95
   Hercules 95
   Lord Himalaya 105
   Purensk 106
   Stienta 95
Bohemian Forest 99
Bolivia 38, 39

Book of Revelations
   and traditional Christian prophecy 68
Bordeaux, FRA 47
Boston, MA
   Six Map Scenario
      Map Four 63
Botswana 51
Braham 87
Braun 99, 114
Brazil 39
   Map 87
British Columbia, CAN 34
   earthquake and fractures 62
   Six Map Scenario
      Map Four 62
   west coast 36
Brussels, BEL 47
Buddhism 107
Bulgaria 46, 49
Burkina Faso 52

C

Cabinda 51
Cairo, EGY 49
California 20, 28
   bankruptcy 58
   earthquakes 27, 57
   migrations
      Six Map Scenario 66
   new Grand Canyon 63
   Northern 19
   Six Map Scenario
      Map Four 62
      Map One 57
      Map Three 60
      Map Two 58
Cambodia 43
Cameroon 51, 52
Campbell, Joseph 68
Canada
   Map 34, 35
   New Continental Divide 31
Canadian Golden Cities Map 77
Capehorn 54
Cape Verde 52
Caribbean
   Map 84
Caribbean Sea 36
Cascade Mountain Range 28
   Six Map Scenario 58
Caspian Sea 49
Cayce, Edgar 121
   Atlantean history 121
Cayce, Hugh 120
Celebration Island 24, 30
Center of Fire 23, 28
Central America 82
   Map 37
Central Asia
   Map 43
Central United States
   Six Map Scenario
      Map Two 58
Chad 52
Chengdu, CHN 41

Chicago, IL 31
Childress, David Hatcher 118
Chile 38, 39
chimeras 121
China 40
   Map 41, 44, 105, 106
choice
   "Time of choice."
      Six Map Scenario 61
Christ Consciousness
   definition 133
   Shalalah and Sheahah 92
Christianity
   and the Ruby-Gold Ray 127
Churchward, James 125
Churchward Map
   illustration 117
Churchward, NZL 94
City of Opportunity
   Bismarck, ND 23, 28
City of Purity
   Saint Louis, MO 23, 25, 28
City of Stars
   San Diego, CA 20
Clayje 91
Clear Strait 36
Climate Change 35
Coast Mountains 36
Co-creation
   definition 133
cold weather 57
Collective Consciousness 68
   definition 133
Colonization of the Earth 122
Colorado 22
   earthquake 58
   earthquake belt 63
Columbia 39
Columbia River
   Six Map Scenario 58
community gardens
   Six Map Scenario 59
Congo 51, 52
Connecticut 26, 29, 34
Consuelo Peak, Queensland 90
Continental Divide
   New 23, 28, 31
Continental Drift 117, 124
Cooperation Mountains 23, 28, 36
   definition 133
Copenhagen, DEN 47
Coral Reef, AUS 41
Coral Sea 41
Corpus Christi, TX 31
Corvallis, OR 58
Cosmic Wave Belts
   Six Map Scenario
      Map One 56
Cosmic Wave Motion
   definition 133
Cradleland Map 82
   definition 133
Creation Grid 56
   definition 133

Cretaceous-Tertiary Extinction 123
Croatia
   Map 101
Crotese 83
   Pink Ray 83
Crystal Sea 54
Crystone 29, 30
   definition 133
Cuba 36
   pre-American civilizations 127
Cycle of the Yugas 117
   and Earth Changes 123
Czech Republic 46
   Map 100

D

Dallas, TX
   seaport city 61
Dalles, OR 58
Damascus, Syria 50
Dawson Range, CAN 77
Delhi 41
Delta Area 24
Denasha 96, 112
Denmark 46
Denver, CO 22, 31
descending cultures
   and Prophecy 68
Desiree 92
Detroit, MI 25
Diamond Islands 27, 37
Diamond Sea 34
diet 128
Divine Beings of Faith, Hope, and Charity 106
divine languages
   and the Golden City names 109
Dongsheng, CHN 108
Donnelly, Ignatius 119
   and the Atlantis Map 118
Drigung Monastery
   Star of Zaskar 105
Dublin, IRL 47
Dvapara Yuga
   and the Land of the Plumed Serpent 127
   timing 125

E

Eabra 77
   and Wahanee 73
Earth
   and Ice Age(s) 124
   a second moon 63
   energies change 64
   esoteric history 122
   Prehistoric
      Map 126
   prehistoric geology
      illustration 126
Earth Changes 123
   definition 133
   spiritual insights 68

earthquake
   and the new Grand Canyon 63
   and the Teton fractures 65
   Arkansas 60
   Oregon 27
Earthquake Belt
   Six Map Scenario
      Map Four 63
Earth's Geological Timeline 123
Earth's Grid
   definition 133
   Six Map Scenario 64
East Asia
   Map 40
East Coast, United States
   Map 29
Eastern Europe
   earthquake 47
   Map 50
Eastern Seaboard Islands
   Six Map Scenario 67
East Malaysia 43
East North Central States
   Map 25
Ecological Alchemy
   definition 134
economy
   California bankruptcy 58
Ecuador 39
Edmonton, AB 79
Egypt 49, 52
   migration from Atlantis 119
   Osirian Culture 127
Ehiopia 51
Elders of Lemuria 118, 123
El Morya 55, 71
   definition 134
Elohim
   definition 134
Elohim Angelica 90
Elohim Arcturus and Diana 107
Elohim Astrea 92
Elohim Cassiopea 108
Elohim Hercules 95
Elohim Orion 91
Elohim Vista 102
Emanation-Radiation Process 122
England 47
equator
   Map 31
Essen, DEU 48
Estonia 46, 50
Ethiopia 49, 52
Eugene, OR 58
Euphrates River 50
Europe
   ice sheeting 47
   Map 46
      topography 47
Everglades, FL 58

F

Fairbanks, AK 36
Falkland Islands 38, 39, 54
fear 68
Fermont, QC 77
Fertile Plain 41, 44
   definition 134
Fiji 53
Finland 46
   earthquake 47
Fire Triplicity
   and arcing of Ray Forces 70
   definition 134
fish
   Greenland 36
Five Pagoda Temple, Inner Mongolia 108
Flathead Lake
   and the Shalahah Vortex 69
floods
   Mississippi and Missouri Rivers 31
   Northeast US 58
   Six Map Scenario
      Mississippi and Missouri Rivers 61
   Virginias and the Carolinas 57
flora and fauna
   changes
      Six Map Scenario 64
Florida 29, 30
   Six Map Scenario
      Map Five 66
      Map One 58
      Map Three 61
      Map Two 59
Fourth Dimensional Consciousness 46
France 46, 47
Freedom Star World Map 32
   definition 134
free energy
   and new technology 65
Freetown, SLE 51
French Guiana 39
French Polynesia 51
Fron 92

G

Gahkuch, PAK 105
Galactic Light
   definition 134
Galactic Sun 56
   definition 134
Galactic Web 72
   definition 134
   Six Map Scenario 56
Galati, Romania 48
Ganakra 102
geology
   and Golden Cities 69
Georgia 29, 30
   Six Map Scenario
      Map Four 64
Germany 46, 99
   Map 100
Ghana 51, 52
Gibraltar Island 20, 27, 66

glacier
   Maine 58
Glasgow, SCT 48
Global Warming 35, 47, 53
   Pacific Northwest 58
   Six Map Scenario
      Map Four 63
      Map Three 61
Glory Ocean 45, 49, 50, 52
   and Earth Changes of Africa 51
   definition 135
Gobean 109
Gobi 106, 110
   and Gobean 107
Goddess Meru 86
Goddess SeRaya 99
Goddess Yemanya 87
Godfre 96
Golden Age
   definition 135
Golden Age of Kali Yuga
   definition 135
Golden City Doorway
   definition 135
Golden City Map
   Ascension Valley 75
   Australia 90
   Cradleland 82
   Greening Map
      Asia 103
      Australia 89
   Land of Co-creation 77
   Map of Exchanges 95
   Motherland 85
   Tibet and surrounding areas 106
Golden City Names 109
Golden City of
   Adjatal 44, 105, 110
      definition 131
      Map 105
   Afrom 46, 50, 99, 110
      definition 131
      Map 101
   Amerigo 46, 96, 110
      definition 131
      Map 99
   Andeo 39, 86, 110
      definition 131
      Map 86
   Angelica 45, 90, 110
      definition 131
      Map 90
   Arctura 41, 107
      definition 131
      Map 107
   Arkana 42, 110
      definition 131
   Asonea 37, 82, 111
      definition 132
      Map 83
   Braham 39, 87, 111
      definition 133
      Map 87

Braun 46, 99, 111
  definition 133
  Map 100
Clayje 45, 91, 111
  definition 133
  Map 91
Cresta 54, 111
  definition 133
Crotese 37, 83, 111
  definition 133
  Map 83
Denasha 46, 72, 96, 111
  definition 133
  Map 98
Donjakey 51, 111
  definition 133
Eabra 34, 73, 77, 111
  definition 133
  Map 78
Fron 45, 93, 111
  definition 134
  Map 93
Ganakra 46, 49, 102, 111
  definition 135
  Map 102
Gandawan 52, 111
  definition 135
Gobean 21, 71, 112
  definition 135
  Map 71
  Mongollan Rim 69
Gobi 41, 44, 71, 106, 112
  definition 135
  Map 107
Grein 45, 93, 94, 112
  definition 136
  Map 94
Gruecha 46, 95, 112
  definition 136
  Map 97
Hue 42, 44, 112
  definition 136
Jeafray 34, 77, 112
  definition 136
  Map 79
Jehoa 37, 83, 113
  definition 137
  Map 84
Kantan 42, 113
  definition 137
Klehma 22, 23, 76, 113
  definition 137
  Map 75
Kreshe 52, 113
  definition 137
Laraito 52, 113
  definition 137
Malton 25, 28, 30, 72, 113
  definition 138
  Map 72
  New Madrid faultline 69
Marnero 37, 82, 113
  definition 138
  Map 82

Mesotamp 49, 113
  definition 138
Mousee 51, 114, 115
  definition 139
Nomaking 41, 108, 114
  definition 139
  Map 108
Pashacino 34, 79, 114
  definition 139
Pearlanu 52, 114
  definition 139
Prana 41, 45, 75, 104, 114
  definition 140
  Map 104
Presching 41, 114
  definition 140
Purensk 44, 106, 114
  definition 140
  Map 106
Shalahah 19, 22, 74, 114
  definition 141
  Hells Canyon 69
  Map 74
Sheahah 45, 92
  definition 141
  Map 92
Shehez 49
  definition 141
Sircalwe 42, 114
  definition 141
Stienta 48, 95, 115
  definition 141
  Map 96
Tehekoa 39, 87, 115
  definition 142
  Map 88
Unte 52, 115
  definition 142
Uverno 34, 79, 115
  definition 142
  Map 81
Wahanee 29, 30, 73, 115
  definition 142
  Map 73
Yuthor 36, 81, 115
  definition 143
  Map 81
Zaskar 41, 44, 105, 115
  definition 143
  Map 105
Golden City Vortex
  and Ascension 64
  and geology 69
  and spiritual light 71
  arching of Ray Forces 70
  benefits of living in 71
  channel Earth's energies 69
  definition 135
  doorways 76
  Eastern Door 75
  intervention by Venus 127
  meanings of the Fifty-One Golden Cities 110

  Northern Door 74
  of other times 59
  overview 69
  Protective Field 57
  Southern Door 74
  Star 76
  symbology 73
  the Star 76
  Western Door 76
Golden Port
  Denver, CO 22
Gold Ray
  Adjatal 105
  Amerigo 96
  Andeo 86
  Archeia Constance 86
  definition 135
  Gobi 106
  Godfre 96
  Lord Himalaya 105
  Lord Meru 106
Gondwana 116, 123
government
  changes
    Six Map Scenario 61
Grampian Mountains, SCT 96
Grand Tetons 58
  and faultlines 63
Great Barrier Reef 125
Great Central Sun 70
  definition 136
Great China Peninsula 41
Great Indian Desert 40
Great Lakes 31
  flooding 61
  Map 27
  Six Map Scenario
    Map Five 66
    Map One 56
    Map Three 61
    Map Two 58
Great River
  Saint Lawrence River 34
Great Wall of China 107
Great White Brotherhood
  definition 136
  foundational teachings from Lemuria 118
Greece 46, 49
Greening Map 40
  definition 136
Greenland 36
  deglaciated map 81
  Land of Co-creation Map 77
  Map 36
Green Ray 128
  definition 136
  Elohim Vista 102
  Ganakra 102
  Grein 94
  Marnero 82
  Pashacino 79
  Shalahah 74
  Viseria 94
  Yuthor 81

Grein 94
Grenanda, GRD 83
Group Mind
   definition 136
group souls
   of animals 128
Gruecha 95
Guadarrama Mountain Range 96
Guinea 52
Gulf of Guinea 51
Gulf of Mexico
   Six Map Scenario 58
Guyana 39

H

Haasts Bluff, NT, AUS 92
Hall, Manly 117
Hamburg, DEU 47
Hanalei Bay, HI 115
Hanoi, VNM 41
Harvest Bay 24
   gravitational pulls and high tides 63
   Six Map Scenario 66
Hawaii 51
   and New Lemuria 51
Haymana, TUR 102
Heart of the Dove
   definition 136
   Six Map Scenario
      Map Two 59
Heavenly Islands 41
Hells Canyon 75
Helsinki, FIN 47
high winds
   and pole shift 61
Hilarion 81
   definition 136
Himalayan Mountains 41, 48
Hobart, AUS 45
Hofsjokull, Iceland 95
Holocene geological epoch 126
Holy Island 45
Hopi Prophecy 20
Houston, TX 31
Hsi Wang Mu 123
   Abode of the Immortals 118
HU-man 117
   definition 136
humanity
   and changes 64
   changes
      Six Map Scenario 64
Hungary 46
   Map 101
hurricane
   Georgia 64
   Six Map Scenario 62
Hurricane Andrew 26

I

I AM America Map 18, 26
   definition 136
   four spiritual teachers 55
Iceland 95
   Map 48
ice sheeting 47
I-Ching 123
Idaho 19, 22
Illinois 25
incarnation process 122
India 41
   ancient cultures 59
   Map 45, 103, 105
Indiana 25
Indonesia 43
inland, underground sea
   Six Map Scenario
      Map Three 60
Inner Mongolia, CHN
   Map 108
insects
   ancient 128
Iowa 23
Iquitos, PER 86
Iran 49, 50
Iraq 49, 50
Ireland 46
Island of Vision 26, 29
Islands of Fortune 19, 20
Israel 49
Italy 46, 49
Ivory Coast 51, 52
Izmir, TUR 49

J

Japan 40
   Map 41
Japanese Archipelago 123
Jeafray 77
   Violet Ray 77
Jehoa 83
Jerusalem, ISR 49
Jin Dynasty 107
Jordan 49
Jupiter 122
Jyotish 128

K

K2 Mountain 105
Kali Yuga
   begins 127
   definition 137
Kamchatka Peninsula 40
Kampankis, Patroclus 121
Kampur, IND 40
Kansas 31
Kansas City, MO 23
   Heart of the Dove 59
Karnataka, IND 104
Kashmir Valley 105
Katholis 118, 120
Kazakhstan 44
   Map 106
Kenai Peninsula 36

Kentucky 30
Kenya 51, 52
Khartoum, SDN 49
Kirata
   ancient culture 123
Krakow, PL 47
Kreshe 52
Kreta Yuga
   the last on Earth 124
Krishna River, IND 104
Kuan Yin 83
   definition 137
   Goddess Hsi Wang Mu 123
Kuan Yin Lineage of Gurus 119
Kulu, TUR 102
Kunggar, Tibet, CHN 105
Kuthumi 47, 55, 72
   definition 137
Kuwait 49
Kuybyshev, ARM 49
Kyrgyzstan 44
   Map 106

L

Labrador, CAN 34, 79
Lady Master Nada 47, 96
   definition 137
Lady Master Reya 105
Lafayette, LA 31
Lake Balkhash, KAZ 106
Lake Erie 26, 27, 34
   ruptures 67
Lake Huron 27
Lake Marmion, WA, AUS 93
Lake Michigan 27, 31
   drains 31
Lake of Deep Truth 42, 44
   definition 137
Lake of Mirrors 37
Lake Ontario 26, 27, 34
Lake Superior 27
Lake Tahoe, NV 27
Lake Victoria 51
Land of Brihaspati 123
   definition 137
Land of Light 41, 42
Land of Rama
   and the spiritual elite 119
   definition 137
   Seven Rishi Cities 120
Land of the Plumed Serpent 117
   definition 137
   flora and fauna 127
   lost history of Mu, Lemuria, and Atlantis 117
Lands of Mu 119
Lanzdou, CHN 41
Laos 41, 43
Lao Tzu 123
Latvia 46, 50
Laurasia 116, 123
Laurentia 123
Law of Love
   definition 137

Lebanon 49
lei line
 and Earth Changes 34
 definition 137
Lemuria 51, 116, 117, 125
 ancient peoples 59
 definition 138
 "Map of the Ancients" 116
 Uighur Empire 125
Lepsi River, KAZ 106
Lesser Antilles 83
Lewisport
 Lewiston, ID 19
Liberia 51, 52
Libya 49
Lima, PER 38
Lithuania 46, 50
Livingston, MT 28
Lolo Pass, MT
 and Shalahah Golden City 74
London, ENG 47
Lord
 definition 122
Lord Himalaya 105
 Retreat of the Blue Lotus 118
Lord Macaw 116
Lord Meru 106
 Colonization of the Earth 122
 definition 138
Lord Rama 122
Los Angeles, CA 63
Lost White Brother
 Six Map Scenario 59
Louisiana 24
 Six Map Scenario
  Map Five 66
love 68
 definition 138

M

Madagascar 51, 52
Mahabharata
 describes Rama's splendor 120
Maine 26, 29, 34
 Six Map Scenario
  Map Five 66
  Map Four 63
  Map Two 58
Malawi 52
Mali 52
Manchester, ENG 48
Manicouagan Reservoir, QC 77
Manitoba, CAN 34
Map of Exchanges 47
 definition 138
Map of the Ancients 116
 and Ray Forces 127
 definition 138
 Map
  "The Seven Rays and the Nine Civilizations they have formed." 116
Maria del Or, Durango, MEX 82
Marnero 82
Mars 122, 128

Martinique 83
Maryland 29, 30
Massachusetts 26, 29
Master K.H. 74
Mecca, SAU 50
meditation
 and Golden Cities 69
 Six Map Scenario 64
Mediterranean Sea 49
 ancient 125
Melbourne, AUS 45
Mercury 122, 128
Mexico 36, 82
 Map 37
Michigan 25
Middle East
 Map 48, 49
Midwest United States
 floods 66
 Six Map Scenario
  Map One 56
  Map Three 60
Mighty Victory 99
Milan, ITA 50
Minerva 108
Minnesota 23
Mississippi River 23
 Map 28
 Six Map Scenario
  Map Three 61
Mississippi State 30
Missouri River 23
 Map 28
 merges into the River of Cooperation 31
 Six Map Scenario
  Map Three 61
Missouri State 23
Moldova 46, 50
Mongolia
 Map 41, 44
Monrovia, LBR 51
Montana 22, 31
 Six Map Scenario
  Map Four 63
Montreal, CAN 36
moon 122
Moraine Lake, AB 113
Morocco 51, 52
Moscow, RUS 47
Mother Karunamayi 104
Motherland Map 85
 definition 139
Mother Mary 82
 definition 139
 Swaddling Cloth 87
Mountain of the Silver Cord 22
Mount Baker, WA 28, 57
Mount Glittertind, NOR 95
Mount Gongga, Tibet, CHN 107
Mount Ossa, TAS 91
Mount Penalara, ESP 96
Mount Rainier, WA 28, 57
Mount Redcliffe, WA, AUS 93
Mount Shasta, CA
 and volcanic activity 62

 islands lead to Shalahah 66
 Peninsula 19
 Six Map Scenario 66
Mousee 115
Mozambique 51, 52
Mu 116, 117
 ancient peoples 59
 and Treta Yuga 124
 lost language 123
Mughal Gardens 105
Myanmar 41, 43

N

Nahuel Mapa, ARG 87
Namibia 52
Namtso Lake
 sacred Lake of Zaskar 105
Nanga Parbat 105
Naples, ITA 49
Native American
 ancestor 119
Nebraska 23
Nepal 40, 45
Netherlands 46
Neuschwanstein Castle, DEU 114
Nevada 28
 Six Map Scenario
  Map Five 66
  Map Four 63
New Age
 definition 139
New Brunswick, CAN 34
New Children
 definition 139
 Swaddling Cloth of Mother Mary 87
New Delhi 41
new dimensions
 definition 139
 Six Map Scenario 64
New England 34
Newfoundland, CAN 34, 36
New Hampshire 26, 29
New Jersey 26, 29, 34
New Lemuria
 definition 139
 Map 51
New Madrid faultline 69
New Mexico 21, 31
 caverns and natural gas 63
New Orleans, LA 31
New York City 34
 earthquake 58
New York State 26, 29
New Zealand 45, 51, 89
 new lands 45
Niger 52
Nigeria 51, 52
Nomaking 108
North America
 Laurentia 123
North American Craton
 illustration 125
 Map 125
North Asia
 Map 42

North Carolina 29, 30
  Six Map Scenario
    Map One 57
    Map Three 61
    Map Two 59
North Dakota 23, 31
  Valley 23, 28
Northeast United States
  Map 26
  Six Map Scenario
    Map Five 67
    Map Four 63
    Map One 57
    Map Three 61
    Map Two 58
North Korea 40
  Map 41
North Pole 127
Northwest Territories, CAN 34
Norway 46, 95
  earthquake 47
  Map 97
Nova Scotia, CAN 34
nuclear detonation 49
nuclear energy
  Six Map Scenario
    Map Four 64
nuclear weapons
  ancient accounts 120
Nunavut, CAN 34

O

Ocean of Balance 42, 44, 46, 50
  definition 139
Ohio 25
Oklahoma 24
Oliver, Frederick 119
Oman 49
Omdurman, SDN 49
Ontario, CAN 34, 81
Open City
  Kansas City, MO 23, 28
Oregon 19, 20
  earthquake 27
  new coastline 60
Osaka, JPN 40
Oslo, NOR 47
Ottawa, CAN 36
ozone tears 48

P

Pachamama 87
Pacific Northwest
  and new islands 65
  Map 19
  new coastline 27
  Six Map Scenario
    Map Five 65
    Map Four 62, 65
    Map One 57
    Map Three 60
    Map Two 58
Pacific Ocean
  and ancient MU 117

Pakistan 40, 45, 105
  Map 105
Palestine 49
Pangaea the Super Continent 116, 123
  illustration 124
  Map 124
Paraguay 39
Paris, FRA 47
Parvati
  as Lady Master Reya 105
Pashacino 79, 113
  and Grein 94
Patagonia 38
Pathway Islands 19, 20, 27
Paul the Devoted 83
  definition 139
Paul the Venetian 79
  definition 139
Pearlanu 52
Pend'Oreille, ID
  and the Shalahah Vortex 69
Pennsylvania 26, 29, 34
Persian Gulf 50
Peru 39
  Map 86
Peter the Everlasting 82
  definition 139
Petit Piton, LCA 84
Pfrees 118, 120
Philadelphia
  pollution of water system 58
Philippines 43
Phoenix, AZ 28
  Six Map Scenario 66
Pink Ray 128
  Andeo 86
  Angelica 90
  Archangel Chamuel 104
  Braham 87
  Clayje 91
  Crotese 83
  definition 139
  Divine Beings of Faith, Hope, and Charity 106
  Elohim Angelica 90
  Elohim Orion 91
  Goddess Meru 86
  Goddess Yemanya 87
  Pachamama 87
  Prana 104
  Purensk 106
  Tehekoa 87
  Uverno 79
Plateau of the Rising Sun 34
Plate Tectonics 117
Plato 127
  and Atlantis 121
Pleistocene Ice Age 125
Poland 46, 50
Pole Shift
  ancient 118
  Map 31
  Six Map Scenario 61
Portia 77
  definition 139

Portland, OR 57
Portugal 46, 50
  Map 99
Prague, CZ 48
Prana 104
prayer
  Six Map Scenario 64
Prehistoric Earth
  illustration 126
Prehistoric Tectonic Plate 127
Prince Edward Island, CAN 34
Prince Siddhartha 20
Prophecy
  and metaphor 68
  definition 140
  Prophecy is not Prediction 19
  "The focus of prophecy is to heal this planet." 55
  timing and timelines 21
Protection Bluff 45
Protective Field
  definition 140
  Six Map Scenario
    Map One 57
Purensk 106

Q

Qatar 49
Qilin Mountains, Tibet, CHN 110
Quaternary Ice Age 124
Quebec, CAN 34, 36, 79
Quetzalcoatl 76
  Ameru and the Incan Christ 117
  civilizations 127
  definition 140
Quilian Shan Peak, Tibet, CHN 106
Quinghai Lake, Tibet, CHN 107

R

rain and windstorms
  Europe 47
Rama 116
  Ancient India 118
Rapid Climate Transformation 26
Ray
  definition 140
  Emanation-Radiation Process 122
Ray(ces) 122, 127
Ray Force(s)
  and Golden Cities 70
  and "Map of the Ancients" 127
Ray Systems 128
Reconciliation Bay 26, 29, 34
Red Sea 49
Regeneration Bay 41
Republic of Czech 50
Rhode Island 26, 29
Rift Valley 51
Right Hand Path
  versus the Left Hand Path 117
Rim of Eternal Balance 41
Ring of Fire 63
  definition 140

I AM AMERICA ATLAS *157*

Rio de Janeiro, Brazil 38
River of Cooperation 23, 25, 28
   Mississippi River 31
River of Opportunity 23, 28
Riyadh, Saudi Arabia 50
Rocky Mountain States 22
Romania 46, 49, 50
   Map 101
Rome, Italy 49
Ruby and Gold Ray 128
   roots of Christianity 127
Ruby Ray
   definition 140
   Gobi 106
   Lord Meru 106
   Malton 72
Russia 40, 42, 50, 127
   Map 44
     topography 50
Rwanda 52

S

Sahara Desert 51, 127
Saint Germain 55, 73, 96
   definition 140
Saint Lawrence River 36
Saint Louis, MO 25
Saint Lucia Island 83
Salem, OR 58
Salt Lake City, UT
   coastline city 65
Samarkan, Uzbekistan 49
Samoan Islands 53
Sananda 55, 74
   definition 140
Sanat Kumara
   definition 140
San Diego, CA 20, 63
San Juan Islands
   Six Map Scenario 58
Santa Clara, CUB 82
Santana, ROU 99
Sapporo, JPN 40
Saskatchewan, CAN 34
Saturn 122, 128
Saudi Arabia 49, 50
Scotia Ridge 53
Scotland
   Map 98
Sea of Calm 44, 45
Sea of Clarity 42
Sea of Eternal Change 49, 52
Sea of Grace 48, 49, 50
   definition 140
Sea of Great Mercy 41
Sea of Okhotsk 40
seasons
   seasawing of 57
Seattle, WA 58
Sedona, AZ 28
Senegal 52
Sequoia National Park 27
Serapis Bey 76
   definition 141

SeRaya, the White Buddha 101
Serbia
   Map 101
Serenity Bay 44, 45
Seven Rays of Light and Sound
   definition 141
   human consciousness shaped through
     "Map of the Ancients" 116
   Nine Civilizations 117
Seven Rishi Cities 120
Seventh Manu
   definition 141
Shalahah 111
   connection to Sheahah 92
Shalmali 117
Shaman
   definition 141
Shamballa
   and Gobi 107
   definition 141
Sheahah 92
Sherffield, ENG 48
Shimmering Islands 45
   definition 141
Shiny Pearl 49, 50
   definition 141
Siberia 42
Sierra Leone 51
Sierra-Nevada Mountains 27, 60
Silk Road 107
Silver City
   Albuquerque, NM 24
Silver Crystal Mountains 36, 37
Singapore 43
Sitchen, Zecharia 125
Six Map Scenario
   definition 141
   Map Five 65
   Map Four 62
   Map One 55
   Map Three 60
   Map Two 57
   Mystic Message
     Map Five 67
     Map Four 64
     Map One 58
     Map Three 62
     Map Two 59
   probabilities 56
   the message of Map Six 67
Slovakia 46
   Map 101
Snake Lake 19, 22
Snake River, WA 111
Soltec 79
   definition 141
Somalia 51, 52
Somoa Islands 51
Sonoran Desert, AZ 109
South Africa 50, 52
South America 36, 38
   ancient history 127
   Map 39
   Motherland Map and Golden Cities 85
South American Plate 117

South Carolina 29
   Six Map Scenario
     Map One 57
     Map Two 59
South Central United States
   Map 24
South Dakota 23, 31
Southeast Asia
   Map 43
Southeast United States
   Map 30
South Georgia Island 54
South Island, NZL 94
South Korea 40
   Map 41
South Orkney Islands 54
South Shetland Islands 54
South Sudan 52
Southwest United States
   fires and natural gas 63
   Map 21
   Six Map Scenario
     Map Four 63
Spain 46, 47, 50
   Map 99
Spiritual Awakening
   definition 141
spiritual change
   Six Map Scenario 59
Spiritual insights on Earth Changes 68
Spokane, WA
   coastal city 62
Sri Lanka 45
Stanovoy Mountains 40
Star of a Golden City 76
   definition 141
Sterlitamak, RUS 49
Stienta 95
Stockholm, SWE 47
Sudan 49, 52
Sun 128
Swaddling Cloth
   definition 141
   four points
     Map 87
Sweden 46, 95
   earthquake 47
   Map 97
Switzerland 46
Sykes, Egerton 120
Syria 49

T

Tablet Islands 19, 22
Tacoma, WA 58
Taiwan 41
Tajikistan 44
   Map 105
Tanzania 51, 52
Tao Te Ching 123
Tasmania Island 45, 89
   Map 91
Tasman Sea 94
tectonic plates
   Atlantic Ocean 47
Tectonic Plate Theory 127

Tehekoa 87
Tehran, IRN 49
Tel Aviv, ISR 49
temperature changes 57, 60
Tennessee 30
   new west coastline 67
Texas 24, 31
   Six Map Scenario
      Map Five 66
      Map One 56
      Map Three 61
      Map Two 58
Thailand 43
thermohaline current
   Atlantic Ocean 48
Thessaloniki, GRC 49
Thirteen Star seeds 34
Thirteenth School 123
   and the Lemurian Elders 118
Three Sisters
   definition 142
Tibet 44
   Map 103, 105, 107
   Region
      Map 45
Tibetan
   ancient culture 123
tides
   Six Map Scenario
      Map Four 63
Tigris River 50
Time Compaction 56
   definition 142
Time of Change
   definition 142
   pollution
      Six Map Scenario 65
   transportation
      Six Map Scenario 61
Timing and Timelines 21
Tirana, Albania 49
Tokyo, JPN 40
Toltec
   and Atlantis 119
   and reincarnated Americans 121
Tornado Outbreak
   1992 26
Transmigration of Souls 122
transportation
   Six Map Scenario 61
Transportation Center/Vortex 19, 22, 75
   definition 142
Treta Yuga
   timing 124
Tripoli, LBY 49
Tropic of Capricorn 92
tsunamis
   Australia 45
Tunisia 49, 52
Tunis, TUN 49
Turkey 46, 49
   Map 102
Turkistan, KAZ 49

U

Uganda 52
Ukraine 46, 50
   Map 101
Uluru/Ayers Rock, Northern Territory 92
underground caverns 60
Ungava Peninsula, CAN 36
United Arab Emirates 49
United States
   destiny 59
   new capital
      Six Map Scenario 66
Unity Lake 23, 25, 28, 34
Unte 52
Upper Lake
   new lake in PA 26
Ural Mountains 49
Uranus 122, 128
Uruguay 39
Utah 19, 22
   Six Map Scenario
      Map Four 63
Uverno 79
Uzbekistan 44

V

Valle Grande, ARG 88
Vancouver Island, CAN 19, 34, 47, 62
Veadeiros National Park, BRA 87
Vedic
   astrology 128
Venezuela 39
   and the Silver Crystal Mountains 36
Venice, ITA 49
Venus 122, 128
   butterflies and bees 128
   not of our solar scheme 127
Vermont 26, 29
Victorian Island, CAN 36
Vietnam 43
Vimana 120
Violet Flame
   definition 142
   invocation at sunrise, sunset 129
Violet Ray 128
   Arctura 107
   definition 142
   Eabra 77
   Elohim Arcturus and Diana 107
   Jeafray 77
   Jehoa 83
   Pachamama 87
   Tehekoa 87
   Wahanee 73
Virginia 29, 30
   Six Map Scenario
      Map Four 63
      Map One 57
Viseria, Goddess of the Stars 94
Vista 102
volcanic eruptions 60
Volcan Irazu, CRI 83
volcano
   Toba 125
Vortex
   definition 142

W

Wabamun Lake, AB 79
Wakhan Corridor
   of Pakistan and Tajikistan 105
Wallowa Mountains 28, 62
Warsaw, PL 47
Wasatch Range 31
Washington, D.C. 34
   and new capital 76
Washington State 19, 20
   earthquakes 27
water
   and disbursement of Vortex energies 69
Weather Crystal 19, 20, 22
Weiden in der Oberpfalz, Bavaria, DEU 99
West Coast United States
   Map 20
   Six Map Scenario
      Map Five 65
Western Asia
   ice sheeting 47
West Indies 36
West Malaysia 43
West North Central States
   Map 23
West Virginia 30
White Buddha 99
White Magic
   and Black Magic 117
White Ray 128
   Afrom 99
   definition 142
   Elohim Astrea 92
   Elohim Claire 99
   Goddess SeRaya 99
   Klehma 76
   Lady Master Reya 105
   Sheahah 92
   Zaskar 105
Willamette Valley 28
   Six Map Scenario 58
Wisconsin 25
Woolong Nature Reserve
   China's pandas 107
Wyoming 22
   earthquake 58
   Six Map Scenario
      Map Four 63

Y

Yellow Ray 128
  Asonea 82
  Braun 99
  definition 143
  Denasha 96
  Divine Beings of Faith, Hope, and Charity 106
  Elohim Cassiopea 108
  Lady Master Nada 96
  Mighty Victory 99
  Minerva 108
  Nomaking 108
  Purensk 106
Yellow River, CHN 108
Yellowstone Caldera 125
Yemen 49
Yining, CHN 106
Yosemite Park, CA 27
Yucatan Peninsula
  and the Silver Crystal Mountains 36
Yugoslavia 49
Yukon, CAN 34, 36, 78
Yum Chenmo
  the Western Minerva 108
Yuthor 81

Z

Zadkiel 77
Zagros Mountains 50
Zambia 52
Zamtag County, CHN 107
Zaskar 105
Zimbabwe 51, 52
Zonguldak, TUR 49

About Lori Toye

Lori Toye is not a Prophet of doom and gloom. The fact that she became a Prophet at all is highly unlikely. Reared in a small Idaho farming community as a member of the conservative Missouri Synod Lutheran church, Lori had never heard of meditation, spiritual development, reincarnation, channeling, or clairvoyant sight.

Her unusual spiritual journey began in Washington State, when, as advertising manager of a weekly newspaper, she answered a request to pick up an ad for a local health food store. As she entered, a woman at the counter pointed a finger at her and said, "You have work to do for Master Saint Germain!"

The next several years were filled with spiritual enlightenment that introduced Lori, then only twenty-two years old, to the most exceptional and inspirational information she had ever encountered. Lori became a student of Ascended Master teachings.

Awakened one night by the luminous figure of Saint Germain at the foot of her bed, her work had begun. Later in the same year, an image of a map appeared in her dream. Four teachers clad in white robes were present, pointing out Earth Changes that would shape the future United States.

Five years later, faced with the stress of a painful divorce and rebuilding her life as a single mother, Lori attended spiritual meditation classes. While there, she shared her experience, and encouraged by friends, she began to explore the dream through daily meditation. The four Beings appeared again, and expressed a willingness to share the information. Over a six-month period, they gave over eighty sessions of material, including detailed information that would later become the I AM America Map.

Clearly she had to produce the map. The only means to finance it was to sell her house. She put her home up for sale, and in a depressed market, it sold the first day at full asking price.

She produced the map in 1989, rolled copies of them on her kitchen table, and sold them through word-of-mouth. She then launched a lecture tour of the Northwest and California. Hers was the first Earth Changes Map published, and many others have followed, but the rest is history.

From the tabloids to the *New York Times*, *The Washington Post*, television interviews in the U.S., London, and Europe, Lori's Mission was to honor the material she had received. The material is not hers, she stresses. It belongs to the Masters, and their loving, healing approach is disseminated through the I AM America Publishing Company operated by her husband and spiritual partner, Lenard Toye. Working together they organized free classes of the teachings and their instructional pursuits led them to form the School of the Four Pillars which includes holistic and energy healing techniques. In 1995 and 1996 they sponsored the first Prophecy Conferences in Philadelphia and Phoenix, Arizona.

Other publications include three additional Prophecy maps, fourteen books, a video, and more than sixty audio tapes based on sessions with Master Teacher Saint Germain and other Ascended Masters.

Spiritual in nature, I AM America is not a church, religion, sect, or cult. There is no interest or intent in amassing followers or engaging in any activity other than what Lori and Lenard can do on their own to publicize the materials they have been entrusted with.

They have also been directed to build the first Golden City community. A very positive aspect of the vision is that all the maps include areas called, "Golden Cities." These places hold a high spiritual energy, and are where sustainable communities are to be built using solar energy alongside classical feng shui engineering and infrastructure. The first community, Wenima Village, is currently being planned for development.

Concerned that some might misinterpret the Maps' messages as doom and gloom and miss the metaphor for personal change, or not consider the spiritual teachings attached to the maps, Lori emphasizes that the Masters stressed that this was a Prophecy of choice. Prophecy allows for choice in making informed decisions and promotes the opportunity for cooperation and harmony. Lenard and Lori's vision for I AM America is to share the Ascended Masters' prophecies as spiritual warnings to heal and renew our lives.

About I AM America

I AM America is an educational and publishing foundation dedicated to disseminating the Ascended Masters' message of Earth Changes Prophecy and Spiritual Teachings for self-development. Our office is run by the husband and wife team of Lenard and Lori Toye who hand-roll maps, package, and mail information and products with a small staff. Our first publication was the I AM America Map, which was published in September 1989. Since then we have published three more Prophecy maps, fourteen books, and numerous recordings based on the channeled sessions with the Spiritual Teachers.

We are not a church, a religion, a sect, or cult and are not interested in amassing followers or members. Nor do we have any affiliation with a church, religion, political group, or government of any kind. We are not a college or university, research facility, or a mystery school. El Morya told us that the best way to see ourselves is as, "Cosmic Beings, having a human experience."

In 1994, we asked Saint Germain, "How do you see our work at I AM America?" and he answered, "I AM America is to be a clearinghouse for the new humanity." Grabbing a dictionary, we quickly learned that the term "clearinghouse" refers to "an organization or unit within an organization that functions as a central agency for collecting, organizing, storing, and disseminating documents, usually within a specific academic discipline or field." So inarguably, we are this too. But in uncomplicated terms, we publish and share spiritually transformational information because at I AM America there is no doubt that, "A Change of Heart can Change the World."

With Violet Flame Blessings,
Lori & Lenard Toye

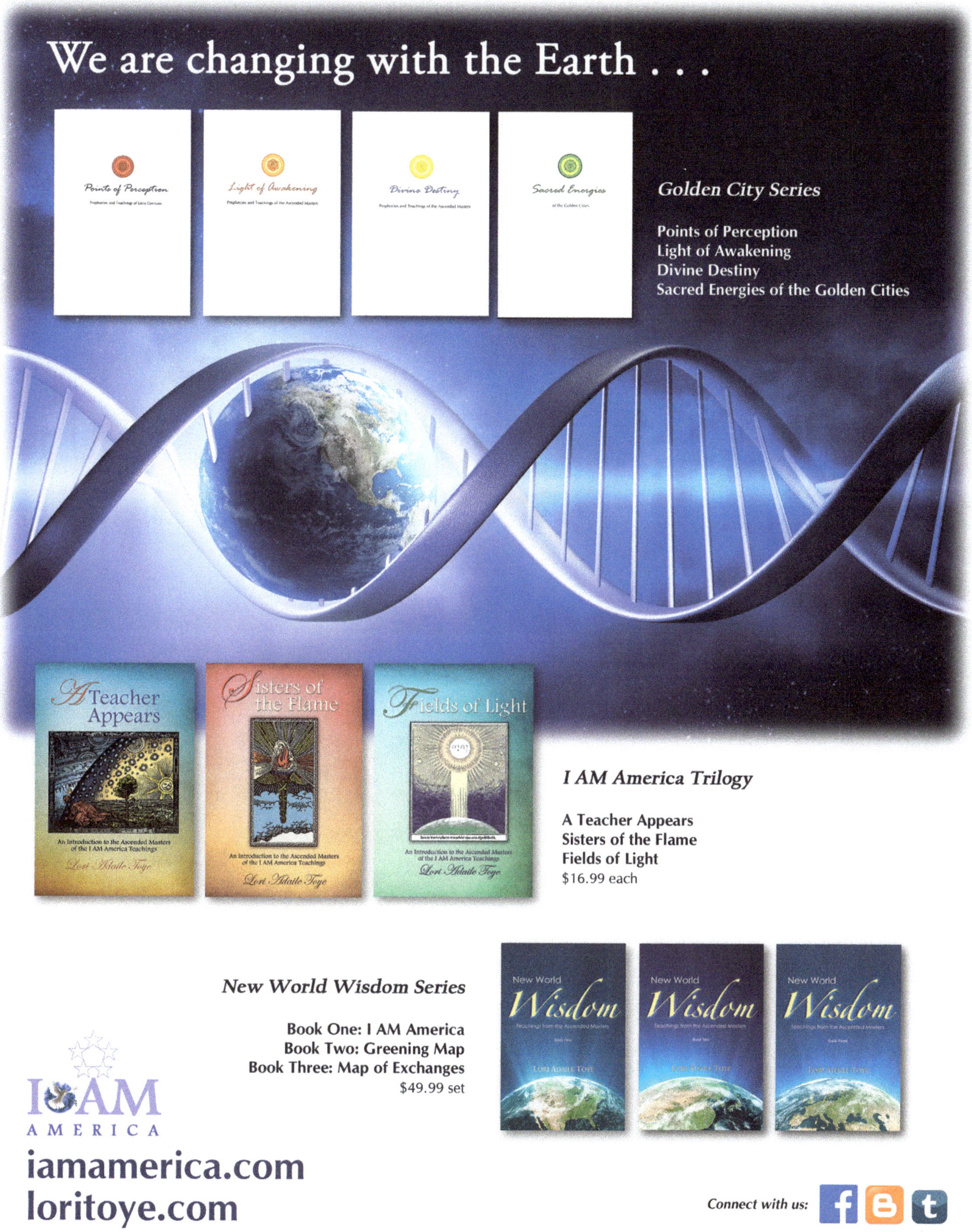
We are changing with the Earth . . .
Points of Perception
Light of Awakening
Divine Destiny
Sacred Energies
Golden City Series
Points of Perception
Light of Awakening
Divine Destiny
Sacred Energies of the Golden Cities
A Teacher Appears
Sisters of the Flame
Fields of Light
An Introduction to the Ascended Masters of the I AM America Teachings
Lori Adaile Toye
I AM America Trilogy
A Teacher Appears
Sisters of the Flame
Fields of Light
$16.99 each
New World Wisdom Series
Book One: I AM America
Book Two: Greening Map
Book Three: Map of Exchanges
$49.99 set
New World Wisdom
Teachings from the Ascended Masters
I AM AMERICA
iamamerica.com
loritoye.com
Connect with us:

[Above: I AM America Map, Freedom Star World Map, 6-Map Scenario, and US Golden City Map]

iamamerica.com
loritoye.com

www.ingramcontent.com/pod-product-compliance
Lightning Source LLC
Chambersburg PA
CBHW041228240426
43661CB00013B/1169